Trust and Risk in Internet Commerce

Trust and Risk in Internet Commerce

L. Jean Camp

The MIT Press
Cambridge, Massachusetts
London, England

First MIT Press paperback edition, 2001

© 2000 Massachusetts Institute of Technology

This book was set in Sabon by Wellington Graphics.

Printed and bound in the United States of America.

Library of Congress Cataloging-in-Publication Data

Camp, L. Jean.
  Trust and risk in Internet commerce / L. Jean Camp.
    p. cm.
  Includes bibliographical references and index.
  ISBN 0-262-03271-6 (hc : alk. paper), 0-262-53197-6 (pb)
  1. Electronic commerce—Security measures. 2. Internet (Computer network)—Security measures. 3. Business enterprises—Computer networks—Security measures. I. Title.

HF5548.32.C355 2000
005.8—dc21
                                                              99-052520

Contents

Preface

This book was inspired by the recognition that risk has new dimensions in electronic commerce and pushed forward by my experiences with those who are evaluating and assessing these new dimensions using inappropriate traditional business practices as models.

Each month produces a new model for success on the Internet. First Yahoo! was a search engine and now it is a portal. First it was marketing and now it is service. Yet many consultants and businesses offer a single approach to a variety of businesses and opportunities.

I had a most illuminating conversation with a senior consultant from a major consulting company. I asked her to enumerate the times when, after reviewing their own work, the consultants' solution was found to be wrong. I asked her to explain the company actions in response to this discovery of error. There were no such cases. Such flawlessness for a single integrated solution in the face of rapid change of businesses and wide variances within the business community was stunning, too stunning to be believable.

Thus this book is based on some unmentionable facts in business: Internet commerce is a change in business; some businesses will do everything "right" yet be destroyed; some businesses will make mistakes yet thrive. There is no single right model for Internet commerce. There is no single right answer that can be bought with certainty by paying the most expensive consultants. For every business there are different choices. Although some businesses have obvious price advantages (e.g., Big Lots) or advantages in consumer confidence (e.g., Crayola), these businesses are not destined to succeed. When the business is in code, not in concrete, there are an infinite number of forms. There will be an explosion of business models in the near term.

There are of course some excellent consultants, who offer many solutions and endeavor to create not a marginally customized product, but a truly tailored solution. As with all that is excellent, these are rare. The vast majority of customers get a set of viewgraphs and documents prepared for the mythical generic firm. The generic firm is as mythical as the unicorn. The unicorn was a transmutation beginning with the rhino and resulting from the textual drift inherent in hand-copied documents. As scribal copying embodied human error and inherently resulted in slow transformation of documents, so mass production embodies the understanding of economic actors as generic units. The mythical firm is a creature of technological limits, beginning with common institutional constructs and resulting from the requirements of mass production. The mythical firm results from the need for a standard compatible with the mass-production model of business and business consulting. In the information age everything is malleable, customized, individual. Thus the texts that propose generic solutions are flawed. Texts that educate and enable individuals to make their own tailored choices are needed for the post-print age. I have endeavored to create one of these: a text that explains some basic parameters.

There are some stable factors in electronic commerce—the towering power of the browser bookmark being one—but every business has its own model. The browser bookmark promises that a site will be the first place checked for news or shopping. But if that site is badly designed, offers bad service, or is unreliable, it is unlikely to get a second look.

Expecting a single monetary form to emerge from Internet commerce is as reasonable as expecting a single paper currency to come off the printing press. Movable type created fundamental changes in knowledge production: standardization, the ability to compare systems of knowledge, and specialization of intellectual labor. With the printing press, complex markets for intellectual goods developed, contracts proliferated, paper money expanded, and the age of quantification took flight (Crosby 1997; Eisenstein 1979).

At the beginning of the age of print there was no clear single path on which to direct those beginning at vastly different positions. Similarly there is no single path forward through the age of electronic information. Every businessperson and consumer has a risk profile that is a function of (to name a few variables) market, market position, and risk aversion; because of this diversity, this book is meant to be not prescriptive but rather descriptive. Just as there was no single way to reorganize business in response to the wealth of paper, forms, and currencies made possible by movable type, there is no single way to minimize risk for every party in light of digital information.

The interdisciplinary nature of this book hints at the magnitude of the changes ahead. The current disciplinary structure was built on the print mode of learning and teaching. Just as a Master's of Information Science degree is a creature of modern change, a future student might get a Bachelor's in Trust. Similarly some modern business structures will be as useful as the medieval guild as the next century approaches and passes. This magnitude of change requires that a detailed book be focused on the near term. Therefore this book inherently has a near-term focus, especially with respect to the Internet commerce systems examined. Trust, risk, privacy, security, and reliability are as fundamental to information commerce as Arabic numerals are to paper modes of commerce. Thus trust and risk are the core of this book.

This book is meant to empower individuals to be their own contractors when shopping on the net, constructing an information business, or building a virtual addition onto their current business structure, to encourage shoppers to tread on the Internet instead of in the mall, and to tell them how to keep their hands tightly on their virtual purses. The Internet has a power to intimidate that is unfathomable for someone who has seen the vast bulk of digital silliness that was the early days of the Web. This book should remove any residual intimidation. Should it fail to do so, a quick tour of Usenet should eliminate any lingering awe for the denizens of the modern Internet. Decades ago, the Internet was inhabited only by researchers, intellectually engaged gentlepersons with shared norms of behavior and common interests. Now, it's everyone—all the myriad human foolishness, wisdom, joy, and grief flow through the wires every day. A widely used acronym on the Internet, IRL, stood for "in real life." Now the Internet is real life. Sign up or miss it.

It is my contention that Internet commerce will truly come of age in the Christmas season of 1999. Allow a digression into personal experience to explain this entirely qualitative, rather unfounded projection. First, I find that I tend to be a moderate early adopter, the first (or third) to try out new technology. Second, I am rare among technical researchers in Internet commerce as I am the one who actually does the family holiday shopping. I attribute this to gender role differences. During the holiday season of 1998, I did my shopping one Saturday morning while my children played downstairs. I had the list, my credit card, and Dogpile. (Dogpile is a metasearch engine, that is, a search engine that searches other search engines.) As I have been shopping on the Web for nearly four years, I was one or two years ahead of the curve. Thus I predict that in the next holiday season working parents and the elderly across the globe will discover this saver of trouble and time, leading to a more relaxed holiday season for everyone (except, of course, the retailers who have not adapted to Internet commerce). I found in my shopping no price (dis)advantage, as the difference in price tended to be absorbed by shipping costs. Shopping on the Internet gave me a price equivalent to the discount store, with no taxes paid, and home delivery.

This leads to the second, more mundane, inspiration for this book. Three years ago at the First Usenix Workshop on Electronic Commerce, I realized I was perhaps one of three people in the room who, by a combination of gender, class, and age, actually shopped. I was the representative of every parent who has the experience of holiday shopping. I was the single person there who understood at a visceral level the need for shopping without catalogues, phone calls, or expensive personal assistance. I live in the gap between mythical SuperMom and actual working parent. That is, I am an actual working parent who needs life to be friction free to meet the demands of the mythical SuperMom. The time crunch and the need for schedule-friendly remote shopping that is oblivious to interruptions will drive Internet shopping. The aging of the population makes a trip to the mall less an effortless jaunt and more a day's event. The reorganization of the modern family demands, and the technology allows, Internet commerce. Together these forces point to inevitability.

This is the ideal moment to thank my family. First, the incomparable Shaun McDermott, a truly wonderful man. A patient and supportive man most supportive in that he is a wonderful father. My daughters, Adonica and Amelia, who have made their own contributions to this book by immeasurable contributions to my life. And finally, Wilson, who taught me many lessons I will not forget.

Certainly my early academic mentors deserve acknowledgment. I would never have started the program of study, much less the book, without the support of Michael Feldman. Early on Hudson Welch and James Morris were endlessly intellectually engaging. I am deeply indebted to Granger Morgan for following his own dreams and beginning the department where I had the honor of studying. Pam Samuelson provided irreplaceable insight into the subtleties of the law, and despite a schedule that is frightening even in retrospect, always found time to provide detailed comments. Mary Shaw has offered valuable time and insights from her technical and personal wisdom. Bennet Yee has given both professional counsel and patient consideration. I wish his office were still across the way, rather than across the continent. Finally my dissertation advisors, Marvin Sirbu and Doug Tygar, without whom this text would not have come to fruition.

To my friends who started virtual and ended up more than actualized: Phaedra Hise, Charlotte Chen, Robin Schoelenthaler, and of course Pip. Laura Painton and Tse-Sung Wu: Thank you. Rosy Chen shared her heart, wisdom, and office. Milind Kandlikar provided passionate occasional doses of perspective. Indira Nair, for whom mention is necessary but not sufficient. Donna Riley shared her rare gifts of strength and kindness, bestowed with a discerning wit. Ian Simpson provided continued intellectual engagement. Richard Field offered his very relevant expertise and the kindness of his heart in reviewing and commenting on my work. Cathleen McGrath offered engaging debate or empathy, as appropriate, over uncounted cups of tea. Phoebe Sengers reminded me to like myself, and hold my work just dear enough.

Barbara Slater, Andrew Russell, Denise Murrin-Macey, Patricia Steranchak, Janice Trygar, and Victoria Massimino assisted in a many ways, the greatest of which has been in the sharing of their company and friendship.

At Harvard, Jane Fountain, Susan Cooper, Rob Jensen, and Lewis Branscomb have provided moral support and given me the gift of their time. Harvey Brooks was kind enough to be a reader, and gentle in communicating his sharp insights.

Introduction

Consider a dollar bill. Newly minted bills have a unique texture and even a distinct odor. A dollar is the measure of money. It is the most readily accepted monetary form on the globe. To exchange that for a machine-readable data stream seems a great leap. It is not.

The value bound to the paper abstraction of wealth is not a result of mass hysteria or a widespread delusion, as an examination of the purely physical components of paper and ink might suggest. Rather it is a reflection of trust that is widely shared and built over centuries. The dollar is worth as much as there is trust in the solvency and continuity of the U.S. government; trust in the ability of law enforcement to prevent counterfeiting; trust that a merchant or bank would not knowingly pass on a counterfeit bill; trust in the foundations of the American economy. These trust decisions are deeply embedded and unexamined in daily transactions.

Trust in American monetary instruments is not an eternal national constant, however. American commercial instruments were marked by early failures, the Continental dollar being the obvious example.[1] In Internet commerce people are once again embarking on a long-term trust commitment. Internet moneys are both like and unlike the dollar. It is one thing to build on the trust of generations past on a monetary instrument, and another to be among the first to take the risk that trust implies. The adopters of the Continental were not rewarded by the eventual global adoption of today's greenback.

1. After the Revolutionary War it was necessary for the U.S. government to print money to pay its bills, including the wages of soldiers. The United States printed Continental dollars, leading to the common saying, "not worth a Continental."

Internet moneys are like the modern greenback and historical Continental dollar in that all are based on invisible trust bindings. The trust-binding value to the dollar depends on the physical difficulties of reproducing the paper monetary instrument and a centuries-old governance system; Internet commerce depends on the difficulties of calculating mathematical functions and decades-old networks. An Internet commerce system may require trust in the merchant's goodwill as well as his technical competence. Another system may require only faith in risk management of major financial institutions.

In this book the trust relationships in electronic commerce are examined and illuminated. The focus is on trust, but it is equally on risk. Trust is the positive view of exposure: whenever there is trust, there is risk. I focus on these two interrelated topics, for trust is risk.

The focus on trust as well as risk not only stresses the continuity of the evolution of money from gold bars to electronic bytes, but also provides the broadest explanation of Internet commerce. This focus further distinguishes this study from a consultant's, who might consider risks in a specific scenario to the mythical generic firm.

The determination of risk can be found in an examination of who trusts in Internet commerce transactions. Who will pay, in terms of both money and data, if trust is misplaced? When the inevitable early failures occur, who will be at risk? Who is liable? In many commerce systems there is a trusted third party. Who is this trusted third party? Why is it necessary to trust this party? What exactly is this party trusted to do? Answering these questions means understanding risk allocation in electronic commerce. Answering these questions requires understanding security, record-keeping, privacy, and reliability.

No single currency or transaction system is certain to dominate the future Internet. The answers to the previous questions vary across the multitude of protocols proposed for electronic commerce on the Internet. However, an examination of a broad range of these protocols makes clear that in electronic commerce, there is considerable opportunity to lose both money and data. Customers can lose money and privacy. Merchants can lose money, proprietary information, and reputations. There is much to be gained. It is worth the necessary risk, but only that risk which is necessary. It worth extending trust, but narrowly.

In this book I translate from the technical protocol to the financial risk. There are three basic sources of risk: security failures, data misuse, and reliability failures. This book is placed to illuminate the space defined by these three axes. I do not attempt to address every possible risk inherent in electronic commerce. Electronic funds transfer can magnify the weaknesses of cash-control systems (Fischer 1988; Mayland 1993). If a company has problems with cash-control mechanisms and misplaced trust, electronic commerce can make it worse. This is obvious, and is not the focus here. The purpose of this book and set of system evaluations is to illustrate risk allocation when a customer, merchant, Internet service provider, or commerce service vendor misplaces trust in outsiders, not those within their own organizations. (Note that I refer to sellers of all goods but Internet commerce systems as merchants; I refer to those who offer commerce systems as vendors.)

Vendors, banks, consumers, and merchants have different interests. Market and legal mechanisms will assure that all needs are met in the long term. But one takes risks in the short term. Today the legal environment is uncertain. The market requires information to function, and many are functioning without any better sources of information than the vendors themselves. Thus there are systems that place risks on participants that might better be left with the vendor. This text should provide the tools to determine the sources of risks, identify what risks are of greatest concern in a few specific systems, and evaluate other similar systems.

Understanding risks in Internet commerce requires integrating an understanding of money, network technologies, information security, and the potential for data appropriation and misuse. Thus this book begins with definitions and discussions of money, the Internet, security, and privacy.

I consider the Internet as a framework for commerce. Much of the argument for Internet commerce is essentially information on the growth and population of the Internet. The history of the Internet is included, as it is more than academic. There was at one point an alternative vision of the Information Superhighway—citizens as consumers of 600 channels with feedback limited to a single button labeled "BUY." Instead the open Internet has prospered. With respect to shopping and selling, the open nature of the Internet creates trust issues. An open Internet with millions of "channels" has far different trust implications than a centralized broadcast model with orders of magnitude fewer choices.

In short, I address the terrain of Internet commerce, rather than trying to lay out a specific path or roadmap. Here are identified the avoidable hazards likely to be found on the road to Internet commerce. And thus we begin by considering the nature of the Internet.

1

The Internet

This chapter illustrates the importance of the nature of the Internet. It includes a brief description of the protocols that are at the core of the Internet and that give the network its characteristics. Understanding these protocols, along with an understanding of money, will provide the foundation for understanding Internet commerce. This description is written for the layperson, with use of analogies and examples.

What Is the Internet?

This text focuses on protocols, or communications standards, suitable for commerce on the Internet. Why the Internet? The complete answer to that question depends on the set of questions here: What is the Internet? Where is the Internet? Who's out there? Why Internet commerce? What distinguishes Internet commerce from telephone and mail-order commerce?

The Internet is a set of networks connected using protocols that are open and portable, and that enable the entire research community to share information. That the protocols are open means that there are no secrets about how the software works. That the protocols are portable means that they can function on more than one operating system.

In the corporate tradition, software is protected by patents, secrecy, and licensing prohibitions against reverse engineering. Under the Internet model, software is very different, which has important implications. Open software progresses faster than proprietary software, because the body of developers is larger. The code or protocols are available to all hobbyists, academics, and anyone else who can study the code, improve it, and share the results. The code has an installed base and is available to all start-ups who would add functionality. Thus those solutions that are most likely to keep up with the rate of change on the Internet are those that are as open as possible. Thus a popular innovation will not leave your site behind.

"Open" does not imply a lack of security; in fact the opposite is true. More closely controlled code requires a greater extension of trust than open code. Because software is open, and anyone can examine or modify it, it is often presented as less secure. But no one modifies the code that a particular site is using. Rather modifications extend the menu of options for the software. The modification of the code is relevant for upgrades. The ability of anyone to examine the code assures that there is not likely to be widespread disagreement about its functionality or features. Open code is examined for security flaws by a community of impartial but expert observers. Greater transparency means a lesser need for trust, in the software business as in the stock market.

What Are Its Origins?

For those for whom the Internet has exploded onto the scene in the 1990s, it may come a surprise that the Internet has been developing for decades; it began as the ARPANET, a U.S. government project for connecting scientific research sites.

The tools for networking networks of computers were developed by scientists and researchers for use in their own nonhierarchical heterogeneous computing environments. The techniques developed were designed for distributed support, using an iterative process that included seeking and considering comments from the user community. Although the ARPANET connected only a couple of hundred computers at that time, it created the core of compatible internetworked computers that became the Internet. By 1983, all the networks connected to the ARPANET used the same protocols for communication.

After the release of Berkeley UNIX 4.2, these protocols were was included in every UNIX workstation. The UNIX standard created a commercial opportunity for network products. Although the vast majority of these machines were not initially connected to what we now know as the Internet, the ability to internetwork networks became a standard feature for high-end operating systems.

In 1986 ARPANET became NSFNET. Eventually the protocols that ran over networks existing at the same time (e.g., the IBM/VMS-based BITNET) ran over the Internet wires as well. Students, researchers, and librarians were all now connected. The purpose of NSFNET was to connect all the supercomputers. As part of connecting the supercomputers, the regional networks were also connected. The T1 lines connecting these machines were the first Internet backbone.

In 1990 the first commercial email provider, MCI Mail, was connected to NSFNET. Also in the 1990s, the National Science Foundation began to reduce subsidies, and gave the responsibility of the NSF backbone to commercial providers, thus enabling a commercial Internet without the limitations borne of federal funding. As long as the Internet was funded from tax dollars, its primary purpose should be research and not the enrichment of corporations or domain name speculators. As the Internet became increasingly commercial, the support for the Internet from research funds became increasingly inappropriate.

Along with commercial email providers, commercial information providers came onto the Internet. Early adopters of Internet technology for information marketing included Dow Jones and Dialog (Cerf 1993). Thus began Internet commerce.

By 1990 the growth of the Internet was too profitable for information providers to ignore. However, the market remained primarily individuals with a technical background, as access to information on the Internet required either some understanding of UNIX or proprietary software provided by an Internet service provider (ISP). Figure 1.1, from the annual Internet Domain Survey, illustrates how the user community has expanded (Internet Domain Survey 1998). Note that the left-hand axis represents millions of Internet hosts.[2] Thus an estimate of 45 million

---

2. "Host" is merely a fancy word for a user's machine. Since there are many types of machines connected through the Internet (for example, messages go through IP routers, telephone switches, and cable modems), the word "host" is used to distinguish a general-purpose computer. A host can be a supercomputer or a used Macintosh LC II, so long as the machine is a general-purpose machine.

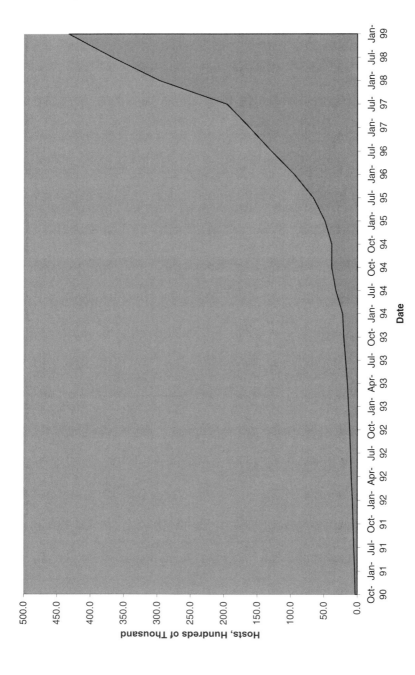

Figure 1.1
Exponential growth of the number of computers connected to the Internet

Internet users is a reasonable lower bound because it assumes that no one shares computers and that the survey located every host.

A year before the connection of MCI Mail, a European researcher, Tim Berners-Lee, became concerned with effectively transporting the images, postscript files,[3] and text and data files necessary for collaborative physics throughout Europe. The protocol he developed is the underlying technology for the World Wide Web. The Web allows consumers to search for information on the Internet with a straightforward, easy-to-use interface developed first by Mosaic (i.e., the browser). Easy access to information has been the greatest driver of Web growth.

The World Wide Web is a critical element in emerging markets. With the Web any person could access information easily. Mosaic made it as easy as point and click; Lycos made searching as easy as point and search. These tools dramatically lowered the threshold for technical knowledge to connect to the Internet, search, and send and obtain information. Although the Internet began as a specialized U.S. government project, it is now global. The Internet domain survey has expanded to include ninety countries.

Where Is the Internet?

The Internet is on the desktop and in South Africa. The Internet is global and American. Determining the scope and population of the Internet with any certainty is both an art form and an open research question. Attempts to determine profiles have included hosts counts, mailed surveys, phone surveys, and voluntary Web surveys. This section's analysis is based on the estimated number of hosts, because actual machines are easier to count than users. The user-to-machine ratio may vary between and among institutions and households.

Another way to investigate who users are and what they are doing is to consider domain names. These are relatively easy to count and their growth is clearly exponential. A domain name is the part of a Web

---

3. Postscript is the language used by printers. People can use postscript with Ghostscript or some other postscript tool. The important point is that these are widely used, more complex than text documents, but smaller than high-resolution image files.

address that is to the right of "www", or the part of an email address that is to the right of the @ sign. A domain name is a mnemonic for humans who would rather not remember emails by numerical Internet protocol (IP) addresses such as: Sue_Smith@128.196.93. Domain names are designed entirely for user interface. Because domain names are the only ubiquitous form of identity information on the Internet, a detailed discussion of them is included in chapter 2.

As described in the following chapter, IP runs on IP addresses. When a device needs to communicate with, for example, a Web server and knows only the domain name of the server, the device must get the corresponding IP address before communication can begin. Domain names are not limited in number as IP addresses are. The number of IP addresses is limited by the design of the system. The number of domain names is limited by human ingenuity (and, from the evidence, human silliness).

Any number of domain names can point to a single IP address, so that a single IP address can represent many domain names. (Each domain name, however, must point to exactly one IP address.) These IP addresses may be of a single machine, or of a class of IP address that represents an entire network.

A domain name consists at least of two parts: the top-level domain name and the second-level domain name. Top-level domains are .com, .net, .org, .mil, .gov, and .edu. The second-level domain is immediately to the left of the top-level domain (e.g., "harvard" in harvard.edu; "chicken" in chicken.com; "despair" in despair.com, and "slashdot" in slashdot.org).

Conflicts occur most often at the second level, where, for example, an early adopter might own mcdonalds.com by virtue of having this as a last name. Then the fast-food chain would find itself preempted. One of the major issues in electronic commerce today is this ownership of domain names. There is no definitive legal ruling on this topic. A domain name may be a extension of intellectual property whether the company owning the corresponding second-level phrase (e.g., "mcdonalds") has registered the domain or not. Domain names may be a raw material, subject to "gold rushes." In the case of http://www.gwbush.com/, the domain name could be considered important political speech, the property of the Bush campaign that was stolen by the commentator, or valuable electronic space first claimed by an innovative entrepreneur.

Domain names are assigned. Yet only the assignment of IP addresses and the domain name system are centralized. In all other ways the Internet and the protocol on which it depends are decentralized.

There are three top-level international domain names: .net, .com, and .org. Addresses in these domains are currently assigned by Inter NIC of Virginia. It costs $70 to register a domain name for two years. There are three top-level domain names that are U.S.-specific: .mil, .edu, and .gov. Assignment of second-level domain names in the .mil and .gov domains are controlled by the Department of Defense.

It is likely that assignments in the .edu domain will go to EDUCAUSE (http://www.educause.edu/). EDUCAUSE is a nonprofit consortium of higher education institutions that encourages the use of information technology in higher education. It was formed by the merger of EDU-COM and CAUSE, which were nonprofits supporting computing and computing research in education.

Many top-level domain names are geographically bound; these are called country code top-level domain names (ccTLD). Each nation that cares to have its own two-level country code top-level domain name may have that domain. Examples of these include .fr for France and .uk for the United Kingdom. Domain names are registered by continental or national entities.

Every domain name must correspond to an Internet address. IP addresses must be unique for the Internet to function. IP addresses are assigned, but there is no authority that requires that these assignments are honored. In Asia domain names are assigned by the Asia-Pacific Network Information Center (www.apnic.net). In Europe domain name assignment is handled by the "Reseau IP Europeens " (www.ripe.net/). In the United States IP addresses are assigned by the American Registry for Internet Numbers (www.arin.net).

At this point it seems possible that the .us domain name will be supervised by the U.S. Postal Service. The .us domain is still being handled by the original research-support institution, ISI. The .us domain name appears to be used primarily by K–12 schools, which do not qualify for .edu domain names, and municipalities. One reason its use by municipalities is popular is that many of the big city .com domain names were bought in the domain name gold rush in the 1990s. Some big city names (for example, boston.com) were bought by location-specific businesses before the city registered.

Figure 1.2 shows that the distribution of the purposes of the users on the Internet has changed over time. It presents the percentage of domain names registered in the different top-level domains from January 1995 through January 1999, as reflected first by public registration levels and then by the Domain Name Survey.

The .org domain is for nonprofits, for example, sierraclub.org. When looking at this figure, it is important to keep the previous figure of absolute group in mind. For example, clearly the number of universities has not declined. Yet the percentage of domains on the Internet that are universities has decreased. Similarly, the number of domain names registered to nonprofit organizations has more than doubled over the time period. The graph shows that the number of nonprofit organizations has expanded exponentially with the number of overall domains.

The .mil domain consists of addresses for the U.S. military. The military's share of total domain names has not significantly decreased, staying at roughly 4.5 percent. Given the rate of growth of the Internet, this illustrates that the military has built upon its early commitment with aggressive deployment of Internet technologies.

The .edu domain is populated by universities. The number of registered educational domain names appears not to have changed dramatically over the period depicted in the figure, though it has declined in percentage terms. In the years covered by the graph, the number of .edu domains more than quadrupled, rising from 1,133,502 in January 1995 to 5,022,815 in January 1998. The phenomenal growth of international, network, and commercial domains over the same period accounts for the relative percentage decline in the educational domain.

The predominant commercial domain is .com. The network domain was originally for network service providers: the IP address registrars above; ISPs; and providers of other network services. Shortly after the inception of the .net domain it was discovered that .net domains provided more fertile hunting grounds for ideal domain names for late adopters. Particularly for companies that missed the opportunity to obtain the .com

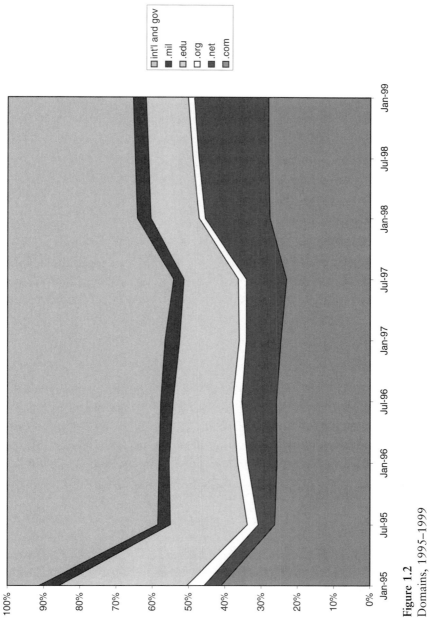

Figure 1.2
Domains, 1995–1999

name of choice, the .net domain provided a second chance. The net domain now serves three markets: traditional businesses moving onto the net, modern net-created business opportunities (e.g., Web hosting), and personal-interest domains (e.g., http://www.momspace.net/).

The top area of the figure shows .gov (U.S. government) and geographical domain names. The increase in regional names, including .us and Asian and European domain names, is reflected by the sharp drop in the total percentages of the other domain names. After July 1995 registration of .net domains increases so dramatically that there appears to be a leveling of regional domain name use. Again considering absolute growth, registration in international domain names continues at an exponentially increasing rate, as shown in table 1.1.

The customer base on the Internet grows as the number of countries and connections grows: exponentially with time. Although the coefficient of growth varies across the continents, the shape of the growth curve remains the same for each region. It is the expectation of the future of these growth curves as much as the current magnitude that so excites the providers of content and commerce services.

Who Is on the Internet?

Profiling the domain is no small task; and profiling of the typical Internet user is more difficult still. Thus any survey-based discussion of Internet users is subject to gross generalization. With this caveat I now consider just such gross generalizations about users. Keeping in mind the tendency of Americans to deviate wildly from any norm, take this discussion for what it is: an examination of trends by a long-time user with an academic bent.

First, the number of female users continues to be smaller than the number of male users. However, the rate of growth in the number of female users is growing faster than the rate of growth for male users. Cultural and economic factors appear to drive this gender imbalance. As the percentage and numbers of female users increase, as they will, gender distribution will eventually stabilize at a level that reflects the differences in incomes and free time between men and women. This will have a number of effects aside from the obvious one of increasing the impor-

Table 1.1
Regional growth of the Internet

Region	Number of hosts					
	Jan. 94	Jan. 95	Jan. 96	Jan. 97	Jan. 98	Jan. 99
North America	1,685,715	3,372,551	7,088,754	11,216,036	20,302,652	33,702,867
Western Europe	550,933	1,039,192	2,699,559	4,352,152	5,537049	9,300,942
Eastern Europe	19,867	46,125	168,142	238,580	443,191	694,723
Middle East	6,946	13,776	44,484	58,930	103,925	211,824
Africa	10,951	27,130	84,715	104,838	199,958	284,912
Asia	81,355	151,773	672,495	1,006,664	1,661,034	3,089,659
Pacific	113,482	192,390	475,505	647,948	916,538	1,066,398

tance of Internet commerce, given that women still do most of the shopping in America.

Certainly men and women, as well as any gross generalizations can apply to billions, will use the Web differently. Will the threshold at which men and women choose to trust their purchases and data to the Internet be different? At what point will Internet commerce break the risk/value threshold of the average shopper? How will the purchasing and marketing decisions of men and women differ and how will theses decisions be similar?

A survey by Harvard's Shorenstein Center on the Press, Politics, and Public Policy[4] noted that the Web is multimedia not only in the technical sense, but also in the sense that it is used differently by different people. This survey classified Web users into four basic types according to what they did while on-line: researchers, political expressives, home consumers, and party animals.

Researchers use the Web for professional purposes. They augment the workplace with news and radio, but the primary interest in their Internet connection is for work-related purposes. (Having been in research environments, I might point out that a simple count of the number of "packets" sent to researchers might place them in the party-animal category, but this is only an artifact of the bandwidth required by multimedia applications. Video and audio require far more packets than text.) The early markets for Internet commerce targeted researchers: books, computer hardware, software, and educational opportunities. Researchers will find that the combination of Internet commerce and the service economy enables them to spend less time at the mundane tasks of life and more time in the lab or office. If not for issues of privacy, researchers would be the ideal target for integrated Web service sites, which lower the overhead of managing one's life by offering housekeeping, grocery shopping, and delivery services. However, integrated services currently sell data about the customers as part of their revenue. Researchers, and others aware of the resale of data, are less likely to embrace such services.

4. P. Norris, *Who surfs? New technology, old voters, and virtual democracy* (Hollis, N.H.: Hollis Publishing, 1999).

Political expressives go on-line primarily for the political information and the opportunities for organization and discourse that the Internet offers. Political merchandise can be obtained readily on the Web. For example, posters from Nelson Mandela's original presidential campaign can be ordered off the Department of Communications' page at the South African government's Web site. The political season is now accompanied by political Web sites that offer platform information and candidates' schedules, and sell goods. Political expressives are committed individuals. The time-saving qualities of Internet commerce are an advantage for this group. Another significant advantage is the ability to evaluate a company or product according to the political information readily available on the Web; searches for products can be easily correlated with evaluations of company performance in areas of social concern. That labor practices, for example, can be reviewed immediately before an athletic shoe purchase could prove beneficial to New Balance shoe merchandisers, who are well known for their fair labor practices.

Home consumers are the obvious point of interest for Internet commerce. The Web's advantages for home consumers are time and convenience. Shopping can be done while the children are napping or absorbing their television ration downstairs.

Party animals are a major target of entertainment sites on the Web. It is a reasonable supposition that suck.com is not aimed at the research audience. Similarly reams of sites exist for even the most obscure television show, cult movie, and bad habit.

The Internet offers different advantages to different groups of users. For young people, for example, it provides endless playmates and a variety of games and chats. It allows them to discuss potentially frightening topics, such as sex, religion, politics, and drugs, in the safety of their homes. The anonymity of the Internet allows young people to explore new personalities, subcultures, and roles. Users can even change their gender on-line if they so wish. Teenagers can safely hurtle obscenities and debate adults, with heady feelings of anonymity and equality. All these things draw high-schoolers and young collegiates on-line. Once there, they can shop at all hours, without the need for permission or transportation to go to the mall. It is simple to implement a site aimed at teens so that shopping and chatting can coexist. (A parallel disadvantage is, of course, that they can impersonate their parents and order merchandise that is later disavowed by cardholding adults.)

Users change their profiles over time. Early users will play, because young people play and there is no reason young people should become suddenly serious when presented with a keyboard. Some of these young people will go to college, and if previous trends prevail, they will become both more intense party animals and political expressives. Perhaps they will even manage to graduate from college. This will lead to a move into the researchers' group at first jobs or graduate schools. When people have families, the extra time gained from use of Web-enabled services will (one hopes) be spent playing with their families. These people will then move to the home consumers group in terms of Internet commerce, although they may generate the bandwidth demands of researchers at work.

How Does the Internet Work?

Why Internet commerce? Why play now when the hazards are undetermined and systems untested on a large scale? Certainly the obvious answer is, "That's where the customers are," as illustrated in the previous discussion of Internet growth. But Internet commerce also offers the potential to greatly reduce transactional overhead and remove the constraints of geography and time.

Understanding how the Internet supports varying information markets requires understanding the layers of the Internet. Discussing Internet transactions requires understanding of different network applications (news, Web browser and clients, chat) as well as layers of protocols underneath these applications.

Changes in markets, especially information markets, depend on the nature of the Internet. When publishers and advertisers pay to provide information, they are paying for attention span, increasingly referred to as *mind share*. In the information economy, attention span is going to become an increasingly valuable commodity. University Professor and Nobel Prize winner Herb Simon stated that the most valuable products in the coming years will be those that decrease information flow: filtering, rating, organization, and evaluation of products. At the time of that statement the Web was still an obscure engineering feat, but its power in organization of information has since become apparent.

The Internet Protocol

A protocol is a communications standard. A protocol defines a series of messages and the syntax for evaluating those messages. The beginning of any datastream identifies the protocol used for formatting the data for transmission. With humans, for example, the greeting will denote the tone of the following conversation. With Internet connections the protocol will define the nature of the connection: streaming high bandwidth content, store and forward text, chat, etc. The receiving machine identifies the protocol and therefore knows how to parse the rest of the data. People use standard sets of exchanges and closures for conversations that are not all that different in function from protocols. When a greeting in a human conversation is businesslike, or friendly, or aggressive, the participant who receives each of those types of greetings has information on what is to follow and how to proceed. When a network protocol is described, each message has a purpose and a form.

Consider if a human greeting was defined as if it were part of a formal protocol. Included might be standard forms for identification, mood evaluation, and topic introduction. For example, the mood evaluation query—a.k.a. friendly greeting—might be defined as:

query-> How are <pronoun> <time period> <status identifier> <Proper noun>

(e.g., How are you today, Professor Lia?).

Protocols may look complex but are only abstractions of simple, and at best graceful, underlying standards.

Imagine greeting the Queen of England with a non sequitur such as "FISH!" She would not know how to respond. Essentially this is what happens when network protocols are not interoperable. When systems lack interoperability, the connection is there, but neither machine can make sense of what the other is saying. The machines are, in a sense, speaking different languages.

The fundamental technology of the Internet is the Internet protocol. The Internet is the network of networks that are connected using IP. There is only one Internet as distinguished from *intranets or internets*, of which there are many.

IP is a connectionless protocol. That is, in IP the routes by which each part of a message will travel to reach its destination are not predeter-

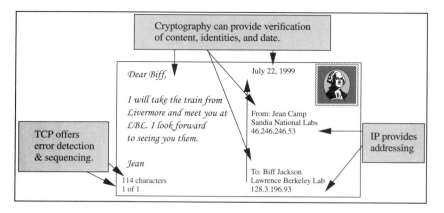

Figure 1.3
Uses of protocols

mined and the resources for message delivery not reserved. In contrast, telephone networks have traditionally been connection oriented. Connection-oriented protocols establish a point-to-point connection, from one phone to another, when communication is requested. This gives the connection-oriented protocol the ability to ensure quality of service before the connection is established.

Sending information using only IP is not unlike sending a postcard. A postcard is excellent for a discrete message. Of course it is in no way private—despite legal controls, it could be read by many. IP provides only the addressing and a best effort in delivering the data.

Figure 1.3 illustrates the analogy between packets and postcards. On the Internet, data is broken down into packets. The packets are dated and each sent independently. The packets are not encrypted; there is no virtual envelope protecting the contents. Each packet is addressed. Other protocols, including cryptographic protocols and the transmission control protocol, add other features as illustrated by analogy in this figure.

IP addresses have two parts: a network identifier (netid) and a host identifier (hostid) (see figure 1.4). The network identifier is like the state and city in a postal address: it identifies an area. The host identifier is like your house number: it identifies a specific destination in a general region. Considering at the sheer length of an IP address, it would seem virtually

class	netid	hostid

Figure 1.4
An Internet protocol address

Table 1.2
Classes of Internet protocols networks

Network class	Number of networks	Number of nodes	First bits of IP address	Min/max
A	127	16,777,214	0	0/126
B	16,383	65,534	10	128/191
C	2,097,152	254	110	192/223

impossible that there would be a shortage. After all, addresses are 32 bits long, suggesting that there are 2^{32} possible Internet addresses. In fact, the addresses are separated into different classes of networks: A, B, and C. The higher the letter designation, the shorter the network ID. This means that different size networks could be easily connected to the same network.

Table 1.2 shows how many networks of each class it is possible to have. Looking at the table and then returning to the postcard example, it is clear that Sandia National Laboratories has a class A address and Lawrence Berkeley Laboratory has a class B address. This is because the address is within the appropriate minimum/maximum range shown in the table. The number of networks and the number of hosts is limited by the size of the IP address; it is $2^{(\text{number of bits in netid})}$. The number of nodes is $2^{(\text{number of bits in hostid})}$, which is the same as $2^{(32 - \text{number of bits in netid})}$.

All this means that the number of Internet network addresses is a little over 2 million, rather than the excess of 4 billion that the simple length of the address suggests. Since the network addresses were separated into classes so that all machine could have individual addresses, the number of networks that can have addresses is limited. So, despite the simple observation of the length of the address, it is possible to have a shortage of IP addresses.

Considering that IP was developed in 1974 (Cerf and Kahn 1974) when there were sixty-two computers—not networks, but computers—on the ARPANET, allowing 2 million networks to easily connect shows foresight and the grace of fine design. The next version of the Internet protocol, Ipv6, will have mechanisms to address the shortage of IP addresses.

An IP address provides a guess on the size of a network. Of course such a guess does not always prove correct. A network may be connected to the Internet at only one point, so that it really needs only one address, and host routing can be handled behind this point of connection. This is very common with commercial sites that have firewalls[5] and extensive local area networks. Or a connected institution may use dynamic IP address-ing[6] so that they need fewer addresses than machines (so a large internal network does not require a correspondingly generous IP address).

Coincidentally, with the expansion of the ARPANET there was the emergence of BITNET. BITNET was an early network that consisted of dial-up terminals and IBM mainframes. (The UNIX-based NSFNET grew to embrace and obliterate this concurrent network.) By 1985 BITNET experienced its first exponential growth in mainframes, to seven "confer-ence machines." Mainframes ran distribution lists and forerunners of

5. Firewalls are special-purpose machines that filter traffic at the network pe-rimeter. Firewalls may manage connections by serving as a proxy for the client. Firewalls may seek, and refuse, specific patterns of connections. Within connec-tions, firewalls may search for types of traffic, in particular active content (e.g., filtering CAFE BABE (Martin, Rajagopalan, and Rubin 1997)). Firewalls may implement security policies for the institution as a whole (e.g., no unencrypted telnet sessions).

Firewalls assume two discrete sets of resources and identifiable connections between the trusted internal resources and the untrusted external resources.

6. Dynamically assigned IP addresses means that an IP address is used by a machine only during the time the machine is connected. When one machine disconnects, some other machine can use the IP address. This allows many machines that are not always connected to the network to share IP addresses.

The original design concept of IP was that a machine would have an IP address. People then kept on their own machines lists of their friends' machines (e.g., bob1). Later this did not work so well, and the Domain Name System was designed and implemented. This still assumed one machine, one address. When most machines are not connected to the Internet, this results in a waste of addresses. This is particularly true in the case of dial-up ISPs, who were the first to use dynamic IP addressing.

Usenix groups and could be considered ancestors to today's servers. In addition there were hundreds of machines that could connect to BITNET, including machines at Yale, the University of Maine, State University of New York-Stony Brook, Brown University, Harvard, MIT, and Tufts University. BITNET allowed users from hundreds of machines to run terminal emulators to come together and chat synchronously. Daniel Oberst offered the followed evaluation of the network in the BITNET monthly newsletter: "BITNET is still by and large a voluntary, cooperative network that only exists to the extent that people work together . . ."

That this comment came from BITNET illustrates an important point: networking is connectivity, it is sharing, it is trust. The following rough description of Internet routing shows why this previous evaluation remains arguably applicable. Routing provides an excellent example of trust. Routing is how a machine (given that a machine has an IP address) connects to others. Routing is, specifically, how a packet (small information chunks, like postcard greetings) gets from machine A to machine B. Routers are special-purpose machines that direct packets. Routing is also a function of a general-purpose desktop machine. Here the primary focus is on the mechanisms, not the machines. However, envisioning only a router as performing the function might make this explanation easier to follow.

Routers keep a list of all the machines or hosts to which the router is directly connected, and a list of machine to which all the physically adjacent routers are directly connected. A network to which neither the router itself nor any of the physically adjacent routers are directly connected is a remote network. For remote networks, the router keeps a continually updated list of the first step of what it believes to be the shortest path to that remote network. Routers do not store complete paths to remote destinations; they store only enough information to send the message to the next router, under the assumption that the next router will direct the message properly, and so on until the message reaches its destination. The trip between two routers is called a "hop"; regardless of the physical distance between two routers, the distance between them is still one hop. Thus routers trust the message to other routers.

Routers are always updating their beliefs about the network. At any time a router may receive a broadcast from another router about that router's stored information. The receiving router always trusts the

Table 1.3
Router database

Machine	Connected to these networks	Connected to these machines
122.46.77.32 (me)	122.46, 113.22	122.46.77.31, 122.46.77.35
128.22.36.81	128.25, 126.14, 115.22	128.25.233, 126.14.122, 115.22.004
128.14.46.98	114.7	128.14.56.33, 128.14.77.22
113.22.88.45	default	

Table 1.4
Your address book

Name	Accessible locations	Can connect to
Carlos	Chicago, Milwaukee	George, Beth
Cathy	Dallas, Austin, San Francisco	Karin, Juan, Ali
Catlin	Charlotte, Atlanta	Margaret, Sanjay
Carter	Oklahoma City	almost everyone

received information about routes and updates itself appropriately. Because of the constant updating, it is quite possible that a message consisting of several packets will travel on different paths and possibly arrive out of order. Table 1.3 illustrates this idea. The addresses on this table are imaginary numbers; the point is to illustrate the type of knowledge a router would have.

Consider the network of routers on the Internet as analogous to a social network. Imagine a world with no central information for people in various regions—in other words, no telephone directories. Imagine searching for a person—say, Gene Eric Person in San Francisco—in the way a router searches. First you would go to your address book (see table 1.4). Consider a region a subnetwork and a person a machine to make this analogy function. You would know all the regions to which you can send directly—Chicago, Dallas, Charlotte. You who also know the regions to which your direct contacts can send. Here is how a page in your address information would work if it were analogous to a router. In this

Table 1.5
Your revised address book

Name	Accessible locations	Can connect to
Carlos	Chicago, Milwaukee, San Francisco	George, Beth
Cathy	Dallas, Austin	Karin, Juan, Ali
Catlin	Charlotte, Atlanta	Margaret, Sanjay

case, you would send your message to Gene Eric Person in region San Francisco to Cathy. She would look at her address book and send it to someone in San Francisco, and that person would send it to Gene Eric.

If you did not have him in your address book, you would send the message to Carter, knowing that Carter is well connected and likely to be able to get a message to any location. Carter is your default router.

Imagine later you get an updated address book from your friend Carlos. Carlos notes that it takes him one friend, one hop, to get to San Francisco. You notice that it took three hops to get to San Francisco through Cathy. You would update your address book as shown in table 1.5.

You may find also that Carlos is two hops separate from Carolyn, who lives in Portland. You would not add Carolyn to your address book because you are not trying to build a complete and global database of every location. You just want to update your information on the best way to get to any location from your location. But the next time you looked for Gene, you would send your postcard to Carlos instead of Cathy.

The address book is your local routing. If the person you wanted to contact was not in your address book, you would call someone who would be likely to know him or her because of their location. That is, like the router, you would make your best guess from your most recent information about your network of peers as to the shortest path to the person you want to reach.

Three critical observations arise from the discussion of routing: there is no optimal physical location, there is no single point of failure, and routing is a cooperative exercise in trust.

First, there is no optimal physical streetcorner on which to reside. Customers will come from all locations, and the appearance of a Web presentation depends upon the path between a browser and the information. It is not possible to be adjacent to every browser—there is no ubiquitous next-door location. Yet there is valuable real estate in the Internet: not on the network but on the customer's desktop. A good place to be on the Internet is in the Web surfer's bookmarks. The ideal place to be is in the bookmarks that the user trusts.

An ancillary implication of this lack of optimal physical location is that there is limited possibility for monopoly control of distribution.[7] In traditional media markets there is limited competition. Consider newspaper, television, and radio markets. The ownership concentration results from expensive or exclusive distribution channels. Most towns have one newspaper because the start-up costs are too expensive in a market with an existing newspaper. The newspaper chicken-and-egg problem is that one must have a subscription base and a distribution network to have a paper. Only one radio or television station can exist at one wavelength. On the Internet there is no single advertising venue. There is no reason that multiple competitive search engines as well as multiple meta-search engines can not continue to thrive and compete. Because there is no center to the Internet, because of the routing, there is no way to ensure that every person entering a market sees one product first.

Second, in a connectionless network each packet is delivered independently, so that there is no single point of failure. So if packets are not getting through on one route, the following packets will try a different, more likely, route. Packets are routed independently of each other, and therefore are not stuck repeating previous mistakes. Because there is no central directory of addresses, there is no single point of failure. This means that connectionless networks are survivable—that is, hard to disrupt. One business implication of this is that such networks are reliable.

7. Monopolizing content control would require software at all user endpoints (for example, built into the operating system). The Internet protocol provides only transport—only distribution. The protocol does not distinguish between sources and destinations. Any user can be both. On the other hand, if Microsoft controls the browser, Microsoft may have the power to determine acceptable content and limit and prioritize selection of Web content. Especially if there were no competition in the browser market, consumers could lose the ability to set their own bookmarks. In my opinion, no other party has a chance of controlling distribution. I do not expect Microsoft or any entity to be able to create a single hierarchy or priority scheme for the Internet.

Third, routing is an exercise in social cooperation. Social networks break down from lack of cooperation. Routing could similarly break down. The widespread routing failures that I know about (there may be classified information, but a routing failure tends to be noticeable) resulted only from errors in router configuration, not from malevolence.

Transmission Control Protocol
Postcards are perfect for short bursts of information, yet they would be a terrible way to send a novel. The pages would need to be in the correct order. Every page would have to get through. If the recipient's mailbox got too full (if, for example, the recipient went on vacation), it would be important to know this and stop sending for some time. It would be important to ensure that the writing did not get smudged, torn, or covered with postmarks. The transmission control protocol, TCP, provides all of these services for messages traveling through the Internet.

TCP provides orderly and reliable delivery of data by providing flow control, sequencing, and error detection. When packets are lost, TCP backs off (which is a fancy way of saying, "slows down by slowing the transmission rate"). Recall figure 1.3, which shows some of the functions of TCP.

Flow control means that TCP prevents the recipient mailbox from overfilling or the load from crippling the mail carrier by sheer volume. Sequencing means the postcards are numbered and can be ordered into a coherent document. Error detection means there is some certainty that what is sent is what is received. (The level of error detection TCP provides is meant only to detect random network failures, however, and can be easily defeated by malicious action.)

TCP provides a virtual connection that is unlike a traditional connection in two ways. First, the information transmitted via TCP/IP does not all flow along the same path, as routers along the way are constantly updating information about optimal paths. Second, information that is transmitted later or cannot be prevented from sharing resources being used by earlier arrivals. To contrast with a traditional connection, if enough phone calls are in progress that a phone company's local switches are being used to capacity, the next person requesting service will get a busy signal. A phone call cannot connect if the connection is already in use. With TCP, on the other hand, if the service is at capacity, the service for everyone slows down as others begin to use the same resources, but no one is refused access simply for arriving late. Many Internet users have noticed this, particularly on the East Coast, where the Web slows noticeably in the afternoon as those on the West Coast begin their day.

TCP transmission begins with a three-way handshake: the caller, or initiator, calls; the receiver, or respondent, replies; then the caller verifies that the receiver has replied. This initiation includes synchronization (SYN) and acknowledgments (AK), thereby defining several important limits on the communication. First, the amount of data the receiver is willing to hold and organize is determined. This is called the *window size* in TCP and is analogous to the size of the mailbox in postal service delivery of a postcard. Returning to the postcard analogy: consider the acknowledgments in TCP short postcards in which the reader tells the writer how many pages have been successfully sent. The window size tells the writer how many can be in transit at any time. If the reader tells the writer through an acknowledgment that the first 150 postcards of the novel have been sent and the window size is, say, 50, then the writer can have sent up to 200 postcards and reasonably expect that all these cards will be received.

Second, the speed of the replies ("acknowledgments") determines the "time-out," after which a packet can assume to be lost. In the postcard example this is analogous to the time it takes for the receiver to receive a postcard, send an acknowledgment, and have the acknowledgment delivered by the postal system. Figure 1.5 shows the beginning of a TCP/IP connection.

This example provides important illustrations of trust on the Internet. TCP requires trust. TCP/IP is ubiquitous. TCP/IP requires cooperation. By 1991 the TCP/IP protocol suite consisted of about 100 implementations, and there were more than 700,000 machines using TCP/IP to connect 4 million users (Cerf 1993). TCP/IP remains the core protocol suite on the Internet, connecting all 40 million users in 1999. When people say that the Internet is inherently unreliable, they are referring to IP transmissions, as TCP, IP's almost constant companion, provides reliability.

The trust implications of the Internet, not the Internet itself, are the focus of this work. The previous descriptions were required for understanding and answering the question: What are the trust features of the

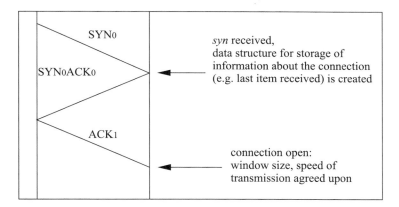

Figure 1.5
The beginning of a TCP/IP connection

Internet and Internet-like networks (i.e., packet-switched networks)? Begin with evaluation of information. Whether one is on the Internet for amusement or commerce, questions of how to evaluate information are important. Thus a brief set of questions to use in determining how to evaluate a Web page is placed in the remainder of this chapter.

I also discuss here the effect of the Internet on the practice of setting prices because pricing illustrates how the nature of the Internet can change what would seems to be unalterable facts in off-line commerce. Fixed prices for all are a basic part of the American retail tradition: changes in price discrimination hint at the fundamental changes to come. Currently prices are set on all retail products except at the high end. Prices of houses and automobiles are subject to bargaining, but those of food and entertainment are not. This is primarily because determining what each individual is willing to pay requires haggling, which is quite expensive off-line. On-line data about purchasing practices and searching enables sellers to price for the particular customer.

Barter markets and town markets allow participants to have face-to-face interaction where negotiation is possible. Internet commerce can bring back face-to-face negotiation in its virtual form. How else will money change with the electronic market? To begin to ask the question requires asking why money is what it is. Therefore an extremely brief history of money (chapter 2) is included to place information money on

Table 1.6
Hierarchy of protocols on the Internet

Protocol	Connects	By providing
Internet commerce	Consumer to merchant	Payment, possible delivery verification
Hypertext transport	Application to application	Location and presentation
Transmission control	Machine to machine	Reliable delivery of multiple packets
Internet	Network to network	Delivery of packets between networks

the evolutionary timeline. But first I continue my consideration of protocols, the stages of a transaction, and the scope of a transaction, all of which can be a function of the monetary form.

Layers of Protocol and Stages of a Transaction

The hypertext transfer protocol (HTTP) is a protocol that provides seamless delivery of different types of data and, since the Mosaic project, offers a user-friendly graphical interface. HTTP is the data formatting protocol of the World Wide Web. It allows users to easily publish and obtain information on the Internet. A browser used with HTTP provides a simple user interface that highlights other files using color or graphics. Browsers using HTTP catalog locally available applications for file display, and automatically provide the text, sound, or graphic using these local applications.

With the development of the Web, the Internet became fully capable of supporting user-friendly distributed commerce, just as previous protocols had enabled functionality from simple communication to file transmission. Table 1.6 illustrates how Internet commerce protocols have built on previous protocols, which has in turn expanded the pool of possible merchants and consumers. Without the ability to locate goods, consumers would not shop on the Internet. Without the ability to easily present goods, merchants would have difficulty selling their wares on the Internet even if they could be located. Of course, Internet commerce does not depend entirely on HTTP, as some protocols include options for users with only email and no HTTP capacity.

HTTP works on a simple client/server request and response mechanism. The Web is indeed the "killer app." Not only is it the killer app in business terms, it could have "killed" the Internet by having many short, and therefore potentially ill-behaved, connections ill-suited for TCP/IP. That the investment to ensure that the Internet will succeed and thrive has been made despite the suboptimal design of HTTP offers promise that the informal governing structure of the Internet can handle future problems that may arise.

Internet commerce has increasingly become possible with the advent of the World Wide Web. The Web is growing at many times the rate of overall Internet host growth. The Web allows the consumer to locate information of interest on the Internet without requiring any technical expertise.

All Internet commerce protocols can be used with the Web. In addition, some commerce protocols (Mastercard 1995; VISA 1995) are comprehensive and include the ability to transfer funds using only email. (For a detailed discussion of network protocols, see Schwartz 1987 and National Center for Supercomputing Applications 1995).

Commercial Transactions

Despite the demographic and geographic diversity of people on the Internet, all electronic transactions will share some features. Which elements of Internet commerce will every transaction share? On the individual level, probably nothing more than that all possible buyers will have the same number of chromosomes. At the business level, however, transactions share a structural similarity.

To understand business implications requires defining the scope of an electronic transaction and the market structure for information. These issues have each been the subject of entire texts (e.g., McKnight and Bailey 1997), so clearly only an introduction will be presented here.

Every transaction has multiple stages, from account acquisition to dispute resolution. The scope of a transaction limits the capacity of a transaction to provide reliability. If a protocol considers only the transmission of payment, then discussions of reliable verification of orders will arguably be biased against that protocol. However, customers would agree that delivery of goods is a critical element of all transactions. Because theft is theft to the consumer regardless of the framing of a protocol designer, the discussion of reliability is appropriate for every protocol, just as discussion of anonymity is appropriate for every protocol. From the perspective of the customer, if money is stolen, there has been theft. If goods are lost, there has been failure. To discuss every protocol only according to the definition of a transaction as provided by its designers would be of limited service. For risk considerations, it is appropriate to consider the entire transaction and not limit the discussion to the framing provided by the designers.

The stages of a transaction are:

1. account acquisition
2. browsing or discovery
3. price negotiation
4. payment
5. merchandise delivery
6. dispute resolution
7. collections and final settlement

Most Internet commerce protocols do not include all of these stages explicitly. In many ways comparing Internet protocols is like comparing apples to oranges. Yet such comparisons need to be made for consumers deciding among very different commerce protocols. Thus the use of consistent language, notation, and transactional scope is itself a subtle but real contribution to the understanding of Internet commerce.

Transactions begin when the customer obtains the means of payment, that is, account acquisition. Depending on the commerce protocol this may mean signing up with a transactions provider (e.g., First Virtual), obtaining a credit card account (e.g., SET), or purchasing digital coins (e.g., Digicash).

But many transactions begin with discovery, since most merchants do not have accounts per se with every customer. Both for the sake of consistency, and to reflect the strongest interest in electronic commerce research, discovery is assumed to happen through the Web, so that every transaction begins with information that can be obtained through standard HTTP requests and responses.

With these assumptions in mind, consider how each stage of the transaction is enabled or altered on the Internet. Product discovery is enabled through advertising and electronic word-of-mouth. Product information is dispersed through Web pages, distribution lists, and Usenet groups. The Web enables individuals to locate specific information and search by product or company name. Search engines, such as the World Wide Web Worm and Lycos corporate Web, which often exist solely for the purpose of distributing product information, can be located. With distribution lists, or dlists, individuals who share a common interest form a closed group and transmit messages, including product announcements and evaluations, to all members of the group. (It should be noted that distribution lists are usually motivated by a desire for general discussion, with product announcements accounting for a small fraction of the traffic.)

Usenet groups are topical discussion areas open to all. Usenet groups are well designed for topical discovery. The title of the group conveys the subject; for example, rec.pets.cats is for those who like to talk about their cats or cats in general; thus discovery of cat-related products is discussed. Usenet group members announce new products, but such product announcements are secondary to discussion. Direct advertising across Usenet groups is often considered offensive by Internet users. A business that decides to advertise by sending many messages to many Usenet groups and lists is likely to find more sworn enemies than new customers, as this violates the social ethic of the Internet. It is not trivial to effectively advertise. Distribution lists, Usenet groups, and the Web overlap. URLs (uniform resource locators, or Web addresses) of products and services are sent over distribution lists and posted on Usenet. Web sites connect to archives of Usenet groups and discussion lists. The Web is excellent for merchant-initiated information. Usenet is ideal for electronic mouth to mouth.

Price negotiation is supported by email and electronic data interchange. Information about goods can be delivered on-line. Customer support can be offered on-line through email and via Web pages.

Payment is the core issue in Internet commerce, and the protocols examined here are concerned with payment. There will evolve as many electronic payment types as exist paper payment types today. The following chapter on money discusses how digital money differs from paper monies.

Merchandise delivery is simple on the Web—for information goods. Otherwise delivery is difficult to ensure. The anonymous purchase of goods that must be accompanied by a delivery address is of limited use. The purchase of goods that are not delivered is not a reliable transaction, no matter how smoothly the monetary transfer flowed. Delivery guarantees can be integrated into payment for information goods; otherwise the situation on the Internet does not differ from mail orders.

In part because of the issue of dispute resolution, Web commerce can be superior to telephone orders. The techniques used to bind payment to merchandise delivery on the Web can be used to bind payment to receipt delivery. So, although the box may not be delivered, the customer at least has a binding promise. While this does not address issues of outright fraud, it will simplify dispute resolution by decreasing cases of miscommunication.

Collections and final settlement are both simpler and more complex in electronic form. The issues of collection and settlement are tightly bound to the nature of money and are thus clarified in the next chapter's discussion of money and reliability.

Every phase of a commercial transaction has associated costs. Figure 1.6 shows distribution of costs in a credit card transaction (Sirbu and Tygar 1995). The rate of adoption of Internet commerce partially depends on how automation can decrease the cost in the figure. The Internet allows administration of customer orders, payment or payment authorization transmission, and production of an invoice to be automated.

In addition to cost advantages through automation, the Internet allows services to be provided, around the clock, around the globe, in multiple languages, and in multiple currencies. Catalogs of merchandise can easily be found by interested shoppers at negligible cost to the merchant and can be updated immediately as prices and inventory change.

Internet commerce was used initially primarily by those already familiar with catalog marketing. Increasingly diverse types of business ventures are

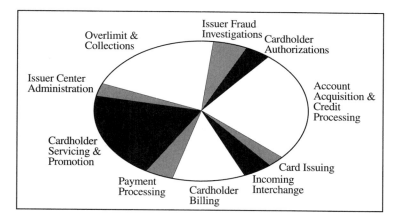

Figure 1.6
Cost distribution in a credit card transaction (Sirbu and Tygar 1995)

Table 1.7
Structure of information markets

Market structure	Electronic example	Paper example
Publisher pays	WWW catalogs	Mail-order catalogs
Advertiser pays	Lycos, Yahoo	Free weekly papers
Club pays	Clarinet, site license software	Corporate library
Customer subscription	Web magazines, dlist	Professional magazines
Customer pays per item	First Virtual	Storefront sales
Customer pays for time	AOL, CompuServe	Rental items
Mixed ads and customer payment	Prodigy, Netscape business sites	Newspaper

now on the Internet. Table 1.7 shows examples of businesses on the Internet and corresponding paper information markets (Goradia et al. 1994).

The standards that will determine how money and information flow around the Internet are being determined now, and some of the fundamental decisions about the risks businesses and consumers will take are being integrated as details in technical specifications. Examination of those specifications and enumeration of the risk is particularly timely while the standards are still in flux.

Evaluating Information On-line

Product discovery is the greatest current commercial use of the Internet. Yet the lack of validation of services and the uncertainty of the quality of information are serious issues in discovery and shopping. How trustworthy is information provided during discovery?

When a business is presented on the Web, there is no tangible information about that business. Slander, fraud, and misinformation are not confined to the Web, but relative anonymity and the lack of a need for physical presence makes misinformation easier. Those who lie can hide behind Web sites with noble faces, including words like "Justice" or "Consumers for Freedom" in their names. Because of the importance of open discourse, American judicial traditions of respecting speech, and the patchwork of jurisdictions over the Web, the reader—not the state—must take responsibility for detecting what is false and not accepting information on the Web at face value. Conversely, it is the responsibility of the creator of a Web page to show why that page should be believed.

Misinformation is the hazard in any medium of communication. In this section I discuss ways to evaluate a site to determine whether it is reliable. There is no certain test to determine from afar the quality of a product or trustworthiness of a site. However, some factors can signal falsehood or identify misrepresentations.

A competent computer science student who has been insulted, been ill-served, lost money, or had his or her affections dismissed can easily put up a Web site illustrating how the a former employer, business relation, or love object is an enemy of good—and with some small skill can make that site look quite believable. On a larger scale, an activist during the 1996 presidential race made Clinton, Dole, and Buchanan attacks through bogus sites at www.clinton96.org, www.dole96.org, and www. buchanan96.com that were sometimes clearly mocking, sometimes subtle and vicious. The casual Web browser was likely shocked by the policies and quotes found at these sites—and understandably so, as these fabrications were beautifully and professionally presented. In the 2000 presidential election, the Bush campaign has requested that the Federal Communication Commission force removal of the www.GWBush.com site on the basis that it has the same look as the official Bush campaign site and may confuse voters.[8]

Companies and organizations have so far been able to respond to Web-based broadsides such as www.netscapesucks.com (which includes the "Sucks 500"). But just as the Web has been the mechanism of angry students in the past, it will increasingly become the mechanism of angry customers and employees in the future. In learning how to deal with this, companies can take a note from those who have been subject to harassment on the Internet long before the explosion in the .com domain.

The first thing to consider when evaluating information is the source. Can you determine the source? In my hobby space, Mom's (http://www.momspace.net/), I clearly identify myself as the creator. In the presidential race examples above, however, only a search of registered domain names would have identified the source of the bogus political pages. Is it really a nonprofit organization fighting for right, or a talented undergraduate at a technical school? Who is the source? Look for the ability to contact a physical person, not through email but with a street address or phone number that connects to an actual human. This information provides jurisdiction information; that is, there is a forum in which to sue should things go wrong.

When evaluating information, look at the domain name. Does it end in .edu, .com, or .org? A real-world nonprofit organization, such as the Sierra Club, will have a domain name ending in ".org." A real company

8. The URL for searching on domain name ownership is http://www.network-solutions.com/cgi-bin/whois/whois. This should provide contact information for the domain name owner.

domain name will end in a ".com," or less likely a ".net" (or even less likely, a geographic name). The absence of a top-level domain may be a good indicator of a bogus organization—but its presence is meaningless.

When evaluating a site, consider the tone. Especially look for "loaded," or derogatory link names. If a link says "Evil Smith Hobbies is owned by the vile Bob Smith, he who stomps worms and hates flowers" and connects to Bob's page, look for evidence in Bob's own words. That the link naming him as a worm-stomping flower hater goes to his page is no evidence that he does in fact loath flora and fauna. Is the "evidence" of Bob's practices fake email from Bob? It is very easy to write text and pretend it is an email, or to edit an actual email. Which Bob Smith is it? Search the Web for Bob's own words. If an organization advocates a truly hateful idea or loathsome policy, it is probably documented somewhere, if not openly advocated. If a contribution to a hate organization results from a purchase, there will likely be mention of it elsewhere, certainly as a tribute or a shopping suggestion on the hate organization's page.

Purported Internet viruses should be subjected to critical scutiny as well. The Department of Energy incident response team, the Computer Incident Advisory Capability (http://ciac.llnl.gov/ciac/CIACHoaxes. html), offers valid virus warnings at its site, as well as advisories concerning selected Internet hoaxes. For example, it discusses the famed and bogus Good Times Virus.

The CIAC identifies several critical elements of a hoax:

• *Technical-sounding language* is not necessarily correct technical language. The very entertaining technobabble of Star Trek illustrates this fact nicely.
• *Claims of association* are easy to make. Anyone can claim that IBM or Bell Labs is sending out a warning. Yet for any credible source, check with the source before responding to the warning.
• *Exhortations to alert friends and associates* encourage recipients to forward without thinking. Checking the source will naturally lead to not forwarding hoaxes.

Always look for links to independent sources. Who links to this page? Is this just a page with many headers that will get selected often by search engines? Or do verifiable organizations link to this page? If such an organization does link, does that constitute a general endorsement of the information contained therein (e.g., "more information here"), or a specific statement of a single example of cooperation (e.g., "Smith Hobbies Haters & The Society to Loathe Bob joined us in this lawsuit for free roses.")? None of the Clinton, Dole, or Buchanan pages linked to other organizations. They were self-referential. They should have linked to political parties and, more important, the political parties should have been linked to them—and would have if they were real! Who links to pages that evaluate businesses? Virtual Better Business Bureau stickers should connect to the Better Business Bureau, and references to *Consumer Reports*' positive evaluations should link to the appropriate story in *Consumer Reports*. The ability of watchdog groups to use bozo filters[9] makes the link far more important than the image (which is simple to copy).

Of course, consider the content. Information too ridiculous to be believed should not be believed. If the things claimed are too bizarre to be true, they may well be false. Being outrageous to lure customers is not as effective on the Web. A huge $20 Levi's jeans sign and no $20 jeans will probably not work as well on the Web as in real life because it is easier to leave the virtual store without further browsing. There is no price to leaving the virtual store. There are no large plastic "Going Out of Business" banners on the Internet, because these would decrease trust and not lure customers.

Beyond evaluating businesses and organizations, one can determine if an irate consumer or angry gadfly is presenting reliable information. Consumers can effectively provide information and companies can respond. There are social and technical mechanisms with which to respond

---

9. A bozo filter is software that can be added to a Web page. A bozo filter evaluates the page that referenced the browser, that is, where the surfer clicked to come to the page with the bozo filter. Then the filter selects a responding page if the referring party is determined to be unreliable (i.e., a bozo). For example, if the referencing page has a loaded link name, the responding page explains why the link name is misleading as opposed to loading the normally selected introductory page. Better Business Bureaus cannot take the stickers out the windows of shops that violate their practices, but they can use bozo filters on the Web. Theses filters are not widely used at this time, but their obvious potential application makes their adoption probable.

to harassment or mere editorials. First, the mythical Smith Hobbies can copy the Meta Data of the complaint page so that searches that result in the complaint page will result also in Smith Hobbies' response page. Meta Data is the information about the Web page that helps the software used by search engines classify pages. To view the Meta Data for any page, just select "view source" from the browser menu. For example a page on parenting might have the following Meta Data:

<META name="keywords" content ="" birth, mother, parent, baby, child, father, child rearing, kids, family">

Of course, this also works in reverse. If a business treats a consumer badly, that consumer can take action to ensure that all searches that find the company find the irate consumer's page as well.

When a browser hits a page, it is easy to determine the referring page. If the referring page is a complaint page, use simple commands and direct that browser to a response page. This is a way to respond to complaints without pointing them out to individuals who would not otherwise be aware of them.

Pricing and Quality in Internet Commerce

Companies that use the Internet are often attempting to attract customers with "consumer surplus," or the difference between the amount a consumer would pay and the price actually paid. Companies can come closer on the Internet than off to charging every customer the most that customer would conceivably pay for any item the customer purchases. Anyone who has ever found a bargain has experienced the joy of consumer surplus.

A leader in real-time differential pricing (before its puchase by Barnes & Noble) was books.com, which offered customers the ability to compare prices easily. If Barnes & Noble or Amazon.com offered a lower price on a particular item and the buyer chose to use books.com's automatic price comparison feature, then books.com automatically matched the competition's price. On average, books.com had a slightly higher price than Amazon.com or Barnes & Noble. The consumer who did not bother to compare would pay the higher price. (Often, however, the prices were the same.) The consumer who shopped at books.com and always compared paid the lowest price if the other servers were immediately available. Of course sometimes the Barnes & Noble or Amazon.com sites were not available. In those cases books.com charged its usual price, regardless of whether it had searched for the object before and had some knowledge of a lower price. Books.com offered differential pricing between those who compare prices and those who do not.

There are social as well as business implications to pricing on the Internet. First, discrimination in markets is not inherently bad. For example, in clothing, upscale stores discriminate against bargain buyers by pricing them out of their stores. Bargain buyers go to TJMaxx instead. This better suits both buyers who will pay top dollar for selection, timeliness, and atmosphere and buyers who want lower prices. Similarly high-feature or brand-name Web sites can charge more, as Amazon.com's continued success in the face of books.com's strategy illustrates.

Second, differential pricing on the Internet cannot be based on the demographics on which socially destructive price discrimination is based. For example, in traditional markets with price discrimination, women pay more for cars. This argues for women to shop on-line for cars. Mortgage approval rates vary based on ethnicity. Yet Web pages offer the same mortgage rates to all. If the perceptions expressed by Fukuyama (1995) are widely shared, the variance in mortgage prices is a function of trust. That is, the lender and seller have less trust in certain demographic groups. This is expressed as higher rates, higher frequency of credit refusal, and higher prices.

The trust of the customer in the merchant is as much an issue in on-line markets as in off-line markets. On-line, however, trust is likely to be based on browsing habits and credit lines, not gender or ethnicity.

In Internet commerce, customer trust is the critical variable. The more a customer trusts a site, the higher the price the site can charge for what it sells. This does not suggest that differential pricing is a matter of customer betrayal; rather, it is a function of merchant reliability. Customer trust is belief that the merchant will fulfill the terms of the transaction (e.g., deliver quality goods in a timely fashion). Any customer on or off the Internet has a price/reliability sensitivity. Thus the lower price of second-hand goods. Differential pricing may mean offering a lower price to obtain a sale rather than offering a targeted higher price, based on preferences exhibited by the customer at the site at the time of purchase.

Misguided merchant attempts to make a certain amount of money on every transaction can lead to lost sales, and sometimes to sour business relationships that can last a lifetime. Consider a real-life example. I went shopping intent on buying a new car, but ended up not doing so. I very much wanted a yellow Geo Metro convertible. (This admission of personal taste should not reflect upon other recommendations in this book.) I investigated the price. I was willing to pay slightly above dealer cost and sign a long-term maintenance contract. The offer I was making was fair. When I found no takers for my offer, I bought a used Volkswagon Beetle. This is an example of imperfect differential pricing based on mistaken trust. The salesmen had greater trust in the veracity of their gender-based evaluation of me than in my ability to set a price. I had the option of sending in a male friend to make the deal—in fact a possibility I investigated. Yet I decided the business relationship was too sour. This has negative social implications, of course, but also has negative business implications for the merchant. I would not seek the friction involved in attempting to buy from a GM dealer again, based on my arguably unrepresentative experience. On the Web, it is even easier to leave the lot. Yet on the Web, there will be some merchant to take a fair offered price.

Internet users can respond to differential pricing by using the power of the Web to search; thus arises the market in mortgage rates and offers for mortgages in which there is a perception of difference. In any such market the Internet will have a distinct advantage in terms of customer trust over traditional marketing mechanisms. There is similarly a significant market for information on automobiles.

The user who would rather have a listing of selected books rather than the option of a price comparison will go to Amazon.com. The most price-sensitive user willing to do price searches on every purchase will go to books.com. Consumers will respond to price discrimination by changing how they use the Internet. Pricing will become increasingly dynamic. With Internet purchases, as with automobiles, there is much competition. If a customer experiences poor differential pricing on the Internet, it is likely that the customer will never return to the site where the error in pricing was encountered. Thus sellers must make differential pricing decisions carefully on a case-by-case and product-by-product basis.

Convergence and the Internet

Internet commerce is a subset of telephone and mail-order commerce. In a few years, Internet commerce will be distance commerce because of the technologies of convergence. (Here mail orders and telephone orders are referred to as "distance" commerce to distinguish them from emerging models of electronic commerce.) Packet telephony, advanced television, and cable modems are all artifacts of digital convergence.

What is convergence? Previously, technology has provided policymakers with three distinct platforms for speech: print, air, and wire. This resulted in the creation of four media types: publisher, distributor, common carrier, and broadcaster. These types began to converge with wireless telephony, multimedia services, and television delivered through cables. Now all tradition media types exist on the Internet: the *Wall Street Journal* is a publisher, Amazon.com is a distributor, ReMix Radio is a broadcaster, and AT&T MediaOne is a common carrier.

All media types will ultimately converge onto a single network of networks using IP switching. All these media play different roles in distance commerce. Here I compare and contrast the uses of traditional media with the Internet.

Broadcasting is especially useful for advertising and information distribution (e.g., discovery). Obviously its one-source-to-many-recipients model makes it unsuitable for purchasing; rather, broadcasting is used to encourage a purchase. Discovery is supported in multiple modes on the Internet, as previously described. Now everyone has NTSC[10] televisions and will slowly adopt digital high-definition television. With high-definition television, the television image will be as good as that on a computer screen, so WebTV will be truly useful and possible.

---

10. NTSC is the standard that defines the broadcast. Because changing the standard requires changing every television now capable of accepting broadcasts, changing the NTSC standard is a major policy and economic decision. Notice that this is in contrast to computers, where my decision to upgrade does not require that anyone else do so; nor does a decision to upgrade require a standards change.

With "Internet broadcasting," companies need to be cognizant of the recipient's capabilities in a manner that is not necessary with traditional broadcasting. Disney provides an excellent example of a failure to understand the distinctions between traditional broadcasting/advertising and the Internet. On its Web site, Disney offers much paid content and that seems reasonable, given its market power. However, to view the free part of the Disney site requires fast hardware, a very high-speed connection, and multiple helper functions. The Disney site contains every form of content: video, audio, animation, etc. This probably looks wonderful at Disney Studios. Based on my experience as a Web surfer, I would guess that Disney used its regular internal team to develop its state-of-the-art Web page. But exclusive use of the best high-end graphics—which are excellent for television—is an error on the Web because of the resources they require. Disney's site is so state-of-the-art that it is time consuming (if not impossible) to use over a 56.6 modem. Children do not like waiting for downloads and will likely not install multiple helpers. There is little or no easy-to-download content (for example, pages to print and color). The use of video and animation is excessive. Clicking around the Disney page is an experience in frustration for users who do not have the latest equipment and at least cable-modem speed connections. Finally, Disney does not have the dominance on the Web it enjoys on television, so frustrated users can easily visit the sites of competitors. Thomas the Tank is as easy to locate on the Web as is Disney. There are multiple Thomas sites with free coloring-book pages and simple interfaces suitable for a wide range of connections and machines, which are nonetheless very entertaining. Disney does not understand that the distribution dominance it has on television does not map perfectly onto the Web. Thus Disney has used a flawed publishing model for its Web site.

Distributors are the category of media most perfectly replaced by the Internet. The Internet is likely to greatly reduce the need not only for bookstands and newsstands, but for all types of distributors. Desktop computing reduced the number of middle managers previously needed to watch the books and handle the paperwork. Sales forces will be the most notable population reduced by Internet commerce. As the Disney example illustrates, dominating the distribution channel has been to this point critical in selling information goods and obtaining "mind share." The music and movie industry structures are built upon the assumption of expensive distribution channels that tend to be controlled by a few major players (i.e., natural oligopolies). This will continue to change.

Publishers of material that is not broadcast are the second category to undergo fundamental change due to the Internet. In the case of newsprint, such publishers have monopolies in most cities. The Internet promises democratic strength in that there is no natural monopoly in distribution. Limited competition in newspaper, television, and radio markets results from expensive or exclusive distribution channels. Most towns have only one newspaper because start-up costs are too high for potential competitors. One must have a subscription base and a distribution network before one has a newspaper—clearly a bootstrapping problem. Only one radio or television station can exist at one wavelength.

In contrast, on the Internet anyone can be a publisher. The network is the distribution channel and it cannot be monopolized. Monopolizing content control would require software at all user endpoints; for example, built into the operating system. IP provides only transport—only distribution. IP does not distinguish between sources and destinations. Any user can be both.

Traditional publishers, of course, find this unnerving. However, traditional publishers will also dominate on the Internet if they fulfill consumers' trust criteria. Users will go first to established sources of information because they have some preexisting trust in these locations. This fact will serve the interests of established institutions that provide product and advertising information along with the opportunity to purchase. Outrageous claims and ill-considered priorities will, however, decrease this trust and undercut their natural advantage.

The rise of the on-line magazine *Salon* (http://www.salonmagazine.com/) in the midst of the Starr investigation illustrates the role of trust in the established media outlets. The traditional print and broadcast media had consistently chosen to honor the privacy of Rep. Henry Hyde by not disclosing what they knew of his sexual conduct while simultaneously publishing the details of President Clinton's personal life. *Salon* broke with the pack by reporting the sad tale of a family destroyed by Rep. Hyde's sexual infidelity. Such reporting increased consumer trust in *Salon* and decreased trust in the traditional media. Certainly major media players have much trust remaining among consumers, but the vaunted Watergate press corps of the 1970s has evolved into the Lewinsky press corps of the 1990s, with a corresponding decrease in trust. This leads to the question: how much of market control is based on trust and how much is based on established distribution patterns? Only long-term Internet use will answer this question.

Common carriers transmit any material, regardless of the message. Telephone companies and the U.S. Postal Service are common carriers. Clearly the Internet can provide the services of common carriage. Currently the mails are used for both transactions and discovery. On the Internet mail can be more tightly targeted, for example, by asking people to sign up at a Web site for a mailing list. Because of the low cost of sending email, however, some companies send spam, or unsolicited advertisements. Yet spam is as likely to result in impassioned recipients' refusals to be customers as it is to result in additional sales.

Digital convergence usually includes broadcast televisions, radio, telephony, and cable transmissions. But more than traditional communications signals run across the wires—payment also goes through the Internet. As video, voice, debates, and newspapers converge, payment for these will converge as well. Internet commerce illustrates that money itself is converging onto a digital, Internet-transmitted form.

2

Money

Why are reliable transactions important? What are the properties of a reliable electronic commerce protocol? Who will be trusted as a reliable creator of money on the Internet? To answer these questions, we must first address a more basic issue: What is money? One may say that electronic commerce relies on electronic money. But electronic money may not retain all the properties of money. Thus a careful definition of what money is, and how that definition relates to e-commerce, is in order.

Functions of Money

What is money? As defined by its three elemental functions, money is a store of value, a unit of account, and a medium of exchange. Ensuring that electronic commerce maintains money's functions as a store of value and a unit of account is not a trivial matter, but is certainly manageable. In contrast, ensuring that electronic commerce maintains money's function as a medium of exchange is difficult. The Internet's power lies in its lack of need for physical presence. This creates a difficulty for electronic commerce, however, in that because there is no physical presence, there are also no handing of papers, no tactile examination of goods, and no certainty of receipt.

Money as a store of value requires durable storage. For money to be a store of value, it must not be easily destroyed or created. If money decays or is destroyed in storage, then it obviously does not succeed in storing the value it represents. In contrast, hyperinflation illustrates the failure of money as a store of value when it can be too easily created. Under hyperinflation, entire nations are forced to abandon money and return to

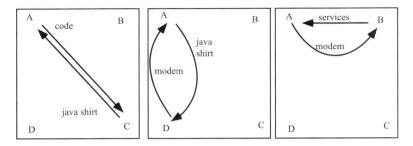

Figure 2.1
Exchanges with no medium

barter. Durable storage is a critical factor, but one that is not difficult to achieve in electronic commerce. Unlike physical money, electronic money is merely bits, and thus can be trivially duplicated. Note that this duplication of money is the same as the creation of money if the duplicates can be spent. Ease of duplication eases durable storage, but can simplify fraud. Thus ease of duplication is a double-edged sword.

Money as a medium of exchange provides a simple triangulation for all transactions. Consider the sheer number of transactions that may be required to obtain a desired good in a barter economy. A complicated series of trades may be required so that some final barter could be arranged. That is, if one person had some good (say, flour) and wanted some other good (say, software), there would be a series of transactions until the person who had flour had the goods desired by the person who had the software. Essentially this is how the Internet ran for many years.

Consider the series of exchanges illustrated in figure 2.1. A has code and wants services. B can provide services but has no need for code. A has to go through a series of trades to get what B wants, in this case a new modem. D has a modem and wants the latest Java logo t-shirt. So A has to go to C to get the Java shirt and then process a series of trades to finally be able to obtain the desired services. Using money, A and B can trade one item wanted by both, rather than a series of exchanges of goods. The comparison of the lines in the boxes in figure 2.1 and the simple exchange in figure 2.2 illustrates why this is called triangulation. Electronic money must provide for this triangulation by setting a unit of account. This is currently being done by pegging electronic moneys to a particular cur-

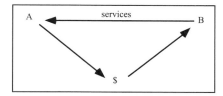

Figure 2.2
Triangulation with a medium of exchange

rency or set of currencies, so that electronic mechanisms can be used to trade dollar equivalents over the network.

Money as a unit of account also requires interoperability;[11] that is, to serve as a unit of account, any specific form of money must either be itself widely used (a standard) or readily convertible to another form that is widely used.

Money as a medium of exchange requires special transactional properties. As a medium of exchange, money must have transactional durability; that is, money must be conserved in transactions, not created or destroyed. Monetary transactions must be consistent: the amount received by the seller must be the same amount paid by the buyer, with no change in that amount occurring during the transaction. The transactional properties that enable money to serve as a medium of exchange amount to transactional reliability. Reliable transactions in electronic commerce are necessary to the proper functioning of electronic money as a medium of exchange.

What are the properties of a reliable electronic commerce protocol? The study of distributed databases has defined the characteristics of reliable database transactions as atomicity, consistency, isolation, and durability. Atomicity means that the transaction fails or succeeds completely. Consistency means that both parties know the outcome of the transaction. Isolation means two payments do not interfere. Durability means that the transaction cannot be undone without the consent of both parties. I will address these in detail in chapter 9; for the moment consider how physical transfers of money illustrate the properties of a reliable transaction. [Please note that during this and all future analyses, I take

11. This does not imply interoperability in the software engineering sense.

advantage of gender-specific language to simplify my discussion. The customer is assumed female; the merchant male; and the bank neuter. This allows me to use she, he, and it without worrying that the reader may confuse the noun referenced by the pronoun.]

Consider a customer's physically handing a dollar bill directly to a merchant and how it exemplifies each of the properties referred to above.

Atomicity: The dollar bill will not be lost as it leaves the customer's hand and is transferred to the merchant. There is always exactly one dollar; it is never duplicated or destroyed. If the dollar is dropped, then the customer can pick it up and return the transaction to its previous state.[12]

Consistency: After the transaction is completed, the merchant knows he has one dollar more; the customer knows she has one dollar less. At no point in the transaction is there ever any confusion over who has the dollar.

Isolation: That dollar bill will not be confused with a previous dollar bill, so the merchant cannot falsely claim failure to have received payment, and the customer cannot escape her obligation to make payment.

Durability: After any party receives the dollar bill, he or she retains the dollar bill until he or she transfers it in another transaction.

None of these simple physical safeguards to reliability necessarily applies in an electronic transaction. Like purchases with a dollar bill, some Internet commerce transactions are anonymous. When a merchant receives a anonymous payment using an anonymous system, it is as if the customer has thrown a dollar bill across a dark room. Who should the merchant credit with this payment? How can this payment be linked with a specific purchase if there is no customer standing in front of the merchant? Who should receive the goods? In this case, the electronic dollar cannot be identified with a specific purchase or purchaser. So the trivial issues in a face-to-face anonymous purchase are significant problems in a networked anonymous purchase. Overcoming these problems

12. If this seems impossible, consider writing two checks for the same funds. After the first check is written, the first merchant believes he has been paid, and so he has. But if a second merchant receives a check for the same funds, and gets to the bank first, the first merchant's payment has been invalidated. This may work with electronic as well as physical checks. Similarly with electronic cash, the customer could spend the same dollar twice via copies, and the first merchant to the bank gets the payment.

depend on a cryptographic public key to verify identity for a promise of payment (as described in detail in chapters 3 and 4). A public key is a mathematical way of proving identity and signing messages. If a public key is used to sign for a payments, who is at risk if the key was not valid: the verifier, the merchant, or the consumer? Right now the answer to that question depends on the physical location of the transaction. However, questions of jurisdiction are far from simple on the Internet. Knowing that the rule of law varies between Florida and Utah does not determine which law is binding. Furthermore, neither the Florida nor the Utah statute has been tested.

In electronic commerce, the payment message must travel over an open network (that is, a network without security) from the customer to the merchant. Without verifiable acknowledgment as part of the protocol, the customer has no way of knowing whether the merchant received the payment message sent by the customer. Under the Internet's standard transmission control protocol, a payment message may be duplicated if the communications protocol believes the packet containing the payment message has been lost on the network. This happens, for example, when there is congestion and messages get dropped at the congested router. Moreover, network failure may destroy a payment message. If a payment message is lost, delayed, or destroyed, confusion may result. If forced or faked network outages can create confusion profitable to someone, then such outages are sure to be created.

In sum, ensuring transactional reliability is not a trivial matter in electronic commerce. Thus the provision of reliable transactions is critical in the analysis of risk in electronic commerce protocols. Difficult technical matters involving reliability assurance may obscure business decisions and risk allocations.

Digital Information Money

In its form, money reflects the economy in which it is found. Cowry shells are the money of an inland society that trades with the coast. Tobacco is the money of an agricultural nation in which producing something that is not food illustrates wealth. Internet or electronic money is the money of an information economy. Those left holding only paper moneys, those who do not make the evolutionary leap in business practices and consummation of transactions, will be passed by.

Historically, early money in most economies was commodity money. A commodity is something that can be consumed. Commodity money fulfills the role of money as a unit of account but is less useful as a medium of exchange. After all, who could carry around an estate's worth of grain or tobacco? Commodity money is also a poor store of value. Very few commodities can be stored indefinitely, especially agricultural commodities that can rot or be consumed by rodents. Commodity money is also subject to inflation on the basis of the quality of goods. For example, after tobacco became the standard of exchange in colonial times, the streets of Virginia were flooded with quantities of inferior leaf. This dismayed the holders of money as much as the smokers. Leaf or grain may conceal impurities, such as stones, which have relatively great weight and no value.

A return to commodity money usually results from hyperinflation or economic collapse. A well-documented case of returning to commodity money is the use of cigarettes as money after World War II in Europe. Two decades later, public phone tokens were used for money following hyperinflation in Israel. In this case the commodity was arguably a service—a phone call.

Metal money typically displaces simple commodity money in most economies. Metal money is the interim money, situated between money that can be consumed and money that has no intrinsic value. It can be argued that metal money is a commodity money because metal can be turned into instruments of warfare (e.g., bronze) or used in decoration (e.g., gold). Metal money can fill all three monetary functions previously identified: it can serve as a store of value, a medium of exchange, and a unit of account. It is more easily transported in large amounts than is commodity money. Metal money can be transported over long distances—another improvement over commodity money. In particular, metal money can be transported on ships and through inclement weather in circumstances where grains and other consumables might rot. Metal money was particularly useful for international commerce in the nineteenth century.

Like paper money, metal money is subject to inflation, although certainly with stronger constraints. To wage war and finance empires, rulers through history have lowered the purity or weight of the coins of the realm. Yet not even the most creative ruler using only metal currency could not produce the hyperinflation possible with paper moneys.

The recognition that there is no actual need to hold the metal money itself in order to possess the value it represents has given rise in the modern economy to convertible paper money. Convertible paper money began with merchants and banks, who would write out notes of credit for customers declaring that they had adequate deposits to enter into a particular debt. The money specified in the note could then be converted into metal at the trustee institution. Yet the holder of the money still had the certain feel of paper in hand. These paper guarantees of deposit were the first Western trust money. The holder of the money trusted the buyer not to abscond with the gold represented by the paper money, and similarly trusted the guarantor of the deposits to hold sufficient gold in the depositor's account to cover the notes when presented.

The concept of symbolic money was a necessary (and not uniquely Western) invention before taking the next step—intangible money. Some vendors currently offer forms of electronic money that can be converted into tangible money, or greenbacks. Others offer money that can be changed into notational credits—on credit cards, for example, where changing to greenbacks can have a high overhead.

Fiat money is paper money with no guarantee that it can be converted to any other form. The U. S. dollar has been fiat money since 1971, when President Nixon took America off the gold standard. Fiat money is trust money on a larger scale. Some vendors offer electronic fiat, which works in a closed environment where it can be exchanged only for goods sold for that currency or for credits within the system of the vendor that issues it. For example, proposals for sharing computer code based on ratings of individual contributions are fiat money. In that case, one could use code based upon what was previously distributed but on a token system instead of a reputation-based system. As I describe later in detail (see chapter 11), First Virtual credits are fiat money for a matter of weeks, but there is a guarantee that if both parties (customer and merchant) act in good faith, the money will eventually be altered to notational money in the form of credits on a depository account.

Arguably one consistent trait in all these forms of money is their difficulty to produce: the labor associated with the creation of money is appropriate to the economy it serves. Thus when agricultural production was the standard, agricultural goods were standard money. As wealth increased with trade, the standard of harder-to-produce metal came to replace consumable goods. After the Industrial Revolution, when steel could be rolled out and sliced like cookie dough, the creation of detailed paper money was required. Now, anyone can produce photo-quality paper. Paper is too easy to produce, ill-suited for remote commerce, and risky to carry. Thus for moving money in an information economy, only bags of bits will do.

Social scientists would argue that all money except immediately consumable commodities are networks of trust, not just fiat money (Coleman 1990). This argument would suggest that Internet commerce is nothing new. I believe that Internet commerce is something new; never before has there been the need to establish a trusted currency for so many on the basis of such intangible connections. Further, the implications for the supply of money, for a private creator of global money, and for global commerce cannot be foreseen. Yet the historical examples of shipping, private banking, and long-distance commerce offer some guidance. Essentially history offers the lesson of caution. Even the most trusted entities may fail. Early Internet moneys may hold their value no better than did Dutch tulips in the seventeenth century. Putting the technical ability to prevent risk in the same hands as the contractual ability to distribute risk calls for careful consideration and oversight. That is, those who can best prevent risk should be the ones to bear it. And as the regulation of credit cards tells us, limiting the ability to exploit the customer may be a precondition for an explosion of the next generation of commercial instrument. So, with that in mind, now consider the risks of selecting a vendor for an electronic commerce protocol.

Money Vendors

Today the creation of money is seen as a national right—an inherent function of the nation-state. Yet this was not always the case, and there is no reason it should continue to be in the long term. As the phrase "not worth a Continental" reminds us, bankers and state governments were more broadly trusted with the ability to uphold commitments to convert money than the U. S. government in the early days of this republic. The U.S. government was able to successfully declare its national monopoly on coinage only after a century of repeated instances of financial speculation became intolerable to the public at large.

Who will offer electronic money? It appears that the first parties to offer successful electronic money have been multinational financial services corporations. These companies have several advantages. One of the greatest is that they have already established trust, or at least customer relations, in many nations. Second, they have a diversity of resources to protect their entry into the potentially risky market of electronic commerce: other financial services they provide will remain profitable while the budding Internet commerce market unfolds. They have scale in number of users; that is, there are already many consumers who use their services, and the corporations have the ability to manage all these accounts. And finally, they can offer easy interoperability between national currencies through their current international market relationships.

Another potential player in the setting of standards for electronic money is Microsoft. There is an efficiency argument for integrating the wallet into the operating system, which is the same argument for integrating the browser, ftp, and many other functions into the operating system. By integrating the standard for electronic commerce into the operating system, Microsoft can set the default standard for Internet shoppers. Integrating the wallet into the operating system has many potential advantages. The wallet can be seamlessly integrated into the browser, enabling every user to browse and buy. This will allow Microsoft to control the risks as well as set the terms. Of course, if any single company holds the coin of the information realm, consumers may find post hoc negotiations about the distribution of risk inadequate for self-protection. In any case, merchants and consumers must take care in selecting their options and reading their software licensing agreements.

Computer chip manufacturers may also set standards for Internet commerce, or at least influence those standards that function optimally. Why is integrating the wallet into the hardware such an obvious next step beyond the browser? First, Moore's law says that chip density doubles every eighteen months. But what will be the use of all those transistors now that every desktop machine can handle multimedia? Security remains computationally intensive and slows even the best desktop machines. Security is therefore the next obvious application for the denser, more powerful chips predicted by Moore's law. A fast encryption chip could determine which systems works fastest and is therefore most acceptable to the consumer.

Of course there is no reason for a single money with today's complex global financial markets. There will be specialty money and custom currencies. Small firms can offer the quick time-to-market and responsiveness necessary to serve lower-volume niche markets. There are many forms of specialized money today, such as frequent-flyer points and discount cards linked to store purchases. It is extremely unlikely that the types of money will decrease with the expansion of Internet commerce and the ease of creating new buying or point systems. Scrips, points, options, and many more as yet unimagined forms of money will proliferate as Internet commerce grows in use and popularity.

3

Basic Cryptography

Cryptography refers to numerical algorithms, implementations of those algorithms, and various mathematical and programming tools used to meet security goals. Cryptanalysis, or the study of those elements, is an ancient science, certainly thousands of years old.

Cryptography can provide authentication and integrity for electronic transmissions if properly implemented. Information protected using cryptography can be transmitted confidentially, dated reliably, signed verifiably, and be simultaneously private and verifiable.

Figure 3.1 shows analog equivalents of the functions of cryptography. Recall that the Internet example is not unlike a postcard—a postcard written in pencil where data can be easily changed. Continuing with that analogy, imagine that cryptography can provide an envelope to prevent snooping (in other words, ensure confidentiality). Cryptography can provide the seal on the envelope to assure the message has not been changed (i.e., assure integrity). Cryptography can provide the signature on the bottom of the letter (this stands for nonrepudiation and authentication of the sender). Cryptography can also provide the lock on the envelope—assuring authentication of the recipient.

There is no single foolproof way to ensure that a cryptographic function is secure and hard to subvert. Schneier's *Applied Cryptography* describes many algorithms, for what they are suited, and how they may fail. Thus when considering a purchase of a product for encryption of data, it is good to have some rules of thumb. (I recommend the Snake Oil FAQ, at http://www.cis.ohio-state.edu/hypertext.faq/usenet/cryptogrpahy-faq/snake-oil/faw.html. Much of this discussion is adapted from that more extensive document.)

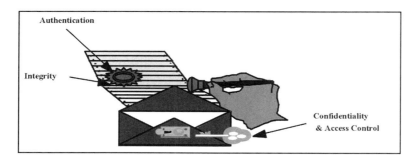

Figure 3.1
Analog equivalents of cryptographic capabilities

Two claims reveal with near certainty that a cryptographic algorithm is not to be trusted: it is proprietary and it is advertised as "proven secure." Owners of proprietary cryptographic algorithms argue that theirs are superior to other algorithms because they are secret. This argument is clearly specious because every product that uses the algorithm must contain it. Even purveyors of secure hardware should be wary of reverse engineering. Consider the difficulty involved in keeping an algorithm widely used in many products secret, versus the effort required only to keep a company or personal set of cryptographic keys secret. If readers of this book take only one recommendation to heart, let it be never to buy a secret, proprietary cryptographic product.

Algorithms can be proven to be immune from certain specific attacks, yet cryptographers are always working to find new methods of attack. For example, there is no attack on full data encryption standard (DES) more effective than just trying keys over and over until the correct one is found. (This is called a *brute force* attack.) Proving that an algorithm is secure is beyond merely daunting. Consider that the most widely used public key algorithm, RSA, is based on a premise that large numbers are hard to factor. But although mathematicians have been working on this question for centuries, it is still only a hypothesis; it has never been proven.

Other warning signs of cryptographic products to avoid:

• Technobabble: the use of copyrighted or new terms to describe the system suggests that common terms would be less than flattering. If even the description of the product is veiled in sales rhetoric too dense to understand, how easy can it be to use?

• Products that claim revolutionary breakthroughs. The vendor who claims revolutionary breakthrough in cryptography is either lying or ignorant.

• Testimonials from experienced security experts and rave reviews. Ask for biographies of the experts. Television interviews do not a cryptographer make. Hackers who understand telephone systems are not necessarily cryptographers; these are two very different sets of skills. Examine the rave reviews and ascertain that they were given for the product's cryptographic strength and not something like the graphical user interface.

• Any implementation that depends on humans for randomness is fundamentally flawed, as humans are a notoriously bad source of randomness. One-time pads[13] are the strongest possible type of cryptography. Unfortunately they are very hard to make. The source of the numbers has to be truly random, like radioactive decay, not some fancy function that tweaks the bits.

• Claims of key recovery that point to system flaws. The vendor may have escrow[14] systems that obtain and copies of the key. Escrow systems add complexity and require that the vendor be trusted with all personal and business keys generated. If there is no key recovery feature, then the vendor must break the system to recover the key, which means someone else can too. Thus, if key recovery is absolutely required, escrow is preferable to a flawed system, but neither is best.

• A claim that the system is "military grade." This is babble. There is no such classification. Again, the vendor is either dishonest or ignorant.

• The assertion of exportability. There is a joke in some cryptographic circles. Q: How do you prove an algorithm is not secure? A: Export it. There is some truth in this jest. For an implementation of a cryptographic

---

13. A one-time pad in electronic communications is a stream of bits that is random and as long as the messages sent. A true one-time pad cannot be broken—without the key it is a random string of numbers and any one plaintext is as likely as any other. One-time pads are rumored to be used on the U.S.-Russian hotline. One-time pads are incredibly expensive. Thus most "one-time" pads either use pseudo-random generators (generating predictable keys) or reuse very long keys (making it possible to break the code).

14. Key escrow means that there are copies kept of the cryptographic keys on which system security depends. This requires sending copies of keys to escrow agents whenever keys are generated, and storing those keys for as long as required by the vendor's escrow guarantee.

algorithm to be exported, either the keys have to be sufficiently short that they can easily be broken through brute force, or the system has to have some form of key escrow. Make sure any exportable algorithm uses the latter. Since security is not simple, any escrow feature will make a system less secure. (Thus another relevant engineering phrase is KISS: "Keep it simple, stupid.") Of course domestic strength from U.S. vendors is widely available, or cryptography with no escrow features with keys of any length can be imported. Thus there is no reason to make this difficult choice between system weaknesses.

Private Key Cryptography

There are two basic types of encryption techniques: private key and public key. Private key encryption uses one key that is shared between various parties. A physical analog of a private key system is a shared lockbox; that is, a box with a lock to which a particular set of people have the keys. Those who have the keys can add contents to the box, and the same people can remove contents. Thus the presence of something in the box does not prove that a particular person put it there, only that one of the people with the key put it there. Private key cryptography uses one key for both encryption and decryption and is therefore sometimes called *symmetric key cryptography.*

Recall figure 3.1. Symmetric key cryptography (figure 3.2) can be used to provide a envelope—shielding what would be the Internet postcard from the eyes of observers. This means symmetric key systems provide confidentiality.

Private key systems can be used for authentication between parties who share a key. Thus if Alice, Bob, and Carol share a key, Alice can present the key to Bob and claim to be Alice. However, Bob can also present the key to Carol and claim to be Alice. Thus private key systems create the opportunity for *replay attacks* (see figure 3.3). Replay attacks are attacks in which information used for authentication is literally replayed, over again, enabling the person who replays the data to masquerade as another. In this case Bob got the information by talking to Alice. Bob could also have gotten the information by watching Alice's communications across the wire and copying the bits, like listening to a telephone call and recording the conversation.

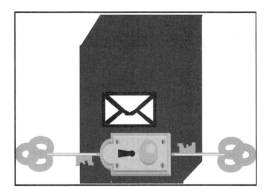

Figure 3.2
Symmetric- or private-key systems

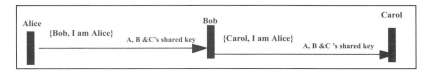

Figure 3.3
A replay attack

Public Key Cryptography

In public key cryptography there are two mathematically related keys. The publication of one key provides no information about the other key. Anything encrypted with one key can be decrypted only with the other key. One key is held secret, shared with no one. The other key is widely publicized. This is why public key cryptography is sometimes called *asymmetric cryptography* (see figure 3.4). Information encrypted using the secret key can be decrypted only with the other, public, key. Information encrypted with the public key can only be decrypted with the secret key.

Secret key encryption can function as a digital signature in two ways. First, if a document can be decrypted with the published key, this proves that only the person with the corresponding secret key could have made the original encryption. Since anyone can access the publicized key, this

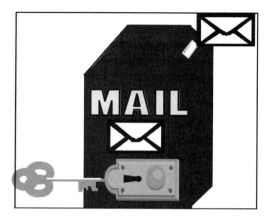

Figure 3.4
Asymmetric or public-key systems

verification can be performed by anyone. Second, the odds against transferring a signature on an electronic document to another document are astronomical.

Information encrypted with the published key can be widely broadcast, but remains unreadable to everyone except the holder of the secret key. This characteristic can create a virtual sealed envelope.

Public key cryptography is based on *one-way functions*. A one-way function is easy to do, but hard to undo. In the physical world, for example, pouring milk from a glass onto the floor is easy to do but impossible to reverse. Cryptographic one-way functions, on the other hand, always have a trap door. Opening this trap door requires the cryptographic key. It is much easier to multiply two large numbers (do) than it is to factor one large number (undo). The public key encryption algorithm RSA (Rivest, Shamir, and Adleman 1978) is based on the difficulty of factoring numbers. A second common cryptographic authentication technique (Schnorr 1990) is based on the discrete logarithm problem. Other techniques (Feige, Fiat, and Shamir 1987; Rabin 1978) are based on the difficulty of finding square roots, which is a special case of factoring.

Public key systems have several advantages in providing authentication, one of which is that replay attacks are more difficult. Simple replay attacks do not work with public key systems, as shown in figure

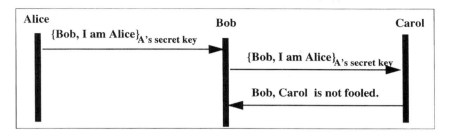

Figure 3.5
Simple replay attacks fail with public-key cryptography

3.5.[15] Here Carol is not fooled because Bob addresses her as "Bob." Bob cannot take the message apart as he could with the private key system because he does not have access to the key Alice used to encrypt her message. Bob cannot break the message into parts and send only the part of the message he wants because the signature encrypts the entire message—not bit by bit. This is because modern cryptography systems act upon the entire message, or on large blocks of a message, not on easily separated small message blocks.

Public key systems can provide authentication, access control, and integrity. Public key systems provide integrity through the use of digital signatures: messages encrypted with the secret key. It can be decrypted with the publicized key, so anyone can verify that the accompanying message has not been changed. Anyone who might open and alter the document cannot then re-sign it with the secret key, so integrity and authentication of the initiator are ensured.

Hash Functions

A third type of useful cryptographic functions is *hash functions*. Hash functions are one-way functions with the property that, given the output, it is difficult to determine the input. Hash functions transform information so that it can be used for verification but not read. The output of a

15. Man-in-the-middle-attacks, where Bob can get Alice to encrypt any message, do work against public key systems, but these attacks are more complex than simple replay attack as they require the oblivious but active cooperation of Alice.

hash function is typically much smaller than the input. Think of hash functions as unpredictable compression functions. When data has been transformed by a hash function, it can be said to have been hashed. The output of a hash function is called a hash value.

Hash functions are subject to attacks based on the *birthday paradox* (Mosteller 1965). How many people must be in room to have a 50 percent chance that two people have the same birthday? If you did not already know the answer, it was probably fewer than you thought: only twenty-three.[16] This holds across all values—for example, there need be only 100 people in a room for there to be 99.99 percent certainty that two people share a birthday, although an initial guess might be closer to 365. This is because calculating corresponding birthdays in a room is a special case of sampling with replacement. Thus to calculate the probability that out of x people, two have the same birthday, the formula is:

$$1 - \frac{365!}{(365-x)!\, 365^x} \; .$$

This same principle applies when trying to calculate hash value collisions. In a sample of all numbers of x bits, collision occurs when two have the same value. Thus the birthday paradox is an example of a collision of birthdays. To find hash values by trial and error alone, an attacker must hash exponentially fewer values than might be expected (on the order of $2^{n/2}$ values, where n is the size of the hash value). Thus even though hash values compress larger files into smaller amounts in an unpredictable manner, hash values less than 128 bits are not considered secure.

In sum: hash values compress data in a unpredictable way. This makes it possible to verify large files by signing small hash values of the file. Since a hash can take a large file and make a verifiable output, hash values are occasionally called thumbprints. This can be defeated not by running the hash function backward, but by making hash values of so many different alternatives that there is a collision. Some hash functions are designed so carefully that this approach is remarkably unlikely to work. This class of hash functions is called collision-free.

16. This requires two assumptions. First, all births on February 29 are ignored. Second, a uniform birth rate across all remaining days is assumed.

4

Security Goals

In this chapter I define the goals of computer security and introduce some tools used to meet those goals. Some of these goals cannot be realized without reliable transactions as well. Reliability, and related transactional characteristics, are described in the following chapter. Security, privacy, and reliability are not entirely separate. Security requires reliability. Security can provide authorization, authentication, and integrity. Security and reliability are both required to ensure that a system is available to legitimate users even when under attack. Yet a system without security can offer reliable service to consummate users' fraudulent transactions. Properties of secure and reliable systems, and the tools used to ensure security and reliability, are defined in these next chapters. Appreciating the technical analysis and its implications requires an understanding of security, privacy, and reliability in electronic commerce. This chapter will provide the necessary definitions of some fundamental security tools and concepts.

Security is the control of information. In a secure system the ability to view, change, and distribute information is controlled by the technologies that implement the security policy. Usually security is the control of information by the owner of the information; however, as systems become increasingly decentralized, security may mean that the user or the creator of the information can control the information. Intellectual property controls would allow the creators of information to control its distribution.

Security ensures that authorized parties are properly identified and their messages sent through a network unaltered. A secure system ensures that the origin of a message is as stated and that the intended content is sent only to the intended recipients. The ability to ascertain the validity of a message is clearly necessary when the information transmitted is a promise to pay or deliver merchandise, or a confirmation of payment.

Note that security is not privacy. Privacy means that the subject of information can control the information. Thus privacy requires security, since security is control over information. However, security is not sufficient for privacy, since the owner and the subject of information may have different interests in and uses for the data. In fact, security may preclude privacy by ensuring that the subjects of information have neither control nor knowledge of the uses of that information.

Later in this book, during the analysis of specific protocols for Internet commerce, I discuss security strengths and flaws. This is not meant to imply that design issues eclipse implementation issues; as in the physical world, a good design does not guarantee a good outcome. However, even the best implementation cannot overcome a design flaw. To learn more about practical approaches to implementation issues, see Garfinkle and Spafford 1986; Denning 1982; and Pfleeger 1989.

Threats to Electronic Information Systems

As in the physical world, in electronic systems security is never absolute. In no case is it impossible to undermine the security of a system. It is important when estimating the cost of security in electronic commerce systems to recognize that these breaches, once they have occurred, can go undetected for some time. In addition, the physical difficulties and dangers that limit the attraction of repeated robberies and break-ins in the physical world do not exist in the electronic realm.

The difficulty of defeating the security mechanisms in a system is referred to as the *work factor*. A system's work factor is the processing time and cost in processing power necessary to defeat the system. A system is considered strong, or a message verifiable, if the cryptography used to protect it has a prohibitively high work factor.

Fundamentally there are three ways to obtain electronic information without authorization: copy it during transmission, access it during storage, or obtain it from an authorized party. Attacks on data transmission include eavesdropping, replay attacks, and cryptanalysis. Eavesdropping is the act of surreptitiously monitoring a communication. A common criminal application of eavesdropping is the theft of calling-card numbers as they are punched into publicly visible phones. Cellular fraud (which is most often implemented by programming one phone to charge calls to another) depends on ease of eavesdropping to obtain the identification codes of the targeted victim's phone. Once electronic information has been stolen, it can be easily and anonymously transferred over a network. Encrypting transmissions can reduce or eliminate the benefit gained by eavesdropping over a network.

Replay attacks take advantage of the ease of duplication of information. Merchants can attempt to be paid twice by replaying electronic messages that authorize payment. This is similar to the use of a credit card number to make additional, unauthorized charges after an authorized transaction. Similarly, individuals can defraud legitimate users of a system by replaying authentication sequences to authorize illegitimate payments. The general problem of replay attacks can be solved in two ways. First, authentication techniques impervious to replay attacks— called *zero-knowledge authentication techniques* (Feige, Fiat, and Shamir 1987; Tygar and Yee 1991)—can be used. Zero-knowledge authentication techniques are mathematically graceful and underused.

The other solution to preventing replay attacks is to add information, analogous to a receipt number, to each message to make it unique. To add information to make transactions unique requires that the information be random. Adding predictable information does not prevent replay attacks because attackers could guess the information to be added and replace it for the next message. Such added information is usually presented as a random number and called a *nonce*. Sometimes nonces have two roles, such as transaction identifiers or identity challenges. Nonces are simple to the point of trivial, as well as multipurpose, and are therefore widely used.

Encrypted transmissions can be attacked using cryptanalysis, or the analysis of encrypted transmissions to break an algorithm or obtain a key. It can be defeated by using secure algorithms with well-chosen keys. It is not possible to protect against cryptanalysis by using a secret algorithm because a cryptanalysis can guess the algorithm by looking at the input and output, unless the algorithm is flawless. If the algorithm is flawless, then it can be published without being broken. In fact, using a proprietary algorithm can be very risky, because algorithms not subject to widespread review are more likely to contain a flaw.

Cryptanalysis is also used in attacks on the authentication systems that protect stored data. Such attacks are the electronic equivalent of an attack on a bank's vault. Building a secure server is difficult, and the concentration of valuable data in one virtual location can make the value of a successful assault extremely high. Weaknesses in operating system and windowing environments can undermine apparently secure applications. If an application is running on an operating system that is not secure, then the files the application needs to trust can be altered. Finally, unlike the case with a physical vault, a successful attack on a secure server may go undetected.

Secure information is commonly protected by passwords. One form of attack on password-protected systems requires that encrypted copies of users' passwords be available to the attacker. Attackers then encrypt popular passwords, such as dictionary words, and compare these values to those in the encrypted password files. By encrypting and looking for a match, the attackers do not have to decrypt anything.

The third method for illicitly obtaining electronic information, the subversion of security through the confidence of a trusted party, is in no way unique to electronic commerce. The most that security can offer in such a case is the ability to track the individual who improperly released the protected information.

Finally, there are denial-of-service attacks. In denying service the attacker does not obtain information, but instead prevents anyone else from obtaining information. These attacks limit the availability of a commerce system, denying access to both merchants and customers. Analogous denial-of-service threats—that someone will damage your business premises or threaten your customers—exist in the physical realm.

Confidentiality

Confidentiality is secrecy. When a message's confidentiality is preserved, only intended recipients can read it. Eavesdropping is either prohibitively difficult or useless against confidential transmission.

Yet confidentiality alone is not adequate for security, as illustrated in the following example. A classic problem in computer science is called the Byzantine Generals problem. (The historically inclined might recognize it as the Spanish Armada problem, which Lord Nelson handily used.) The scenario is this: two generals are camped on opposite sides of a city. If their armies coordinate an attack, then they will be victorious. If they attack at different times, the forces of the city will defeat them. One general needs to send a message to the other that is confidential (so the city forces will not be prepared) and correct. Imagine they have illiterate messengers, so that any written message is confidential. Yet the messenger could still alter the message. So if a message saying, "Attack Not, Retreat" was altered to read "Attack, Not Retreat," or a one becomes a seven, or the message becomes illegible when the attack was imminent, the communications channel has not functioned securely, because of a loss in message integrity.

Confidentiality is also not privacy. Gossip is a classic example of confidentially communicated but privacy-violating information. The integrity of a message depends on the ability to determine the identity of its initial author. When Carol whispers to Alice that the boss said Bob was a better employee than Alice, Alice knows the soft-spoken conversation behind closed doors is between only two. However, the integrity of the message leaves something to be desired. After hearing this missive, Alice cannot be sure her boss actually said it. The ability to violate with impunity Bob's or the boss's privacy by repeating their words or words about them depends on the cooperation of the listeners to keep the message confidential and thereby not verify the accuracy of the information. This also further illustrates the difference between privacy and confidentiality.

The simple case of gossip also provides a nice illustration of security in transmission versus security in storage. Carol's communication to Alice is confidential, but neither party can be sure that the information will be kept confidential. Alice does not know how many people have access to this piece of information in Carol's head; Carol does do not know to whom Alice will speak.

Different degrees of confidentiality are possible in electronic transmissions, as confidentiality can depend on simple passwords, complex one-time passwords, secure connections, or more advanced technologies.

Availability

Availability is exactly what it sounds like: keeping a system up and running. Malicious hackers, network failures, or commercial espionage can compromise system availability. Denial of service can be costly, whether it results from an attack, a design failure, or an accident. To be useful and marketable, a system must be consistently available.

Availability for the individual merchant or customer is a function of network availability, server availability, and protocol scalability. Availability can be a function of protocol design. The TCP-based attacks called *SYN flooding* are an example of a denial of service attack made possible by inherent requirement for trust in a protocol. (Recall that SYM refers to the communicating parties synchronizing in order to communicate.) TCP has a three-step process for initiating a connection, as described in the previous chapter. The caller calls, the receiver responds, the receiver puts aside some resources to deal with the connection, and the sender then confirms the response. This is analogous to interrupting paperwork and answering the phone. There is some overhead of interrupting work (time wasted, concentration interrupted, etc.), and greetings are exchanged before significant communication takes place. If there is no response when the phone is picked up, most people would query the line a few times before hanging up. If nine out of ten phone calls were prank calls, then the subject of the prank would get no work done. Similarly, the machine that accepts a TCP request for a connection creates a data structure and reserves space for information about the connection. Then the recipient holds this space available and waits for the requester to sender the connection.

Recipients trust that the sender is honest in desiring a connection. In a flooding attack, the sender takes advantage of this trust. The sender does not acknowledge the open connection and thus leaves a *half-open* connection (see figure 4.1). Instead of using the connection, the attacker continues to send TCP requests until the server is unable to serve any new requests but the bogus requests (because connections already established are not affected). Measures to prevent such attacks include refusing many requests from a single domain; increasing the amount of space available to hold half-open connections; refusing requests from obviously bogus

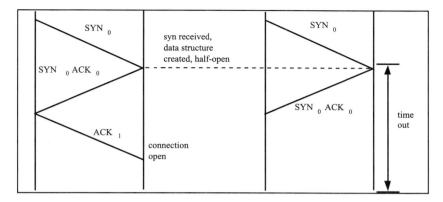

Figure 4.1
A three-way handshake and a half-open connection

domains; and reducing the time a data structure remains reserved when waiting for a message to verify the connection (Schuba et al. 1997). Notice that this is an attack against a server—in the network the increased flooding results in lower service rates for everyone, but no one person can be blocked off.

A commerce system may depend on *real-time* access, rather than providing off-line authentication. Certainly consumers expect real-time responses. System availability is a function of the reliability of the network as well as the number and size of messages required by the protocol used for transactions and transmission. Protocols vary in the ability to confirm information without access to the central server. In Digicash, the merchant can confirm the form of an electronic dollar off-line. This means the merchant can be certain that the digital dollar presented was at one time verified by a bank. The merchant still has to go to the bank, however, to be certain that the token has not already been spent. A later version of Digicash tries to assure that anyone who spends money twice will be caught. This provides some assurance to the merchant, so the merchant does not need to contact the bank at every transaction.

Availability requires reliability, but reliability is not sufficient for availability. Availability requires that a system be scalable in the number of users. Availability and scalability are functions of the need for central processing.

Scalability

Scalability in the context of electronic commerce means scalable in the number of connections, the number of transactions, the size of transactions, and the number of users. I address scalability here because availability is be a function of scalability, not because scalability is a first-level security goal in its own right.

One way to ensure scalability is through *load migration.* Migrating processing load away from the server to the customer or merchant can increase scalability. The design of the automated teller machine system migrates load by requiring terminals to verify personal identification numbers (PINs) off-line before making a request to a remote bank. An electronic commerce project at Carnegie Mellon (NetBill) decreased the central servers' load by making the merchant sign messages using the Rivest Shamir Adleman (RSA) public key system, whereas the central server uses the Digital Signature Standard (DSS) (Cox, Tygar, and Sirbu 1995). Using both RSA and DSS serves to distribute load because DSS signatures require relatively few central processing unit (CPU) cycles, but are complex to verify. Conversely, RSA signatures are computationally intensive but easier to verify. Therefore the merchant server does more work than the central server, ensuring that the central server is available to respond to requests quickly. This illustrates that while a protocol that concentrates the processing in a central server might appear at first glance to be preferable to one that requires more work on the merchant side, the advantage of scalability can outweigh the disadvantages.

A second option in scalability is to offer batching services, so that transactions can be scheduled according to the availability of the central server. The electronic commerce mechanism designed by Visa and Mastercard (Secure Electronic Transactions, or SET) offers merchants the option of batching transactions. Thus the on-line bank server (the gateway) may offer high average response time, but the time it takes to authorize or capture a single transaction may be quite high. In evaluating a protocol that addresses scalability partially though batching, it is important to consider the variance as well as the average transaction response time.

Authentication

Authentication is the goal of knowing that a particular user is authorized to take an action, for example, authorizing a charge to an account. Tools used to meet the authentication goal include passwords, cryptographic keys, and challenge/response mechanisms. Secure systems limit resource use according to user attributes (usually identity). Authentication establishes user identity or other appropriate user attributes. The appropriate user attribute is then compared against a table of permissions (such as read, write, alter) to determine functions for which the user is authorized.

Authentication is implemented either using shared information or the ability to prove unique information. The latter is simplest and requires that one party present information as proof of identity to another party. PINs and passwords are common examples of simple authentication. Authentication techniques that require one party to present verified identification information require that the presenting party trust the verifier.

In the case of PINs, the customer's ability to produce a unique number provides authentication. Since the customer provides that number to the merchant's terminal, this means the customer must trust the terminal. In practical terms, this means that one badly protected or unreliable ATM can harm any bank connected to the network. The requirement for customer trust of ATMs enables attacks such as bogus ATM machines (Davies 1981; Business Week 1993; Johnson 1993); thieves programming ATM cards with others' information (Harrison 1994); and large losses at badly managed machines (New York Times 1995a, 1995b). A similar weakness in the credit card clearing system allows disbarred merchants to use terminals belonging to dishonest merchants (Van Natta 1995).

A mutually trusted authority simplifies the problem of authentication. This authority can either provide verification of authorization upon request or provide electronic letters of introduction. (This is done with digitally signed certificates, as explained in the next chapter.)

Cryptographic techniques and digital signatures using these techniques enable mutual authentication (Rabin 1978; Schnorr 1990; Feige, Fiat, and Shamir 1987; Rivest, Shamir, and Adleman 1978). With mutual authentication, each party can prove authorization to the other and neither party has enough information to later impersonate the other.

Untrustworthy hardware creates problems that can be addressed in three ways: by requiring secure hardware, by requiring merchants and customers to secure their own terminals, and by accepting the cost of fraud. Electronic transaction systems that require secure hardware are called *smart card* systems. Most on-line systems require customers and merchants to ensure the security of their own hardware. Systems that simply trust the user and accept the corresponding losses are called *crypto-less* systems.

Even when all parties are honest, networks are not always reliable. Therefore, the reliability of unauthenticated acknowledgments should not be critical to the security and reliability of an electronic commerce system. Some electronic commerce protocols assume reliable acknowledgments. Although higher-layer protocols can provide acknowledgments that packets are delivered, this does not include the acknowledgment of the contents of the packet. Thus the acknowledgments developed for reliable packet transmission are inadequate for verification for electronic commerce transactions. These acknowledgments are not secure; thus they do not provide verifiable information.

Authentication enables access control. Access control allows different levels of access for individual files or data fields. Table 4.1 offers a theoretical example of access control for a hypothetical credit record. Note that access control can protect privacy as well as integrity by limiting both read and write access. For example, an employer can write information about disability payments if they are made, but there is no reason for the employer to be able to read past disability payments.

Access control also creates privacy conflicts. Access control can protect privacy by keeping records of who used the data about a specific individual. By increasing individual control of the data, access control has the potential to increase individual privacy. Conversely, access control can limit privacy by keeping track of data used by a specific individual, in this example by a financial services worker. For example, if every record viewed or written by a loan officer has been authenticated by that loan officer, it would be a trivial matter to track the loan officer's behavior in detail. Thus access control would increase the privacy of everyone who

Table 4.1
Access control list

Data party	Mortgage status	Income from disability insurance	Employment history	Current debts
Individual	Read	Read	Read	Read
Bank	Read/Write	None	Read	Write
Employer	None	Write	Read/Write	None
IRS	Read	Read	Read	Read/Write

had credit records, but the loan officer's workplace would become a place of constant surveillance, reducing the loan officer's privacy.

Integrity

A recipient of a message with transmitted integrity knows that the contents of the message have not been changed. But integrity alone is not security. For example, if a message that claims to be from an account holder is actually from a thief, integrity can ensure that the message transmitted is the one the thief sent, but integrity does not prevent the theft.

Encryption can provide integrity. A document that is digitally signed is a document that is encrypted. Encrypting a document with a private or symmetric key provides the recipient with some certainty that the document was not altered. Symmetric key encryption provides confidentiality, integrity, and possibly authentication. Symmetric key encryption provides confidentiality because only the holders of the symmetric key can read the message. Integrity is provided because when a message protected by cryptography is altered, it becomes garbled upon decryption. If the key is shared between only two parties, authentication is provided as well, since the recipient knows the sender must have encrypted it.

Using a symmetric key for verification of transmission requires that the recipient and the signer share trust on the contents of the document. With symmetric key encryption, any holder of the symmetric key can modify the document. For this reason digital *signatures* usually refer to public-key signatures, which means that the document is encrypted with the secret key of the sender's public key pair. Public key signatures provide integrity and authentication, and therefore irrefutability. (An action is irrefutable if it can be clearly proven to a third party that the action occurred.) Authentication is provided because only the sender could have encrypted the document with his or her secret key. Integrity results from the cryptographic security of the signature. Because the recipient could prove that the document was encrypted by the possessor of the private key and that the message has not been altered, public key signatures provide irrefutability. Notice that because anyone with the publicized key can decrypt the message, public key signatures do not provide confidentiality.

Clear signing refers to signing a hash of a document and sending that with the original document in the clear (i.e., not encrypted). This is particularly effective with large documents because it removes the need for multiple encryption operations. The transmission in the clear of the accompanying message means that clear signing does not provide confidentiality. Clear signing provides integrity, authentication, and irrefutability.

Nonrepudiation

Nonrepudiation means that an individual cannot reasonably claim not to have taken an action. Nonrepudiation means an action is irrefutable. In physical commerce nonrepudiation is obtained through controlled hardware tokens (such as credit cards) and physical attributes (like physical signatures).

In electronic commerce nonrepudiation is obtained through use of digital signatures. A digital signature is created when a user encrypts a document using his or her secret key. Then anyone with the user's public key can decrypt the encrypted document and thus prove that the encryption could have been done only by the original user.

Thus there are many types of cryptography and all have their prices, in terms of processing power in addition to licensing fees. Choosing the right type of algorithm means picking one to suit your needs, because there is no such thing as the "best" algorithm, just as there is no such

Table 4.2
Cryptographic tools and uses

	Zero-knowledge protocols	Hash functions	Asymmetric encryption	Symmetric encryption
Authentication	X		X	X
Confidentiality			X	X
Integrity		X	X	X
Nonrepudiation			X	
Safe from replay attacks	X			

thing as the "best" paper product. Table 4.2 summarizes the uses of various tools and their relationships to the properties described in this chapter.

Nonrepudiation is possible without identity information. In fact, identity information should be a fail-safe, for the case that there is a system failure. Linking to identity is a second-order attempt at accounting liability. Identity linkage allows a party that has not been served or paid to record this fact. Thus what is really necessary is linking a specific action to a key: the right to an item, the right to spend a specific type of money, etc. It is far better to be certain of payment or service than to be able to report failures to law enforcement. Nonrepudiation of action, rather than identity, should be sought in Internet commerce transactions.

Key management is a critical element of risk management in electronic commerce. The loss of a key should be both unlikely and have limited potential for damage. Linking a key to authorization for only a single action (e.g., authorize a charge to a single account) or a set of actions both limits loss and increases reliability.

5

Key Management Is Trust Management

Cryptographic key management is trust management. This chapter builds on the understanding of cryptographic technology and describes the trust relationships as implemented through key management. Digital signatures depend upon the trust hierarchy that validates that a particular digital key corresponds to a particular signer. Digital certificates are electronic certificates (like electronic driver's licenses) that link identity and attribute, but identity is not a Boolean variable. There are degrees of identity, with new mechanisms available for ensuring anonymity and pseudonymity.

A valuable feature of public key systems is the ability to have digital nonrepudiation. Such systems have another critical feature, however, that also makes them remarkably functional in distributed electronic commerce: the simplification of key management.

The management of public keys consists of linking cryptographic keys to identities or rights and keeping the secret key secret. In cryptography systems, key storage is a critical but often weak link. It depends heavily upon correctly implementing not only the commerce software but also the operating system. Operating systems (rationally) have usability and speed, rather than security, as their highest goals. For example, it is difficult to run a secure server on WindowsNT, because it has a number of security holes. A search of the Web by the wisely wary would reveal some tools for attacking holes in any operating system.

Of course no store is perfectly secure either, or the customers would be unable to use it easily. No house can be both livable and perfectly secure, thus residents have safety deposit boxes and make copies of critical information. The same balance between security and usability should be reflected in Internet commerce.

Symmetric Key Management

In symmetric keys the problem of key management is exacerbated by the need for a unique key for every possible set of people. Consider the problem of managing keys if a company shared a key with every customer, and each of those keys had to be unique. Now extend that problem to when customers are themselves merchants, so that each one of them must further share a different key with every other party. For a number (call this number k) of customers and merchants assuming every entity to communicate with every other using symmetric cryptography, there must be $\frac{k \cdot (k-1)}{2}$ pairs of keys. Not only must these keys be created and organized, to minimize the threat of cryptanalysis or the possible damage from a lost key, they must also be changed at regular intervals.

There are many excellent uses for symmetric keys because symmetric encryption is much faster (less processing intensive) than asymmetric encryption. One such use is session keys, which are keys used for one conversation or transaction. Instead of using processor-intensive public key operations for all encryption, most systems use the first public-key message to set up a session key, and then that is used to protect the transmission from prying eyes.

There are two kinds of symmetric cryptographic protocols: block ciphers and stream ciphers. (Cipher is just an old-fashioned name for a symmetric encryption system.) They are exactly what their names would indicate—one operates on chunks of data and one operates on a continuous flow. Think of the difference between pouring concrete and building with bricks.

Table 5.1 is an example of a simple symmetric cipher. Thus "A" is 16 and "R" is 39. So Jean Camp becomes

57561648 36163819

and

"I want red size eight shoes what is the price"

becomes

Table 5.1
A simple symmetric cipher

	1	2	3	4	5
6	A	B	C	D	E
7	F	G	H	I	J
8	K	L	M	N	O
9	P	Q	R	S	T
*	U	V	W	X	Y
&	Z	E	space	space	space

474&3*16 48594&39 56464&49 47565&56 47273759 5&493758
56493&3* 3716593& 47494&59 37563&19 39473656

Of course the breaks would not be in the coded information, but adding them makes it somewhat easier to read. There is a single key and the information is encoded block by block, where the block size is one letter. This type of simple substitution, called a *digraphic system,* was developed in the sixteenth century. Although far more simple than any Internet commerce encryption, as an example it communicates a sense of what is happening and some of the issues of key management. In this case the key is table 5.1.

The above is a block cipher. A stream cipher works on information as it streams through the encrypting device. Of course every stream must be acted on at some discrete level, for example, at the bit level or at the letter level. Given the same input twice, a block cipher will produce the same output. Given the same input twice, a stream cipher should not produce the same output because the stream is not reset for each encryption. With a stream cipher the key varies as the data goes through. Consider again, "I want red size eight shoes what is the price." With a stream cipher this message is translated into the appropriate numeric, as is the stream shown in figure 5.1. These are added together, as shown here. The point of this rather extended exercise is to show that in this case there are two secrets: one a trivial cipher and the other the source or nature of the stream. The primary secret is the content of the stream. The name of the book, "The Hobbit," from which the stream is taken, is the secret that one must be careful not to share in this example of a stream cipher.

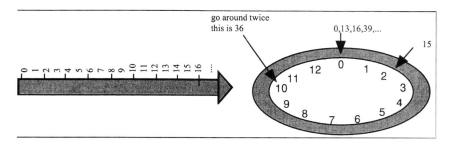

Figure 5.1
The number line and the number circle (p = 13)

Table 5.2
Trivial code for stream cipher example

c	d	e	f	g	h	i	j	k	l	m	n	o	p	q	r
3	4	5	6	7	8	9	10	11	12	13	14	15	16	17	18

s	t	u	v	w	x	y	z	space
19	20	21	22	23	24	25	26	30

Consider the simple code where A = 1, B = 2, . . . (see table 5.2). Now this extremely simple code is added to an equally simple secret and results in the cipher text shown in table 5.3. Were this exact text to be encrypted again, the output would be different because a different stream would be used in the encryption. The key would continue as "nasty, dirty. . . ." to be added to "I want . . ." resulting in a cipher text beginning "2301." Note that this means not only the text itself but also the starting point in the text must be synchronized.

The ideal cipher would be a stream cipher that used a different key for each message, and each key would be as long as the message, that is, a one time pad. In practice the ideal would be a random string of bits (e.g., 100111010100010110), which is combined with the message in a simple technique called *exclusive or*. Exclusive or is a way that computers combine numbers so that the key and the text cannot be guessed from looking at the output.

In the case of using a book to supply the data stream for encryption, someone has already produced the stream. If a true stream cipher were being used, there would be a random number as long as the message. This key would be extremely large, every message would require its own key, and key management would be correspondingly difficult. Thus whereas in theory this is the ideal, it is not remotely practical for price-sensitive communications. Both the stream and block ciphers here are symmetric key systems. The same key is used to decrypt and encrypt the message.

Asymmetric Key Management

The first asymmetric algorithm (Diffie-Hellman, named after its inventors) was invented for the exchange of symmetric keys between users who share no trusted party. In fact, given any asymmetric key algorithm, key exchange becomes a trivial matter—the initiator of the conversation encrypts the desired key in the receiver's public key and signs it with her own key. This provides confidentiality and integrity. It can also provide authentication if the symmetric key is linked to the initiator.

Given the current state of cryptography, the problems of security, authentication, and confidentiality could all be solved in a straightforward manner if the distribution of cryptography keys were elementary (and the related software and hardware perfectly trustworthy). Unfortunately, this is not the case.

Thus with asymmetric keys, distribution of the key itself is a trivial concern, whereas linking a key to an individual is difficult. It is simple for me to post a public key and claim it is mine. Presumably after that only I could read anything sent in that key, for I would have the secret key that decrypts the message sent in the public key. Of course it is equally simple for me to post a key and claim it belongs to Senator Kennedy. Thus the issue in asymmetric key management is linking the public key to the correct individual possessing the secret key. This is done today with *digital certificates*.

Digital Certificates

One early suggestion for managing public key distribution was that digital certificates be used to link keys and attributes (Kohnfelder 1978). This suggestion has now been widely adopted. A certificate in electronic commerce links an individual, an attribute, and a public key. For

Table 5.3
Simple stream cipher

Message	+	Streaming key	=	Cipher text
Msg. value	+	Key value	=	Cipher value
I	9	I	9	18
	30	n	14	44
w	23		30	53
a	1	a	1	2
n	14		30	44
t	20	h	8	28
	30	o	15	45
r	18	l	12	30
e	5	e	5	10
d	4		30	34
	30	i	9	39
s	19	n	14	33
i	9		30	39
z	26	t	20	46
e	5	h	8	13
	30	e	5	35
e	5		30	35
i	9	g	7	16
g	7	r	18	25
h	8	o	15	33
t	20	u	15	35
	30	n	14	44
s	19	d	4	23
h	8		30	38
o	15	l	12	27

Table 5.3
(continued)

Message	+	Streaming key	=	Cipher text
Msg. value	+	Key value	=	Cipher value
e	5	i	9	14
s	19	v	22	41
	30	e	5	35
w	23	d	4	27
h	8		30	38
a	1	a	1	2
t	20		30	50
	30	h	8	38
i	9	o	15	24
s	19	b	2	21
	30	b	2	32
t	20	i	9	29
h	8	t	20	28
e	5		30	35
	30	n	14	44
p	16	o	15	31
r	18	t	20	38
i	9		30	39
c	3	a	1	4
E	5		30	35

example, a Secure Electronic Transactions (SET) certificate links a consumer with an identity, the right to authorize a charge against a Visa account, and the public key used to verify a payment authorization. The certificate may contain a pseudonymous account number (PAN) instead of the customer's account number, or a pseudonym instead of a name. Visa and Mastercard consider the certificate in SET to be the electronic representation of the bank card.

Certificates can be used to connect an individual to any attribute, such as a person to a public key. Examples of off-line certificates include credit cards, driver's licenses, and club membership cards. Just as one person holds many off-line certificates, one person can hold multiple on-line certificates.

With a certificate, key management concerns are the validity of the attribute/key linkage, the length of the root key, the length of individual keys, the number of roots, and the lifetime of the certificate.[17] For a certificate to be valid, it has to have integrity, and authentication must be possible. A signature from the root or any trusted authority can provide both of these, given that the root key is secure and the information in the certificate is still valid at time of use.

An attacker can use an otherwise valid certificate if the associated secret key has been compromised. It is easy to obtain copies of a certificate—just as easy as it is to obtain a phone number, because certificates are public affirmations of attributes. It should be nearly impossible to obtain a secret key. Thus for a certificate to be valid, the secret key corresponding to the certificate must be secure. Also, a certificate may be used fraudulently if the information or the attributes attested to in the certificate are incorrect. This may result from fraud when the certificate was issued, or from a change in information after the certificate was issued (such as the loss of credit privileges).

When certificates are renewed, keys should be changed. The lifetime of a certificate is the time between issuance and expiration. In the case of key compromise, the ability to commit fraud ends with the lifetime of the certificate. This suggests that shortening the key lifetime could sig-

17. The root is the authority that verifies the key. For example, the state department of motor vehicles would have a root key for on-line documentation. Each worker at the DMV may have a key certified by that root.

nificantly reduce fraud. However, if certificate lifetime is too short, the cost of constant certificate issuing and the inability to cache certificates may outweigh the benefits of fraud reduction. (See Simpson 1996 for a discussion of management of caching policies and certificate lifetimes.)

Key length is also an issue in public key systems. When attempting to break asymmetric keys, the attacker attempts to factor the number[18] that is the public part of the key set. However, it is reasonable to compare asymmetric key lengths for systems based on factoring and those based on the difficulty of brute force attacks (when an adversary tries to break a key by trying all combinations). Brute force attacks on symmetric keys consist of guessing numbers to try to find the key. The larger the key, the more numbers one has to guess. Brute force attacks against public key systems consist of trying to divide the key by different numbers. Considering only the difficulty brute force attacks, 56 and 112 bit DES keys are roughly equivalent in strength to 384 bit and 1794 bit RSA keys, respectively (Schneier 1995).

There are two basic philosophies in the verification of the attribute/key link attested to by a certificate: hierarchical and nonhierarchical. Most designers of electronic commerce systems use a hierarchical approach. Hierarchical key management systems for general use have been proposed by the U.S. Postal Service (*Economist* 1996) and Verisign (Verisign 1996). An example of a nonhierarchical system is used in Pretty Good Privacy (Zimmerman 1995).

With Pretty Good Privacy, a user publishes his or her key, and other users can endorse this key using their own digital signatures. First a user generates a key. Then the user publicizes that key and endorses it with the corresponding secret key. This first signature/endorsement proves that the person claiming the publicized key has the corresponding secret key. This ensures that no other person can claim the key.[19] The user publicizes the

---

18. Recall that public keys are a set of numbers. That encryption is based on one-way functions. In the case of public key encryption, multiplication is easy, factoring is hard. To break the encryption requires factoring a very large number. Consider a human-scale example: factor 1,081. Multiply 23×47. Multiplication is easier than factoring, for both humans and computers.

19. Such an attacker could not read your mail or sign documents in your name, but could implement a denial of service attack.

appropriately signed key. Other users then endorse the publicized key/attribute claim by using their own digital signatures.

Public key endorsements create a "Web of Trust" that takes advantage of off-line relationships and reputation. No single hierarchy can verify every user for every situation—only a set of people vouching for one's goodwill. This creates a network in which a person offers her reputation for proof that a key links to an individual. Thus, once someone has established a reputation in a particular electronic community, her endorsement will be meaningful in that community. However, if a reputation has been established on *Salon*, the endorsement is meaningless on Slashdot. (Interestingly enough, there is no monetary market for Web of Trust endorsements.)

In the special case of the Web of Trust, an endorsement means that the endorser believes the holder of the key corresponds to the claimed identity. There is no implication that the endorser supports the endorsed party as being trustworthy on any count other than identity/key link. There is no implication that the endorsed party likes or approves of the endorsing party or has asked for or appreciates the endorsement. There is no implication of honor, agreement, or trustworthiness. No person can be prevented from endorsing another's key. Thus public figures have generally avoided the Web of Trust. To see why, imagine your chagrin at finding your key endorsed by the Aryan Nation hate group. Thus in a Web of Trust each person has limited power to state that an individual is linked to a key. Each additional signature increases the probability that the identity claim of the endorsed is valid. Some signatures are considered more trustworthy than others. Each person evaluating an endorsed key trust the endorsers differently. There is no single most trusted key.

Conversely a hierarchical system begins with the assumption that a single source has complete power in stating that a key corresponds to an individual. This trusted party, called the *root* of the hierarchy, may verify others as having the power to connect individuals to keys; however, every key/identity link is based on the trust of the first party. The mutual trusted party in such a system can provide digitally signed electronic credentials suitable for off-line authentication. These credentials verify that ownership of a public key pair corresponds to an attribute, usually identity.

Multiple parties are planning to operate public key hierarchies. Competitors in the market for the provision of electronic credentials for electronic commerce include Verisign, Banker's Trust, and the U.S. Postal Service (Verisign 1995; *Economist* 1996). If there is a single winner in the competition to be the trusted root, this endows one party with the ability to decide who has a valid existence in the digital world. This would also create a single point of catastrophic failure in what is otherwise a highly distributed system.

The relationship between certificates and trust may develop in an apparently arbitrary manner, as with physical certificates. When the state issues a driver's license, for example, the state intention is to verify that the holder has the right to operate a vehicle. However, to assure that this physical token is not transferred between parties, identity information is added in a human-readable manner. That information includes a photo, age, and hair color. Because of the inclusion of age and photo, driver's licenses are used to verify the right to purchase alcohol and tobacco. Because of the inclusion of the photo, driver's licenses are used to verify identity for, among other things, boarding domestic flights. And because of the unique identity number, driver's licenses are used to verify creditworthiness when the bearer is writing a check, by assuring that the holder has not previously passed bad checks. Likewise, while the relationship between identity, certificate, purpose, and issuer may seem limited and constrained at issuance, digital certificates can be used for many purposes.

Many businesses may choose to run their own certificate servers or add attributes to consumers' certificates. If a business wants to give out limited frequent-buyer discounts of some value, insecure technologies such as cookies[20] may prove too prone to fraud for such a purpose. The business may add an attribute to a particular key/identity pair as bound by a certificate, although the certificate may have been intended for an entirely different use. A group of businesses may come together, issue certificates, and then share information on consumers in a direct manner.

---

20. Cookies send data—but not programs—about the users on whose machines they reside. Usually they send a password or identifier that links to the merchant's database.

Table 5.4
Information in a digital certificate

Field	Purpose
Version	version 1, 2, or 3
Serial number	unique (within issuer) serial number, assigned by issuer
Signature	algorithm used to sign the certificate
Issuer	trusted entity that signed the certificate
Validity	dates between which the certificate is valid
Subject	identity of the valid holder of the certificate
SubjectPublicKeyInfo .algorithm .algorithmIdentifier	algorithms for which this certificate is valid
SubjectPublicKeyInfo .subjectPublicKey	public key of the holder of the certificate
IssuerUniqueID	unique identifier of trusted entity
SubjectUniqueID	unique identifier of holder of the certificate, assigned by trusted entity
Extensions.extnId	identifies extensions
Extensions.critical	Boolean, use described in .extnId above
Extensions.extnValue	extension data

Currently businesses share unverified information through cooperatives such as Abacus[21] at considerable overhead and with some risk that other businesses may provide altered data. Sharing a customer certificate could provide the same service, enhanced by the existence customer authentication and the potential for data verification.

X.509 is the dominant standard for certificates. Table 5.4 shows the required fields in X.509. The required fields determine the attributes or relationships on the basis of which the certificate issuer believes that the certificate holder should be trusted. Notice that creditworthiness is not a required field. When reading this table, recall the purposes of digital certificates. The distribution of certificates allows the trusted third party to provide off-line verification of multiple attributes. The distribution of

21. Abacus is a data-sharing cooperative organization used by direct-marketing companies. It provides information on customer orders from a range of catalogs owned by member companies. It is but one example of mutually beneficial, but unverified, data exchange.

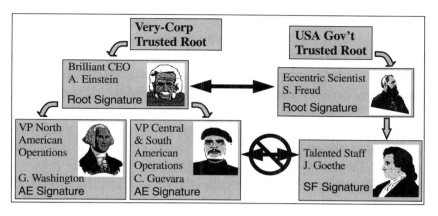

Figure 5.2
Two certificate hierarchies and their trust relationships

the certificate also implies distribution of identity and association information.

The loss of security for the secret root key of a certificate chain results in all certificates in that chain becoming suspect, and all bindings lose their trust. If the secret root key is compromised, an attacker can create or alter certificates; for example, an attacker could copy a public key set of an otherwise valid certificate, thereby obtaining the ability to authorize payments on some other person's account.

The party that verifies certificates is referred to as the verifier. Yet this definition creates more questions than it answers. Who is the verifier? And how much does one business trust the verifier from another business? This problem can be solved by building on the distinct trust hierarchies. (Recall that key hierarchies are trust hierarchies.) Interactions between trust hierarchies can be formalized.

Consider the whimsical example in figure 5.2. The U.S. government and a hypothetical multinational, Very-Corp, may have a relationship based on substantial data sharing at the highest level. Not all the data shared at a higher level, however, will be shared at a lower level. In fact, even work on joint projects might be prohibited at the lower level. The illustration suggests that although there may be trust at the highest level, it is one thing to trust another party and another to trust that party's discretion.

Key Length

The second trust management issue, after choosing an algorithm for an application, is key length. Key lengths are measured in bits (binary digits). One binary digit, or bit, can be either zero or one because digital information is represented in base two; just as a one-decimal digit (base ten) bit can be any number from zero to nine Two bits can represent 0–3, as two decimal digits can represent numbers 0–99. The largest number that can be represented in a key with n bits is $(2^n - 1)$.

Here are some numbers in binary and base ten:

Binary	Base ten
$10 = 10 \times 1$	$1010 = 1 \times 2 + 1 \times 8$
$2 = 2 \times 1$	$1 = 1 \times 2$
$16 = 6 \times 1 + 1 \times\ \ 10$	$10000 = 1 \times 16$
$5 = 5 \times 1$	$101 = 1 \times 1 + 1 \times 4$

Thus representing a number in binary terms requires more digits than representing that same number in decimal mode.

Breaking a key, like breaking a safe, is a function of time and money. The price/speed ratio for key breaking is linear (Schneier 1995). Thus, optimal key length depends on how long information must be protected and the value of that information if the key is broken. Key length is not a function of the duration of the transaction, since information may be stored long after the transaction is over. If a consumer wants to encrypt a credit card number and protect the credit card information for ten years, then she should select a key that will withstand a brute force attack funded by an amount equal to ten times her credit limit. The decrease over time in the cost of processing power must be a part of this calculation. For example: the credit limit is $10,000, the card expires in five years, and the consumer is using the Digital Encryption Standard, or DES (Federal Bureau of Standards 1977). In this case the consumer would want a key large enough that spending $100,000 would not break the encryption in five years (i.e., an 80 bit key).[22] Note that the factor of ten

22. Cryptography using 40 bit keys can be exported under current federal regulations. Greater key lengths may be exported only with key escrow under current proposals. Thus, in practice a consumer gets 40 bit protection.

is a result of the decrease in the price of computing power resulting from Moore's law[23] (Schneier 1995). For example, DES is a widely used symmetric encryption algorithm. As a function of the way in which DES is designed, DES keys must be 56 bits or a multiple of 65 bits, so an 80 bit minimum implies a 112 bit key.

Of course in practice there are off-line controls, including laws that assign the burden of security loss. Thus instead of a credit limit, the consumer might want to substitute $50 in the calculation, since under current law the consumer could lose only $50 if her credit card number were stolen. However, some party will take the loss for unauthorized credit card use, and the maximum value of that loss provides a conservative estimate for key length required to defend against a brute force attack. The fact that any individual credit care transaction will take only minutes is not a guideline for key generation.

Once key length has been determined, how does one distribute the keys? By definition there is not already a shared key. Simply sending the key would provide no security, because any observer of future transactions would have a copy of the symmetric key. This problem has been addressed using a common trusted entity who can generate keys and already has independently authenticated both parties. In practice this would be the bank or financial services provided for a commerce protocol.

Credentials usually link an identity to an attribute. Credentials can also be used pseudonymously. Unlike a pseudonym alone, credentials by definition provide membership information, thereby giving partial identity information. For example, a user of a Carnegie Mellon University discount is one of 7,000, not just one of millions. A user at the Kennedy School of Government is from an even smaller set.

Pseudonymity and Anonymity

The analysis of microdata—fragments of information about us that are distributed in different settings and roles—offers the possibility of obtain-

---

23. Moore's law notes that the density of silicon integrated circuits has closely followed the curve (bits per square inch) $= 2^{(t - 192)}$, where t is time in years; that is, the amount of information storable on a given amount of silicon has roughly doubled every year since the technology was invented.

ing information about an individual's travels, beliefs, financial status, and medical conditions. This information can be collected, however, only if it is possible to link information from a transaction to the individual taking part in the transaction. Two ways to prevent such linkage are anonymity and pseudonymity. (Much of this overview is based on Froomkin 1995.)

Despite its critical role in privacy, identity is merely another data field in an electronic information system. Any information such a system collects may be hidden during a transaction. When the identity of the customer is hidden, then that transaction is anonymous. Identity includes any user attribute that can be easily linked to a specific individual: user id and domain name, Social Security number, or IP address of a single-user machine.

Anonymity means that the identity of a party involved in a transaction cannot be determined during or after that transaction. Conditional anonymity means that a party's identity cannot be determined during a transaction, but may be determined afterward with the cooperation of one or more record-keeping parties. True anonymity is technically feasible for electronic commerce (e.g., one mechanism for anonymous and pseudonymous communication was proposed by Cox 1994), but for reasons of law enforcement such anonymity may not be desirable. In fact, anonymity is illegal for some transactions in many jurisdictions, including the United States. In the absence of legal protection, anonymity offers consumers the only protection against data surveillance. Unfortunately, widespread availability and use of anonymity has its own dangers. A recipient of an anonymous electronic threat knows this truth too well.

Pseudonyms are aliases. Pseudonyms may provide continuity in an otherwise anonymous environment, or they may be a special case of conditional anonymity. Pseudonymity means that a customer can be identified by a pseudonym during a specific transaction or set of transactions, but the user's actual identity cannot be determined. A pseudonym may provide authorization or identify certain attributes (for a discount for repeated use, for example). A user may choose to have a unique pseudonym for each transaction, to use the same pseudonym for multiple transactions, or to have a pseudonym for each merchant. Without a delivery address, or with an intermediary that hides the delivery address, a pseudonym provides no identity information. Traceable pseudonymity means that the chosen alias can be linked to the user's true identity. Many so-called anonymous remailers[24] really provide traceable pseudonyms, since the records of the remailer can reveal the identity of the user of the service.

The value of a pseudonym in terms of privacy protection is a function of the frequency, duration, and breadth of its use. A pseudonym used many times in multiple situations becomes equivalent to identity. For example, the use of Social Security numbers has become so common that these numbers are now equivalent to identity; and like identity, Social Security numbers are linked to many attributes.

Microdata Security

Identity information can be maintained in separate locations. Any data can be maintained in separate locations, even cryptographic keys. Many of us do this in our daily lives. One person may be a member of a school board, a company, and a beer-making group. A person may be a parent, a partisan, a volunteer for the homeless, a stockbroker, and a member of a religious organization. Everyone who is both a citizen and employee should be able to easily shield religious and political beliefs from employers and employer reviews from his or her religious community.

In electronic commerce systems, personal data is distributed transaction by transaction. Information on any one transaction usually provides very limited information about a consumer. However, compiled transactional data can provide a detailed summary of a consumer's habits, preferences, income, and possibly beliefs.

Microdata security is the protection of the identity or attributes of individuals, be they customers or businesses. Microdata security is compromised if information about a specific entity can be obtained either from data sets where such specific queries are prohibited, or from the correlation of information across data sets. Microdata security is an issue of hiding fragments of information in such a manner and in enough different places so that the big picture is hidden as well.

24. An anonymous remailer resends email with the identity of the original recipient removed. Anonymous remailers play a critical role in protecting on-line privacy For example, anonymous remailers have been central in the on-line battle between supporters and opponents of the Church of Scientology. A listing of anonymous remailers can be found at http://kiwi.cs.berkeley.edu/mixmaster-list.html.

Microdata security focuses on disclosure. A disclosure of information is not necessarily a violation of microdata security, and a violation of privacy may not always be a disclosure of information. For example, TRW, a credit information agency, collects data about purchasing patterns of individuals both to provide credit references for consumers upon request and to market that information, which may be a violation of privacy. The first purpose is a arguably a service to the consumer when the consumer is trying to obtain credit. But both uses of the data can be properly referred to as disclosures of consumer information.

Microdata security is concerned with all types of disclosure, without consideration of intent. There are four types of microdata disclosure: identity disclosure, attribute disclosure, inferential disclosure, and population disclosure (Duncan and Lambert 1989). Identity disclosure is the release of information clearly associated with an individual. A university's release of the Social Security numbers of its students would constitute identity disclosure. Given that customers can be identified through their digital certificates, sending certificates without confidentiality-protecting encryption is identity disclosure. If an observer can watch a single person browsing and buying, that observer can determine where that browser client connects to a server. If the person directing that browser subsequently sends her certificate, there has been identity disclosure. When an observer watches a particular server, then the observer can identify all the users who send certificates, assuming those certificates are initially sent in the clear. Thus an observer could collect microdata to determine a customer's browsing and shopping habits, or watch a business to determine a merchant's customer base.

Attribute disclosure occurs when linking a record with an individual provides additional information about that individual. As an example, the Social Security numbers of the students mentioned above may allow anyone receiving that information to obtain the students' credit, employment, or medical history. Attribute disclosure has been a primary concern in the widespread use of Social Security numbers and other universal identifiers. When an IP address can be linked to anything from income range to identity, the result is attribute disclosure.

Inferential disclosure is the release of information that does not identify associated individuals. This does not mean data have no unique identifiers, only that those identifiers cannot be linked to specific people. For example, the records of the New Haven needle exchange program use code names and therefore do not specifically identify a person, but do keep records over time (Kaplan 1991; Kaylin 1992). The concern over inferential disclosure is that given access to a set of attributes, identity disclosure may occur. For example, some databases are made "anonymous" by clearing the names. Yet this does not make the data set anonymous. Merely three datapoints—current location, date of birth, and location of birth—will identify a significant subset uniquely. Thus simple removal of identifiers is not adequate to protect identity information.

In commerce this is primarily a customer concern rather than a merchant concern, as merchants like their identities advertised. Some systems offer pseudonyms for customers who want to mask their identities. Note that pseudonyms are only effective in protecting privacy if the user does not deploy it so widely that inferential disclosure is enabled. For example, politicians and celebrities often seek pseudonyms that replace their names in the minds of consumers and voters. By frequent use, the pseudonyms will become a dominant identifier: Prince, Jesse "The Body" Ventura, Vanilla Ice, etc.

Population disclosure is the release of information associated with a defined population. Depending on the size of the population and the information released, population disclosure can result in privacy violations. In a large population, privacy violations through information releases are unlikely, but release of information about populations that are sufficiently small may enable someone who has the information to link it to specific individuals or make specific inferences. For example, release of the mean and standard deviation of the salaries of five employees risks violating privacy due to sample size. A release of the same information about 500 employees would result in a much lower risk to privacy. A well-documented example of population disclosure of innately sensitive material was the release of the name of a high school with a high number of HIV-positive students. This left students at the high school open to harassment (McGraw 1992). Frequency of disclosure is an issue as well; repeated population disclosure can result in attribute or identity disclosure even with large populations. An example of repeated disclosures that can violate privacy is the release of the average salary in an institution immediately before and after one person joins the staff. A curious colleague could use the change in the average salary and the fact that there is one more employee to calculate the salary of the newly hired employee. For a business, an example would be watching for changes in a competitor's delivery time commitments among purchases to infer stock levels for various items.

The risk of identity disclosure from the release of data is difficult to calculate. This risk can be reduced but not eliminated through masking (Duncan and Lambert 1986). Methods of masking include: adding bogus records that leave aggregate values unchanged, changing values among different people in the data set, and removing identifiers. A significant risk of population and inferential disclosure may remain, however, even after masking. Furthermore, an observer who collects data about personal or business habits through long-term observations certainly has no interest in masking such data. Imagine someone following one person around every day and observing all purchases she makes, or a competitor standing at a business's doorway and noting the attributes and purchases of all customers. Such observation of businesses or individuals can be automated with Web commerce. Businesses and individuals can reduce the risks of observation. Businesses can regularly change catalogue items, protect customer identity through use of secure connections, offer guarantees of delivery times only in encrypted form, or encourage customers to use business-specific pseudonyms after the first visit. (These pseudonyms could refer to a certificate on file, reducing the need to send certificates.) Of course the best approach is to ensure that customers, or rather the chosen commerce systems, protect all stages of the transaction through encryption.

Studies of disclosure offer useful definitions and methods for developing privacy-protecting systems. Microdata security offers insight into the threats to privacy that can result from a data compilation. The microdata security paradigm recognizes the different threats to privacy created by compilations of different types of data and identifies some vulnerabilities of data compilations to privacy-violating misuse. The study of microdata security illustrates that the release of a single element of information must be considered in the context of all other possible data releases and not as an isolated incident. The application to transactional records is clear.

6

Privacy Perspectives

This chapter and chapter 7 focus on privacy. One takes the risk of compromised privacy when one trusts another with identity information as well as attribute or action information. Consumers understand that their privacy is not protected on the Internet. In commerce, a company as well as a customer can be subject to privacy violations. Privacy is repeatedly identified as a concern that prevents consumers from using the Internet for transactions. The Privacy Protection Commission Study (1977) identified electronic commerce as offering a particular strong surveillance threat. The report of the commission stated that a centralized electronic funds transfer system would be "an unparalleled threat to personal privacy" and "a highly effective tool for keeping track of people and enforcing 'correct' behavior." In this book chapter 7 focuses on the legal dimensions of privacy and the values that underlie the legal construction of privacy.

This sixth chapter begins with an abbreviated and generic discussion of privacy with respect to information systems and moves on to a more detailed analysis of what information is available in the specific case of Web browsing. This discussion shows how merchants as well as customers can lose information privacy on the Web. Also discussed on this chapter is the European perspective on privacy: that the issue is one of data protection rather than privacy. The United States and Europe use the same hardware, the same operating systems, the same applications, and sometimes even the same computer science textbooks. Yet fundamentally different assumptions govern the manipulation of user data within the United States and Europe. The United States has a rights-based and property-based concept of privacy. One European country, the

Netherlands, has a greater respect for privacy and less concern for property rights; another, the United Kingdom, has a practical approach based on the goal of data protection. The discussion in this chapter focuses on the European Community's approach to the privacy issue.

This chapter also includes a limited discussion of privacy from the perspective of those who would limit privacy by requiring data collection. The viewpoints of law enforcement, business interests, system designers, and civil libertarians illuminate the conflicts between privacy and data availability. This brief discussion leads into the following chapters by illustrating the need for data collection. Without some data collection there is no accountability: for payment, for promises of merchandise delivery, and for fraud. Thus there exists a tension between privacy and data availability with respect to trust. Complete data surveillance means an extremely wide extension of trust, as data are easily correlated and searched by all observers. An extension of trust is required when accountability is limited by the absence of data concerning the identity of those who perform various electronic actions.

Chapter 8 discusses data collection. Ready availability of identity-correlated data is the opposite of privacy. For purposes of Internet commerce, the focus is on required governmental data collection for financial transactions. The conflict between privacy and accountability is clear in legal requirements for financial transactions: there exist both constraints on and requirements for disclosure. The assortment of statutory and regulatory constraints that can apply to electronic commerce is too immense to discuss here, and the reader is referred to a plethora of publications on regulatory law. Regulatory compliance is achieved through required technical mechanisms, but laws and regulations typically have underlying social motivations that range from providing capital for preferred purposes to preventing money laundering. The reporting requirements selected for discussion here are classified first in terms of their expressed goals and then in terms of the technical means used to achieve these goals. The discussion focuses on the United States, because it is a leader in consumer protection (although a follower in privacy protection) in the world community.

Governmental data collection for law enforcement purposes is explicitly data collection to ensure accountability. Thus law enforcement data requirements make a good baseline for the information available for governance; yet they are only an approximate substitute. To help close this gap, a discussion of alternative methods for achieving accountability follows the discussion of required data collection for governance in the system analyses.

Law Enforcement: Trust Us

Government needs information to accomplish its legitimate purposes. (The range of and reasons for data requirements for governance are detailed in chapter 8.) The greatest source of conflict between privacy protection and data availability has been in law enforcement, perhaps because accountability for criminal acts is an area where the need for accountability is greatest and the desire for accountability among the participants (meaning criminals) is least. Law enforcement opposes anonymity. The law enforcement community is charged with ensuring that individuals responsible for specific acts be identified and held responsible. Increasing data availability makes it easier to detect patterns of illegal activity and pursue the appropriate parties. A range of reporting requirements has been created to serve the needs of law enforcement.

By definition, law enforcement consists of individuals who have committed their professional lives to serving the government by punishing those who commit crimes. Certainly some police become brutal, disillusioned, and corrupt, but few select this employment with the goal of being corrupt, petty tyrants. Ideally the ones who succeed are honest. Having sworn to risk life and limb for law and order, they see every reason why law enforcement should be trusted with detailed surveillance information.

The law enforcement community has a set of carefully crafted requirements for data, as explained in chapter 8. In particular, law enforcement has a clear interest in preventing anonymity. Anonymity and pseudonymity are related to risk because law enforcement views knowledge of identity as a way to reduce risk. Identity information on those who break the law is necessary for punishment. The threat "I know where you live" implies that identity provides an opportunity for retribution, if necessary. It also illustrates that giving another knowledge about one's identity requires trusting the recipient of the knowledge to use it responsibly and not mishandle it. Identity information and privacy are inexorably linked.

Basic safeguards such as a prohibition on anonymous bank accounts and limited anonymity in purchases fulfill the needs of law enforcement to preserve accountability. Anonymous electronic funds transfer mechanisms cannot appropriately be evaluated without the reality of money laundering. In the United States, $500 billion is laundered annually with 80 percent of that being drug money (Bickford 1996). The ease of smurfing[25] makes the traditional upper limits on funds transfers inadequate safeguards in the electronic realm (Office of Technology Assessment 1995).

Although the courts have found general limits on anonymous speech unconstitutional, general limits on anonymous financial transactions have been deemed reasonable. Laws limit the scale of anonymous transactions and impose requirements on record-keeping the maintenance identity information. These have included limits to scale in anonymous transactions. The requirements of law enforcement, however, have not prevented all use of anonymous electronic currency. For example, the anonymous currency Digicash has been offered by Mark Twain—a small regional bank—for years. The approval of Digicash for use in the United States is based on two factors. First, size limits exist on anonymous transfers, including electronic transactions. Second, Digicash can be used only once before deposit. This means that Digicash can go through a single transaction, but cannot go through a chain of transactions. Thus in every transaction Digicash returns to fully traceable banking channels.

The use of anonymous encrypted communication can allow widely distributed individuals to plan and implement illegal activities without fear of surveillance. Modern porous international borders result in an inability to contain regional conflicts, and separatist conflicts may result in deaths on another continent. Internationally interconnected networks have magnified the ability of one individual to cause harm (Baird 1996). In contrast, the ability to seek information without governmental over-

---

25. Smurfing is the practice of taking one large transaction and separating it into multiple small transactions that fall beneath required reporting requirements.

sight is a core principle of democracy. If a citizen cannot listen to another's speech without being subject to surveillance, the right to free speech is undermined (Cohen 1996).

Like legitimate businesses, criminal organizations are becoming leaner and meaner. Because of computing and communications technologies, criminal organizations need fewer people and are therefore more difficult to penetrate (Bickford 1996). Their ability to move money without a trace—aided by these same technologies—makes observing their actions, or even locating them, difficult.

International criminal organizations may be assisted by criminal governments, thus Americans cannot always depend on foreign governments to protect their interests. Law enforcement and national security are increasingly interdependent, and the lack of coordination and information between these two entities can be costly. Collapsing empires result in the rise of organized crime to enforce property and contract rights that the government cannot protect. These criminal organizations can then create international corruption (Rodman 1996).

Criminal governments will use the same tools for built-in surveillance that legitimate law enforcement uses for its purposes. There is no way to build a surveillance infrastructure and prevent its misuse. The most glaring example of this is the use of cryptography by human rights groups in countries with repressive regimes. Records of names of victims, but more important, perpetrators of human rights abuses, as well as information on evidence and informers, need cryptographic protection. Organizations monitoring governmental corruption need secure cryptographic protection specifically from what is for them local law enforcement.

Conflicts between anonymity and the need for information for law enforcement purposes are inevitable. Perfect surveillance makes any crime easy to solve—except for crimes committed by those empowered to watch. Perfect surveillance ensures that criminals are more vulnerable than police. However, in many nations the most violent crimes, including disappearances and torture, are committed by the police state.

Perfect surveillance is an ideal solution for balancing privacy and accountability—but only if those in charge of surveillance can be perfectly trusted. Mandatory reporting of data requires an extension of trust to the government. One must trust the intentions, the judgment, the technical competence, and the data security competence of the data collectors.

Governmental data surveillance assumes that the information monitored or collected will be used only as intended and will not be used to harm the individual. Because of conflicts between government oversight and privacy, however, this assumption has been sometimes proved sadly wrong. Consider two cases in which information collected for financial accounting was used for purposes clearly against the interest of the subjects of the information. In *Minnesota Medical Associations v. the Catholic Bulletin Publishing Company*, the Catholic Bulletin Publishing Company requested the names of all doctors, hospitals, and clinics that had been reimbursed for publicly funded abortions from the state of Minnesota. The company would not state the purpose for requesting the information or describe how it was to be used; it is reasonable to assume, however, that it would be used to harass these health services providers, their practices, and their families. In another case, *Industrial Foundation of the South v. Texas Industrial Board*, the industrial group obtained access to the names of every worker who had filed worker's compensation, probably for the purpose of employment discrimination. In neither case would those who requested information deny these purposes attributed to them. In both cases the data in question had been compiled in compliance with fiscal oversight requirements. In both cases judicial oversight forced the release of the information despite the intent of the recipients of the information to harm the subjects. Information technology made duplicating the information a simple matter; thus arguments used in past decades against compliance with such demands for information (that record duplication was prohibitively expensive) no longer held. Applications of advanced encryption technology would have made these lapses of judicial wisdom less harmful by obscuring identity information in the data compilations.

Clearly when data is necessary to govern, there must be some trust in government. Norms of disclosure that respect privacy conflict with the desire for open government—the "right to know." Even the most reasonable collection of data for billing creates the possibility of misuse in a way that is harmful to the subject. In such cases the common interest in order conflicts with the common interest in privacy and freedom.

The Business Community: Trust Me

Providing data means trusting the watchers, in both the private and public sectors. Companies collect information for uses both primary (their own) and secondary (somebody else's). The most obvious object of primary data collection is repeat purchasers. Amazon.com collects detailed purchasing and browsing information about buyers and then offers them books it believes may interest them based on the information it collects. Again a conflict arises, in this case between customers' desire for tailored service and their desire for privacy. There also exists a profitable secondary market for consumer information. Companies who gather customer information profit from both its internal use and the ability to market it to others. Both companies and consumers profit when targeted advertising results in a transaction.

Businesses most often use customer data to better serve the needs of customers. Those in direct mail consider their services as aids to the consumer that identify opportunities of which customers may be unaware. To choose protecting privacy over the advantages of collecting and reusing customer data, business must perceive such privacy protection as the more valuable. Respect for privacy has long-term benefits, whereas the market for consumer data offers immediate profit.

Regulatory limits on the use of consumer transactional data would create an economic loss for those who market such data. Thus many merchants, including those that sell financial data, would oppose regulatory limits on the collection, analysis, and disclosure of consumer information. What effect limiting the flow of consumer data would have on an information economy cannot be foreseen, and the uncertainty is greater than is usually acknowledged. The order of magnitude and the direction of the effects of privacy regulation on Internet commerce cannot be predicted. Consider the effects of the Electronic Funds Transfer Act, which limited consumer losses in electronic transactions to $50 per credit card. Without this regulation the credit card industry would have never expanded to today's levels, and fear of fraud would have smothered Internet commerce at birth. Yet at the time it was enacted, banking associations opposed such regulation assuming it would dampen the credit card market.

The business community has provided and will continue provide anonymity to those willing to purchase such a service. Customers willing to invest time and effort in such a search can find among a host of credit cards with varying policies for secondary disclosure of consumer transactional information those whose policies offer the desired level of privacy or anonymity. On the Internet, those interested in anonymity can use the anonymous token currency Digicash, for the cost of Mark Twain's services.

The market has not uniformly resisted consumer privacy protections. For example, Microsoft has pledged to follow the standards set forth in the European privacy directive (as described later in this chapter). Netscape addressed the possible misuse of anonymous FTP as quickly as possible after becoming aware of it, in the release of Netscape Navigator 2.01. A possible increase in the use and trust of network services could profit such companies with credible assurances that no company will surreptitiously obtain additional data during transactions. No network services provider or business profits when its customers are subject to third-party surveillance. Thus companies might cooperate to create a floor of minimum privacy protection and provide the equivalent of the Better Business Bureau seal to assist their customers in choosing trustworthy merchants. Currently such efforts are under way not only by the Better Business Bureau but also by TRUSTe.

Externalities may exist with widespread implementation of anonymity. That is, there may be a critical mass that must be reached in terms of number of consumers demanding anonymity before there are profits in distributing anonymous software or providing anonymity through secure intermediaries. Thus new price paradigms that recognize the existence of positive network externalities may be needed. If this is the case, and there is a powerful market for privacy-protecting services, that market may yet be served by market forces. Many customers may be willing to pay a price, but not the premium that Mark Twain would charge, for privacy.

The business community has a fairly uniform perspective concerning the prohibition on the export of encryption hardware or software (United States Council for International Business 1993). Export of encryption allows producers of software, hardware, and systems to take advantage of a traditional American strength in serving the global market. The prohibition of export of cryptography without built-in surveillance hurts business by preventing them from effectively serving these markets. Thus the business community supports the free export of cryptography, which enables anonymity.

System Designers: Ignore Me

In a computer network the ability to observe and record users' choices depends in large part on the configuration of each system. Implicit assumptions about the value of privacy are made explicit in technical details such as file defaults, Usenet newsgroup selection, and provision of anonymous mail.

Electronic information system providers face a fundamental tension. To preserve the privacy of users, information on system use should be as secret as possible. Yet system administrators need to collect detailed information on usage to tune and improve the system. This tension shows up repeatedly in information systems ranging from national census records to private medical information networks (Compaine 1988). System administrators' ability to evaluate and improve software, thus providing user-friendly interfaces, reliable service, and efficient systems, depends on the ability to monitor software use. Because obtaining the necessary information requires observing individual users over time as they adapt to information systems, there apparently exists a false choice between privacy and access to usage data.

When patrons access a Web page, they reveal information about their preferences and ideas. When used judiciously, usage data can provide information that helps administrators improve the performance of the information system, provide tailored service, and ensure faster response times. But collection of such data also creates the risk of abuse: this information can also be used to spy on or invade the privacy of a Web surfer.

Anonymous use is, unfortunately, not a workable solution; information about the ways in which people change their use of the system over time requires a correlation between current and historical system use. Ensuring that changes in usage patterns result from of changes in user habits rather than changes in the user population requires that the behavior of specific users be identified. Masking user identity prevents this type of longitudinal analysis, although pseudonyms are useful.

For the special case of information systems providing access to on-line databases, information providers often require user identification to ensure that the licensing agreement is being enforced. For information services providers, in general, user identification is a necessary part of billing.

Identifying individuals also allows people to be tracked by type. This information can be used to determine, for example, if only members of a particular demographic group are using particular services. The apparent inverse correlation between privacy of personal information and availability of data has been the subject of considerable study from both the technical and sociological perspectives (Herlihy 1987, 1991; Randell 1983, 1986; Marx 1986; Pool 1983; Sproull 1991). Considerable technology can be used to protect privacy, for example, the anonymizer (www.anonymizer.com).

Mathematical techniques can resolve conflicts between user privacy and the legitimate need for access to data in an electronic system within a nation's borders. These same techniques have the potential to prevent international conflict when information regularly available in one nation is defined as private by another. The same technology that creates new conflicts if used without consideration of policy implications can instead resolve old conflicts if innovation is combined with respect for and awareness of international differences. Unfortunately these techniques are expensive and difficult to implement, so they are infrequently used.

Social Critics: Trust for the Common Good

Civil libertarians are both strong advocates of privacy and strong supporters of social goals unrelated to privacy. Both the potential for surveillance and the effect of a perception of surveillance concern them. Consider the impact of the proposal put forth by law enforcement that would ensure access to clear text of all communications (which will increasingly be financial transactions) using key escrow.[26] The estab-

26. Key escrow, like financial escrow, means that the cryptographic keys (recall that these are numbers) are kept by a third party.

lishment of a governmental electronic funds transfer service was considered and rejected by the Privacy Protection Commission. The commission objected that such a system would result in government surveillance and thus enable government to easily prescribe "correct" behavior (Privacy Protection Commission 1977). Key escrow for access to consumer financial transactions poses the same threat.

Secondary disclosure of information includes disclosure to the government. In *Lamont v. Postmaster General*[27] the Supreme Court noted that observation by the federal government has a chilling effect on the pursuit of information. There is no reason for this to change as information becomes electronic and not paper-based. The decision in *Lamont v. Postmaster General* applied to both free and purchased information. Civil libertarians are fighting for a recognition that the idea that freedom with surveillance is not true freedom applies to electronic transactions.

From the civil libertarian perspective, law enforcement requirements have served only to limit the availability of security and privacy through constraints on cryptography. The prohibition of exporting encryption technology has had ubiquitous effects. This prohibition effectively prevents strong cryptography for the protection of privacy from being implemented. The ubiquitous use of public key Kerberos (Davis 1995) would be prohibited. The advantage of public key Kerberos[28] is that it requires no central key authority—and it is precisely this lack of a central key authority that concerns law enforcement.

27. The United States Postal Service was required by §305 USC 40 (the Postal Service and Federal Employees Salary Act) to detain mail considered "Communist political propaganda" and release it only upon the request of the recipient. The recipient had not only to verify its receipt but also sign a statement that the information had been solicited. This not only created a list of suspected Communist sympathizers it also prohibited Communist and far-left organizations from using the mails to widely distribute information to the undecided. Note that the fascist and far-right organizations were under no such constraint in their ability to send out information about Communism and the far left. The court determined that such surveillance undermined the free expression of ideas.

28. Public key Kerberos is an adaptation of the widely used authentication standard Kerberos (Jennifer, Steiner, Neuman, and Schiller 1988), modified so that there is no longer a need for a single access control list that defines access to all resources.

Civil libertarians note that with the proliferation of information technology, cryptography is no longer a predominantly military technology. The list of uses for cryptography now more resembles the broad range of applications for internal combustion than the narrow focus of ballistic missile technology. Cryptography is used in every electronic commerce system. Export prohibition has prevented security from being an integral part of operating systems and software for Internet access from desktop machines, and thus limiting privacy.

From the perspective of civil libertarians, that law enforcement is constrained from unreasonable search and seizure should not mean that citizens have to live with a network designed to make reasonable search and seizure simple. Citizens still have the right to avoid law enforcement access, according to civil libertarians, without a presumption of guilt.

Civil libertarians are also concerned about use of consumer data by the business community as well as government. They would applaud constraints on the secondary use of consumer data. However, they also recognize the need for data to meet social needs, such as preventing discrimination, and thus support some federal oversight that requires some data collection. They also seek to protect consumers' economic rights, so concerns about reliability will affect their support for privacy. Civil libertarians are the most likely supporters of advanced but expensive technical solutions to problems of privacy and reliability such as anonymous certified delivery.

Civil libertarians support the removal of constraints on the use of strong cryptography even for international discussions. While the fight for consumer privacy may often result in conflict between civil libertarians and the business community, they are united in their opposition to the prohibition of the export of strong cryptography.

Europeans: Limit Trust

The European Directive on Protection of Personal Data, released on July 25, 1995, was an attempt to unify the laws on data protection within the European Community. The difference in language here is critical: in the United States the debate centers on privacy concerns, whereas in the

European Community the debate concerns data protection. The conflicts that can arise over data flows between the European Community and the United States may be even more severe than the previous conflicts within Europe if these fundamental differences in perspective aggravate the explicit legal differences. These differences are not insurmountable, but are social and culturally, if not politically, resolvable.

There is some argument as to whether the issue involves a consistent regulatory approach to privacy or a trade barrier. I do not agree, although the opinion that the European approach to data protection is more about the protection of European industry from trade than the protection of consumer data is sufficiently popular that it requires mention. It is also a reasonable supposition.

The European directive has resolved the divergent approaches across the continent to the data protection paradigm. The United States still protects consumer privacy, but considers data corporate property. What do these different viewpoints on privacy and property mean in practice? Can users expect data about their electronic habits to receive the same respect in both regions? Does European law and practice offer users more protection in daily life than U.S. law and practice? How do U.S. and European concepts of privacy provide secure access to electronic media? Is data protection merely a (trade barrier) wolf in (civil libertarian) sheep's clothing?

One weakness of the rights perspective is that once a person freely chooses to disclose information for a specific purpose, information is no longer considered private and can be disclosed generally. Examples of privacy-threatening secondary use of such data abound. One strength of the rights perspective is that certain questions are prohibited. For example, a store cannot require any customer information for a cash purchase of most goods. How have these strengths and weakness extended into and even been compounded by the widespread use of information technology? What policies are needed in this new electronic realm? For example, will the registration information including television viewing, Web browsing habits, and specific daily browsing sent to Microsoft by WebTV be acceptable to the American computer user? Will the appropriation and dissemination of this same data be acceptable to the British computer user? How do attitudes differ?

Even asking these questions suggests significant philosophical differences between European and American approaches to privacy. In actuality, the difference is in the regulation of privacy, not the presumptions of privacy in the two cultures.

European regulation prevents secondary use of data. That is, the regulation requires that data be collected for a specific purpose and not used for another purpose, although with a significant exception for fair use (historical, statistical, or scientific purposes). The regulatory directive requires that information collected be accurate, that only data necessary for the stated explicit purpose be collected (anonymous when possible), and that information be deleted when no longer useful for the original purpose. The directive defines way in which data can be collected and defines the characteristics of mechanisms that will fulfill the principles.

The directive limits the collection or processing of data in the absence of the subject's consent, but presents a large number of exceptions to this requirement: when the subject might want to hide the data to avoid the performance of a contract or entering into contract; when necessary for compliance with a legal obligation; or when the data are a necessary part of tasks "in the public interest." Data can also be processed for the vital interests of the data subject. "Vital" is not defined in the directive, however. Is a commercial interest "vital," or does "vital" apply only for health information? The final and by far the largest exception is "processing is necessary for the purposes of the legitimate interests pursued by the controller or by the third party or parties to whom the data are disclosed."

Although the First Amendment is uniquely an American institution, the European Directive recognizes the conflict between speech and privacy. This conflict arises when speech by one person is about another, for then the speech of one may be a privacy violation of another. The directive states:

Member States shall provide for exemptions or derogations from the provisions of this Chapter, Chapter IV and Chapter VI for the processing of personal data carried out solely for journalistic purposes or the purpose of artistic or literary expression only if they are necessary to reconcile the right to privacy with the rules governing freedom of expression.

The European approach to the issue of data privacy and protection has been represented as vastly different from the American approach, and this is true in a regulatory sense. In fact the debates themselves—data protection versus privacy—are very different in tone. Yet in practice the regulatory solutions to electronic privacy problems in the United States are very similar to those in European.

The American solutions are usually based on the Code of Fair Information Practice and are piecemeal rather than comprehensive. This code, as developed by the Office of Technology Assessment in response to concerns about the potential for electronic surveillance, is close in spirit and function to the European Directive (Office of Technology Assessment 1985). The code speaks of compilations and data collections whereas the Directive speaks of privacy; however, there is a common essence in the two documents.

The code sets forth a minimum set of attributes that all data compilations should share. It states that data compilations should never be secret. For existing data compilations, it requires a mechanism through which individuals included in the compilation to find out what information is stored about them and how the information is used. The code also requires providing to these individuals the ability to audit and correct their information. It mandates a way for the individual to prevent disclosure; however, it identifies prevention of disclosure as the responsibility of the organization with possession of or access to the data. Considering this list of requirements, it is clear that the code, if broadly applied, would parallel the European Directive.

The code has been applied to federal records (Privacy Act of 1974), financial records (Right to Financial Privacy Act, Fair Debt Collection Practices Act), educational records (Family Education Rights and Privacy Act), employee polygraph records (Employee Polygraph Protection Act), and even video records (Video Privacy Protection Act). It offers no protection of medical data because no specific enabling legislation has been passed. In fact an ill-considered plan of assigning each citizen a unique medical identifier, with no corresponding requirements for privacy of the records created, has been proposed.

The lack of an overarching regulatory framework with respect to data protection and privacy invites failures. The plethora of credit card offers one receives in the mail is clearly evidence of the failure of the Right to Financial Privacy Act, which sought to limit the widespread marketing of individual credit data. However, credit offers continue to proliferate because the law was limited in scope, both in terms of the data and the companies to which it applied.

Although the reality of data protection and the surrounding political debate are widely divergent on the two sides of the Atlantic, the basic concepts of how to protect data are the same. It is my belief that there are no fundamental differences in cultural perspective that will aggravate the explicit legal differences between the two regions. The substantive differences are in regulatory reach, not cultural perspective. Thus the distance between the European Directive and American Code of Fair Information Practice is not great in underlying theory. The directive would primarily affect those businesses that make considerable money from the secondary distribution of data. For companies that plan to observe their own customers and use the data to improve service locally, following the code has a high probability of meeting the directive's privacy constraints.

The possibility that the directive will present a trade barrier has been previously noted. It could also serve a positive role with respect to privacy, as a trademark and a verification of trustworthiness. Several mechanisms and institutions propose to show consumers that privacy is protected on the Internet. The largest of these is the TRUSTe effort at www.truste.org, which has a children's program in addition to a general consumer trust product. TRUSTe reads and rates the privacy statements of different sites, but it does not attempt to ensure that these policies are fulfilled, as the burden of work is too great. The directive could offer such a mechanism that would have some legal strength behind it, making the privacy directive a competitive advantage. This would require only that the site be acceptable under the directive. If the logic of TRUSTe is correct, the directive may in fact prove a trade advantage for any merchant willing to abide by its constraints. Verifiable protections of privacy could create opportunities for merchants around the world.

7

Privacy in Law, Privacy in Practice

Although Americans have long valued privacy, the law has been somewhat slow to recognize a right of privacy as such. In a now famous law review article, Warren and Brandeis (1890) made an eloquent case for recognition of a legal right to privacy. They justified this new legal right by pointing to a number of judicial decisions rendered in different fields of law, finding in these decisions the core idea that privacy is an interest that needed explicit legal protection. Warren and Brandeis advocated the right "to be let alone."

Case by case, a new legal right of privacy has been built upon the logical foundation produced by Warren and Brandeis's article. Through common law (that is, case-by-case) developments in state courts, the privacy rights of Americans have slowly been recognized. The result is a patchwork of protections that vary across different states and situations.

Although much of the legal protection of privacy interests remains a matter for state common law, some states have also passed statutes specifically for the protection of privacy. Some statutes, such as New York's, are of a general character; others, such as those that protect the confidentiality of library records, are very specific. A few states include provisions that protect privacy.

The federal government has generally been less involved in privacy law than state courts and legislatures, in large part because of a general congressional inclination—one that has constitutional overtones because of the limited powers the U.S. Constitution confers on Congress—to leave to state law the legal protection of personal interests. Nevertheless, in furtherance of its powers to promote interstate commerce and communications, Congress has enacted a number of special laws, such as the

Electronic Communications Privacy Act and the Right to Financial Privacy Act, that involve protecting privacy.

Furthermore, through a series of cases interpreting the Bill of Rights provisions of the U.S. Constitution, federal courts have come to recognize in the First, Third, Fourth, Fifth, Ninth, and Fourteenth Amendments the basis for inferring a more general constitutional right to privacy. The best-known of the Supreme Court decisions is *Roe v. Wade* (Schambelan 1992), which announced a constitutional right of privacy in relation to decisions about whether to seek an abortion. A number of additional Supreme Court decisions deal with privacy.

Privacy protections offered under state and federal law arise from two fundamentally different sources: rights of autonomy and rights of solitude. Rights of autonomy underlie the constitutional protections of privacy. They are necessary to ensure that the citizenry can take full advantage of the rights provided by the Constitution in practice as well as in theory. Rights of solitude underlie the protections of privacy provided at the state level.

A further complication arises in the fact that privacy rights are not absolute: They often conflict and must be reconciled with other social, economic, or legal interests, such as the right to speak freely. Even the United Nations Universal Declaration of Human Rights (1995) defines a limited right to privacy, recognizing only the right to be free from unwarranted intrusions, rather than all intrusions.[29] In contrast, more fundamental rights (freedom of the press) and the most basic right (to life) are subject to no such constraints. Many industry groups have lobbied against legislation that would expand privacy rights, arguing that privacy interests are better protected through more flexible and consensual efforts such as industry adoption of codes of fair information practices.

Thus, to provide a complete overview of privacy, I consider codes of ethics that have been offered in the absence of law. The discussion of ethical codes is preceded by sections concerning the more binding state law and federal law. The chapter considers federal statutory and constitutional law separately.

29. Article 12 of the United Nations Universal Declaration of Human Rights states, "No one shall be subject to arbitrary interference with his privacy." By comparison, the same document recognizes an individual's right to life with no qualifiers.

State Law

State law is primarily tort law, which is civil law as opposed to criminal law. In criminal offenses the state is the prosecuting agent. By definition, criminal acts are offenses against the state. In civil cases, on the other hand, two parties argue the case and the state serves as the impartial agent for judgment. Civil law is also distinguished from criminal law in that it concerns only those violations that can be addressed with monetary compensation; the state alone has the right to demand imprisonment.

Trying to make conceptual sense of the disparate rulings in the common law cases on privacy, Prosser in his 1941 treatise on tort law identified four kinds of privacy rights cases: intrusion upon seclusion, appropriation of name and likeness, false light, and public disclosure of private facts. Although some have challenged the appropriateness of Prosser's categorization (Halpern 1991; Bloustein 1968; Kalven 1966), the separation of privacy violations into four separate torts is the judicial standard. (The cases I cite in the following discussion of these four torts come primarily from Alderman and Kennedy 1995; Trublow 1991; and Speiser, Krause, and Gans 1991.)

Intrusion upon seclusion is the violation of the right to be let alone. The first judicial definition of privacy clearly singled out the press for intruding into private affairs: "Gossip is no longer the resource of the idle and of the vicious, but has become a trade which is pursued with industry as well as effrontery" (Warren and Brandeis 1890). But what is seclusion when applied to the electronic realm? Is it one's own electronic mailbox where particular messages are unwelcome?

Appropriation of name and likeness is the use of a person's name, reputation, or image without his or her consent. An early and well-known case involved a young woman who found her image distributed throughout the city on bags of flour. She had given no consent and received no compensation. The makers of the flour had thought her face would be commercially useful and that she was owed no compensation for the luck of having such a countenance. The New York courts agreed. Despite the woman's failure in seeking restitution at the time, appropriation of name and likeness has since become universally recognized as requiring compensation when it results in commercial gain. Different states set different limits on the ability to seek restitution in cases involving no commercial gain, but all states recognize at least a limited right to seek redress against those using private information only for commercial gain. Thus far the use of electronic images (such as the Babes on the Web site) for gaining hits (the currency of the Web) has not been tested in court. Furthermore, the selling of data images or data profiles of individuals has not been successfully prosecuted. Most use of imagery in the electronic realm has been pursued in the courts under an intellectual property rubric rather than using a name and likeness approach. Thus this privacy tort remains untested in the electronic realm despite the many instances where it might be applicable.

False light involves the publication of information that is misleading and thus shows an individual in a false light. It is similar to libel. The ability to charge another with depicting in false light depends on the standing of the victim and the role of the privacy violator. Private persons (as opposed to public figures) need show only that the information presented is false in a case of false light; however, concerns over rights to free speech hinder the pursuit of restitution in such cases. Public figures need to illustrate that the information was incorrect, and that the disseminator of the information acted with malice.

What makes a person a public figure on the Internet? Is everyone with a Web page a public figure? What about people who post to newsgroups? How much privacy does one forfeit when one becomes electronically active? Do Internet posts make one validly subject to other posts that disclose private facts? When everyone can be a reporter on the Internet, is everyone also a public figure? These questions do not yet have a definitive answer.

All fifty states recognize false light under one rubric or another (usually under libel). However, some states do not recognize misrepresentation as a privacy violation per se. False light may arise in an e-commerce if, for example, someone claims that another shops at a socially disreputable location. False light against a business entity might involve posting false information about its business practices on the Web, for example, lodging a complaint in a newsgroup, violating voluntary industry standards. (Dealing with misinformation posted on the Internet was addressed previously. As noted, I believe that on-line responses should always be offered to on-line misinformation, but this does not preclude the possibility of legal action.)

Public disclosure of private facts is self-explanatory. Private information is just that—private—and publication of such information can give rise to a legitimate civil action. Information deemed as "newsworthy," however, can be printed even if it is a violation of privacy. Some jurisdictions, including New York and South Carolina, treat public disclosure of private facts seriously; in others, notably North Carolina and Texas, one cannot bring action under this tort (Alderman and Kennedy 1995). The existence of private facts in the electronic realm is yet to be established and defined. For an individual, electronic private facts might include browsing habits or bookmarks. Like a sentence taken out of context, an isolated URL to which one has linked at some point can be used to imply habits or affiliations very unlike one's own. Businesses' private facts are much more likely to be along the lines of customer profiles that they maintain, although the browsing habits of employees can clearly be classified as such.

In addition to tort and case law, some states also offer statutory and constitutional protections of privacy. The level of such protection varies widely among states; it is worth noting, however, that moving to a state with low levels of privacy protection does not with certainty protect a business from privacy suits. In terms of remote commerce with credit cards, the usury laws have been constructed so that the home state of the offering company, not of the consumers, determines the applicable law. Internet laws have not been solidified; thus it is possible for a customer with privacy expectations based on that customer's home-state law to bring a company into court. Understanding the range of state laws involving privacy is therefore useful wherever you may be.

Ten states[30] include privacy as an explicit right in their constitutions. Of those, only Louisiana and California provide privacy protection to private sector employees, while the provisions in the other states deal exclusively with the rights of the state to obtain information. How state constitutional law will be applied to electronic information remains undetermined.

30. Alaska, Arizona, California, Florida, Hawaii, Illinois, Louisiana, Montana, South Carolina, and Washington.

State laws vary with respect to the categories of electronic information they protect. Fifteen states[31] have laws that offer specific protection of financial transaction information. The laws in Arkansas, Massachusetts, and Montana apply only to records of electronic funds transfer. The protections in other states limit disclosure of consumer financial information. In addition, fourteen states[32] protect all financial information, not merely transaction-specific data, from state governments. Those laws offer protection similar to the Right to Financial Privacy Act at the federal level (discussed later in this chapter.)

Forty-one states[33] and the District of Columbia also have specific statutes on the confidentiality of library circulation records. The significance of this protection in the context of electronic privacy is that some of the records of purchases of information goods on the Internet can provide information on a consumer's regular reading habits, much like library records. Though there is clearly a parallel, states have yet to extend confidentiality protections specifically to electronic commerce records.

States also may protect information specifically because of its electronic form. State statutes of interest include both wiretapping statutes and broad computer crime statutes. Computer crime statutes at the state level often focus on manipulation of financial information for fraudulent purposes, and thus resemble the Federal Wire Fraud Act more than the federal Computer Fraud and Abuse Act. (Both of these acts are discussed in detail later in this chapter.) Eleven states[34] offer specific protection

31. Alaska, Arkansas, California, Florida, Illinois, Kentucky, Massachusetts, Minnesota, Mississippi, Missouri, Montana, Nebraska, Pennsylvania, Texas, and Wisconsin (Trublow 1991).

32. Alabama, California, Connecticut, Illinois, Louisiana, Maine, Maryland, Massachusetts, Montana, Nebraska, Nevada, New Hampshire, Oklahoma, and Oregon (Trublow 1991).

33. Alabama, Alaska, Arizona, Arkansas, California, Colorado, Connecticut, Delaware, Florida, Georgia, Illinois, Indiana, Iowa, Kansas, Louisiana, Maine, Maryland, Massachusetts, Michigan, Minnesota, Missouri, Montana, Nebraska, Nevada, New Jersey, New Mexico, New York, North Carolina, North Dakota, Oklahoma, Oregon, Pennsylvania, Rhode Island, South Carolina, South Dakota, Tennessee, Vermont, Virginia, Washington, Wisconsin, and Wyoming (B.S. Johnson 1989).

34. Arizona, California, Delaware, Georgia, Michigan, New Mexico, North Carolina, Tennessee, Texas, Utah, and Virginia (Nimmer 1992).

against abuse of computerized financial information for personal gain. Under wiretap laws, states may protect telephone numbers, which provide electronic location information in a manner that might logically be construed as analogous to an IP address on the Internet. For example, in California and Pennsylvania, courts have ruled that telephone numbers as offered by Caller ID have some protection under wiretapping statutes. Yet courts have limited the reach of wiretapping statutes into other electronic realms. Again consider California, where the courts have ruled that intercepting email is not wiretapping.

A particularly problematic issue in the application of state law is the tenuous nature of location in electronic information systems. Suppose a customer has a credit card account in Wisconsin and an ISP in her home state of California and makes a purchase from an electronic merchant in Delaware. If the purchase information is intercepted and compiled for internal use by a company in Utah, where did the interception take place? Did it involve a wiretap? Is it judged under the local jurisdiction of the credit card headquarters, as would be the case if the customer were concerned with usury? Does it matter if the company in Utah is taking a demographic survey of the customers of the Delaware merchant? If the company in Utah makes no money but is trying to make marketing decisions about general Internet purchasing habits, is that wire fraud or legitimate use? None of these questions is simple, and they are further complicated by uncertainty of jurisdiction.

Federal Law

At the federal level, where privacy concerns are autonomy concerns, special statutes protect privacy and constitutional guarantees of privacy. Those under surveillance are seen as not acting freely even when not otherwise constrained.

Statutory Law

Federal law can apply to electronic commerce on at least three subjects: controls on financial information, controls on electronic information, and laws enabling the regulation of cryptography. The confluence of consumer privacy and cryptography is a recent technologically driven event and is addressed in a separate section. Here I restrict myself to a discussion of laws concerning financial and electronic information.

Specific protections exist for various classes of personal information in analog forms, including medical, video rental, criminal, and financial records. When information in one of these classes is purchase electronically, the purchase falls not only under the rules governing electronic transactions, but also in the category of financial exchange. Laws covering privacy of access to information have a different tradition than laws governing commercial information; these laws are based on the assumption that financial records belong to the bank and not the consumer.

The Right to Financial Privacy Act was enacted in response to a Supreme Court decision that denied rather than defined a right privacy: *United States v. Miller* (1976). In *Miller*, the Court determined that there are no Fourth Amendment constraints limiting government access to personal financial records. The Act extends the Fourth Amendment and the Code of Fair Information Practice to bank records. (Recall the discussion in the previous chapter of the Code of Fair Information Practice and its similarity to the European controls on data protection.) It limits the conditions under which any institution can disclose customer information to federal authorities. Yet the Right to Financial Privacy Act is not as encompassing as Fourth Amendment protection because it contains broad exceptions to the protection it offers. The exceptions of the act include when the bank is acting in its own self-interest, for regulatory proceedings, in response to IRS summonses, and in compiling federally required reports. The Right to Financial Privacy Act also does not apply to individual information included in an aggregate listing. The protection offered by the act is limited in other ways; for example, the Court has ruled that financial records stolen from a third party through the contrivances of a government agency are admissible in court (*United States v. Payner* 1980).

The Fair Credit Reporting Act applies the principles of the Code of Fair Information Practice to credit reporting agencies. Unfortunately, it applies only to those entities that provide credit reports, such as credit bureaus or credit agencies, as their *primary business function*. This means that financial information given to credit card companies, banks, and other institutions can be freely traded without consumer knowledge since these organizations have primary business functions other than providing credit reporting. The Fair Credit Reporting Act has been effective, however, in preventing the proliferation of private credit guides containing information on individuals. Prior to its enactment, companies sold credit guides without the knowledge or consent of the individuals profiled. These credit guides offered detailed, often unreliable, information on easily identifiable individuals. Now only guides that contain encoded information, making it difficult to identify a consumer without the information on a payment instrument (such as a checking account number) are allowed. For example, checking account clearance centers use driver's license numbers and banking information to check the history of a person and an account. The identity of the person who holds the account is not listed. The only information listed is the driver's license number and if that person has bounced checks. Compare this to previous private credit guides that listed names and addresses, along with assorted unreliable information (for example, neighborhood gossip). The status of credit records in the 1970s resembled the status of medical records now: unregulated in the interest of the subject of the record, owned by various parties, often not accessible to the subject, prone to error, and difficult to correct.

The Fair Credit Reporting Act also protects credit agencies from the charge of negligent release in cases involving misrepresentation by the requester. Credit agencies must ask the requester the purpose of a requested information release, but need make no effort to verify the truth of the requester's assertions. In fact, the courts have ruled that "The Act clearly does not provide a remedy for an illicit or abusive use of information about consumers" (*Henry v. Forbes* 1976).

The Privacy Act of 1974 also deals with government collection of data, codifies the principles of the Code of Fair Information Practice, and requires that the practices it prescribes be followed for all government databases and databases of government contractors. It requires that individuals be informed of all government compilations of data of which they may be part and limits the sharing of data among federal agencies. The act also limits the use of Social Security numbers as universal identifiers in federal databases by requiring that citizens be able to select a different nine-digit number as an identifier.

The Fair Debt Collection Practices Act limits dissemination of information about a consumer's financial transactions. It prevents creditors or their agents from disclosing to a third party the fact that an individual is in debt, although it allows creditors and their agents to attempt to obtain information about a debtor's location.

Information exchanged in Internet commerce will be both financial and electronic. Laws that protect electronic information are therefore equally relevant to those that protect financial information. Transmission of electronic information is addressed by the Electronic Communications Privacy Act (ECPA) which establishes criminal sanctions for interception of electronic communication. The act calls for imprisonment of not more than five years, a fine, or both for criminal interception of electronic communication. These are strong penalties, but the ECPA also contains broad exceptions—quite possibly so broad that one could push the entire Internet through. The act offers exceptions for those who act under the color of law (i.e., police officers with a warrant); when the party intercepting the communication is also a party to the communication; or when one party has given prior consent. The first exception gives access to communications to officers with a warrant. The second exception may involve a financial agent, such as a bank or credit card company, that is party to a communication and thus has the right to read and reference that communication. In the third exception, prior consent can be explicit or implied. Consent may be implied by an employee agreeing to work in an environment where system use is required, or it may be explicit in a written request for financial services. Thus the ECPA provides limited protection from law enforcement or employer scrutiny, but it does provide legal protection against observers.

The two exceptions of the ECPA that make it inadequate for protection on the Internet are the assumptions that all parties to a communication are equally at risk to privacy violations and that any event at a business is business related. All parties are clearly not at equal risk for privacy violations on the Internet—the server is far more able to collect aggregate information about visiting clients than the client can normally obtain from the server. By using cookies at multiple sites and spreading advertising widely, an organization can correlate a user's visits across sites

without fear of retribution, rather than prevent the publication of certain types of information as state laws governing privacy do. In fact, privacy rights prohibiting intrusion into seclusion and publication of private information have been limited at the federal level precisely because of the First Amendment's protection of speech rights.

The Supreme Court has determined that there is no constitutional right to privacy or expectation of privacy in financial matters (*United States v. Miller* 1976). Consumers voluntarily supply financial information to financial institutions, the information is owned by those institutions, and there is no reasonable expectation of privacy for such information because by its nature it must be shared in the course of business. Some advocates of privacy rights propose a property law, whereby individuals would be construed to own information about themselves. Thus far property laws have been used primarily to limit privacy by declaring information about one person to be the property of another and not properly subject to the oversight of the subject.

Constitutional protections of privacy have been applied inconsistently. Often a delay exists between the introduction of new technologies and the extension of privacy rights to the users of those technologies. Consider the case of telephony. In 1928 the Supreme Court determined that no person has a right to privacy in telephone conversations (*Olmstead v. United States* 1928), ruling that recording telephone conversations was not a search under the Fourth Amendment because the conversation left the defendant's home on lines that could not be secured. The Court stated that since the technology was inherently without security, people knowingly sacrificed privacy when they communicated using the telephone. The Court reasoned that telephone correspondents knew that the signals went outside their homes and only the most naive would expect privacy. Olmstead reads: "There was no searching. There was no seizure. The evidence was secured by the use of the sense of hearing and that only. There was no entry of the houses or offices of the defendants. . . . The language of the amendment cannot be extended and expanded to include telephone wires, reaching to the whole world from the defendant's home or office. The intervening wires are not part of his house or office, any more than are the highways along which they are stretched."

The reasoning in Olmstead applies to the Internet today. Of course, this reasoning remains true for the telephone network as well. For the decades between *Olmstead v. United States* and *Katz v. United States* (*Katz v. United States* 1967), the law of access to telephone conversations essentially stated that because the system was open, privacy was not to be expected. In *Katz* the Supreme Court ruled that individuals have a "reasonable expectation" of privacy during telephone conversations. The Court determined that a court order, and the basis for suspicion that justified the court order, was necessary for listening into the same global network of wires found open to all in the previous decades. The Court has not determined which judgment applies to the Internet today.

Privacy and Information Technology

The first judicial definition of privacy in Warren and Brandeis 1890 was written in response to technological threats to privacy. Specifically, Warren and Brandeis were concerned with the press's reporting of scandals (aided by advances in photography, telephony, and printing) and its lack of regard for privacy. These jurists felt that the new technologies upset the previous balance between privacy and the availability of information, thus forcing a reconsideration of the right to privacy. A century later information technology—this time in the form of the Internet and the data processing capacities on the networks it connects—is again changing the balance between privacy and data availability.

Electronic information technology changes the balance between privacy and information availability because electronic information is so easy to compile, correlate, and distribute. Monitoring every keystroke of users of information technology requires little amount of effort. Information, once electronically collected, is easy to analyze and distribute (Turn and Ware 1976; Pool 1983; Office of Technology Assessment 1985; Compaine 1988; Computer Science and Telecommunications Board 1994).

Consider the effect of information technology on the four torts discussed earlier in this chapter. In a practical sense, invasions of privacy were once the purview of the press and government by virtue of the difficulty of publication and surveillance, respectively. Most individuals lacked the time and resources to conduct surveillance required to invade an individual's privacy, as well as the means to disseminate the information uncovered. Privacy violations were therefore restricted to those who did, chiefly the government and the press. Information technology, however, has made eavesdropping and publication easy for all Internet users, thus increasing an individual's opportunity to violate the privacy of others. Currently the lack of means of determining the authentication or integrity of information makes the dissemination of false information via electronic media much easier because of the potential lack of accountability.

In the case of intrusion upon seclusion, electronic trespass has been defined as a crime at the federal level. Yet electronic intrusion upon seclusion has yet to be defined. One potential electronic case of intrusion upon seclusion was revealed in the beta release of Microsoft's networking software. Early hackers who had obtained beta versions of Microsoft network software noted that the software would have sent consumers' machine capacities and entire directory structures to Microsoft when consumers installed the product. After this fact was publicized, Microsoft reduced the amount of information to be transmitted and offered the consumer a choice of whether to "register" with the company. Recently it was determined that Microsoft keeps the identifying information of those who register Word and Office, and can use identifiers in the software to determine who has produced Word or Office files. If in the electronic world one's own hard disk is electronic seclusion, then Microsoft's practice of availing itself of consumer information without consumer knowledge could have been a tort violation.

Certainly the capability of distributing other people's private communications, through forwarding email or building Web pages for general distribution, creates new possibilities in the electronic realm for false light. Email may be edited and displayed as "evidence" that an individual has certain beliefs very unlike his or her own. A combination of loaded labels, unidentified sources, and hidden agendas can be used to present an issue in a false light (FAIR 1996). Loaded link names, anonymous email, and misleading domain names make these tools of deception available to everyone on the Internet. Loaded link names incorrectly describe the page to which another page is linked. For example, a link to Swift's "A Modest Proposal" describing it as "a policy under consideration" would be a loaded link name. Anonymous email can be used to make statements without authenticating them. Much like in the newspaper, "an anonymous source close to the situation . . ." can say things that cannot be validated. Misleading domain names can be used to present a person with a gripe as an institution on a mission, as described previously.

To determine the effect of information technology of the appropriation of name and likeness, one must ask, what is one's electronic likeness? What value must exist for use of one's electronic likeness to be considered misappropriation? The difficulty of applying appropriation of name and likeness in the electronic realm is illustrated by the search engine Alta Vista (http://www.altavista.com/), which provides its users withthe ability to search Usenet postings by author or keyword. Alta Vista is using the speech and ideas, the electronic visage of an Internet user, for the purpose selling attention span to advertisers. Yet this is an offense against no person in particular. The only possible "profit" is an increase in the number of hits to the Alta Vista site, and the corresponding increase in ad revenues.[35] No one person can claim that the unique statements he or she placed on Usenet create that value, so no one person has the necessary standing to sue on economic grounds.

Finally, consider the fourth tort, public disclosure of private facts. Public disclosure becomes very easy when everyone is a publisher. For example, at Carnegie Mellon University, one student's homosexuality was revealed on an electronic departmental bulletin board. Communicating such a fact to many of the department faculty and all of the student's colleagues was vastly simplified by the use of information technology. Without such technology, no doubt the student who publicized the information would have been intercepted in the department and been told to leave when he tried to share private information.

In short, information technology has altered the balance between privacy and data availability by giving many people the power to compile and disclose information—powers previously held almost exclusively by governments and the press. The mere existence of a right to privacy that is universally recognized through the UN, in national legal structures, and in common law is important. If privacy is a right, those who gather and

35. A visit to a particular file on a Web server is called a hit. The number of hits on a Web site is a measure of its popularity and a suggestion of its producer's Web-publishing abilities.

disseminate data, not the individual, bear the responsibility for maintaining privacy. Protection of this right has not been implemented in information technology, however: privacy is part of ethical codes but not consistently part of computer code. Unfortunately privacy protection through codes of ethics has proven inadequate (Office of Technology Assessment 1985; National Research Council 1996).

Browsing Information

Any transaction must begin with discovery; information than can be exchanged during discovery is properly classified as transactional information. If a customer uses the Internet for discovery, the merchant can obtain information about the customer as she looks through the merchant's wares. This is the first information exchanged in a transaction and is common to all Internet commerce transactions.

A customer cannot purchase an item unless she knows of its existence. To sell a product successfully, vendors must make their product's existence known to all customers who may want it. This requires information about potential customers. In the analog world, stores obtain information about customer preferences by observing their browsing patterns and set up displays accordingly, or use data on various customers' purchasing habits to target catalog mailings. Electronic merchants will no doubt do the same and can obtain electronic browsing information easily.

The customer must also know the location of the merchant in order to make a purchase from that merchant. With Internet commerce this does not require knowing the exact identity of the merchant, merely the domain name.

The amount of information a merchant can obtain during discovery via the Internet depends on the policies, practices, and physical configuration of the customer's ISP. Other factors that can affect the information available to the merchant include the configuration of the customer's system, the services provided by the customer's ISP, and the software the customer uses to access the Internet. I discuss examples of each of these in this section.

When the customer's client contacts a merchant's server, whether by ftp or Web browser, the merchant can capture the client's IP address. Connecting through intermediaries (remailers or anonymizers) can prevent the release of consumer information. However, most consumers either do not know about such intermediaries or don't bother with them or are even unaware that simply by connecting to a Web site, they are transmitting their IP address.

Recall that from an IP address, the merchant can obtain the name of the customer's host using the Domain Name System (DNS), which provides a mapping between domain names (e.g., miami.epp.cmu.edu) and the corresponding network addresses (e.g., 128.2.58.26).

If the customer's system is protected by her employer's firewall, the IP address may identify only the employer. If the customer is going through the shared IP address of an Internet service provider (ISP), the information available to the merchant depends on the practices of the ISP. An ISP's configuration may prevent any information but the identity of the ISP from being made available—for example, if an ISP dynamically assigns IP addresses as customers access the Internet, as does MCIMail, then only the identity of the ISP is known. On the other hand, if the customer's ISP is MediaOne, then the customer's machine name identifies the user. (A machine name includes a third- and often a fourth-level domain name.) This is because MediaOne uses the userID as the third-level domain names, so for a user with the name, "userName," that user's machine-specific name would be "userName.mediaone.com." Thus the minimum information the merchant will have as a result of the contact by a customer is the name of the customer's Internet access provider, whether that provider be an employer, a place of learning, or a commercial ISP.

Some ISPs provide automatic user identification services; the most widely used are finger services and AOL's profile services. In addition, as described with MediaOne above, ISPs may have a configuration that results in the users name being the machine's name. In these cases the merchant may be able to identify the customer by accessing a common process, such as fingerid, on the customer's machine. Depending on the naming scheme, various user attributes, such as departmental affiliation (if the machine is in a university setting), will be available (for example, math.cmu.edu). In fact, if many users from one company contact a merchant and the company's network transmits the information, a merchant can build a map of the company's internal network and corre-

that they cannot use. This reflects the fact that merchants obtain information that they cannot use, as discussed later in this chapter.

Many electronic commerce protocols are designed to begin with an exchange of digital certificates to assure identity and exchange keys. Digital certificates will become increasingly common. The customer's certificate includes the customer's identity, the issuer's identifier, and its certificate policies. The issuer's identifier can support the customer's claim to be authorized to use the specific payment method she has selected. Any qualifiers on the customer's use of the payment mechanism and the certificate policy identifier provide information on the customer. For example, it may indicate the customer's creditworthiness or identify the customer as a student. The dates that the certificate is valid may indicate the customer's shopping habits or creditworthiness, based on the policies of the issuer.

Availability and Value of Consumer Information

Much of this text focuses on privacy. Yet many popular works on Internet commerce argue the opposite: that the most important thing is obtaining as much data as possible, and privacy is essentially not an issue. One text that advocates aggressive customer surveillance is *NetGain* (Hagel and Armstrong 1997), which presents a linear mechanism for building a profitable Web presence. The building process is based heavily upon the ability to identify and track users, so that they may be classified in various ways. The process is presented as linear and applicable to all firms. Among the various texts in this vein, *NetGain* appears to advocate most aggressively the tracking of consumers. Given that this viewpoint is in direct contrast to the premise of this text, I will address the arguments presented in *NetGain*, as some are commonly accepted.

First, the intense tracing assumes that a single business model exists—that of providing intermediation between businesses and customers. This is the model for many of the overnight wonders one hears of on the Web, including Yahoo. It is the model of AOL, which bundles Internet access with provision of selected content and selection of business partners. This model obviously cannot be applied to the majority of sites on the Web; by definition, only a minority of providers can be intermediators for all other providers.

Second, it is generally recognized that any community created must have some consumer loyalty to be long lasting and viable. Data sites are being built to be sticky—but stickiness through constant intense surveillance and marketing will inevitably have an effect on consumer loyalty. There is a price to refusing customer privacy, and the collection of data must be considered with respect to that price. Privacy is not without costs. If indeed the electronic marketplace shifts the power from consumers to vendors and intermediaries, then constant surveillance of consumers may prove unwise in the long run because consumers may react to that power by changing participation. However, when data gathered in an electronic transaction clearly and directly serve the consumer, it is useful for both parties. The temptation to resell the data must be judged against the desire not to alienate customers.

NetGain advocates that fully 20 percent of a Net business's initial funds go into tracking the consumer, mouse click by mouse click. But is that truly the best way to spend 20 percent of the company's funds for Internet presence for selling a product, as opposed to, say, starting up an intermediary? If the business's goal is to sell attention span, how much information is necessary? The current standard business assumption is that users should be tracked with as much detail as possible. I have not seen this assumption validated, however, by careful financial analysis.

The tracking of Internet users and concentration of customer information is reminiscent of nothing so much as the command-and-control days of the Vietnam War. The White House was involved in centralized control in which staffers thousands of miles from the actual site used data to direct military operations. White House staffers had minute-by-minute information of the sounds and movement of the Ho Chi Minh Trail that they believed enabled them to determine precisely where a bomb should be dropped to destroy trucks. And, as a result they could claim to have devastated traffic on the trail whether or not that was true. In fact, the Air Force claimed at one point to have destroyed a number of trucks that was greater than the total number of trucks believed to be in North Vietnam at the time!

The White House believed it understood the war and collected and analyzed data exhaustively. Because the White House was certain that the data described the real situation, staffers were effectively blinded by their data. By scientifically managing the data, they failed to manage the war. Similarly, merchants collect data exhaustively in order to understand customers. Ironically, the same business plan that would recommend exhaustive data collection usually claims to understand the customer. Data are not information. Too much data and a focus on careful management of customers can lead to a lack of information and failure to respond to customers' actual (often stated) needs and requests.

Why else is this war comparison reasonable? It provides reams of information that may or may not reflect reality, leading to what is termed "information pathologies"—often referred to outside of academia as the inability to see the forest for the trees (Edwards 1997). It is redolent of the centralized, remote operations justified on a statistical basis with no feedback from the ground, as when the Air Force used data to claim destruction of more trucks than were in existence.

Such "information pathologies" are all too evident as firms enter the information marketplace today. Microsoft was going to dominate the Internet by limiting PC-compatible users to the Microsoft network and obtaining detailed information about the users' machines and habits. Clearly this failed. Yet with Yahoo, a pair of graduate students treating everyone as interested and interesting enjoyed great success. Yahoo may capture customers, but the focus is on customer service and customer cooperation.

Scientific techniques of command and control failed in warfare, as innovation was stifled by statistical arguments that created a tremendous amount of data and no real information. Scientific management mechanisms that rely on data in the absence of context have failed to motivate workers and create the nimble productive businesses that advocates claimed would inevitably result from their application. Is it plausible for Internet businesses to think that applying the same failed principles to customers would create loyalty and long-term success when these techniques failed so utterly with soldiers and workers?

In addition to the inherent fallibility of data and its interpretation, the observation of consumers results in information pathology because so much information is collected that is not used. The most important experience on the Web site is the customer experience—to the customer, to the sale, and to the merchant. Capturing data on connection speed

Confirm
Order

Please verify your order information, shown below. If the information is correct, click on the "Confirm Order" button at the bottom of the page to place your order. If you need to change some information, use the "Back" button on your browser to return to the previous page.

Description	Manufacturer	Quantity	Price	Subtotal
Short Double Curved Track	Brio	2	$ 12.35	$ 24.70
Double Track	Brio	2	$ 6.80	$ 13.60
Supports	Brio	1	$ 10.20	$ 10.20
Order Subtotal				$ 48.50
Shipping				$ 4.85
Total				$ 53.35

Billing Information:

First Name: Jean
Last Name: Camp
Street: 1 Anystreet
Apt/Suite#: NO INPUT
City: Anytown
State/Prov: MA
Zipcode: 01234
Country: us
Phone: 123-456-7890

Figure 7.1
Small-screen version of A2Z site

along with monitor size and existence of helper functions is easy, yet few pages are optimized for this particularly useful piece of information. Though many pages are customized to respond to data about a customer's past purchases, I have yet to come across a Web page customized to respond to information collected about modem speed, helper functions, and screen size.

This can be quite a problem as shown by two examples from my personal experience. First, the A2ZTOys page does not fit a smaller monitor well. Consider the image in figure 7.1. As I was attempting to order at the A2Z site, this was the third screen that popped up. Given where the screen is truncated, that it was the third screen, and my impatient shopping style, I considered my order to have been placed and went to the next store on my list. A2Z is bookmarked on my machine, and I went back later to query about my order. Of course it had not been filled. Figure 7.2 shows the entire page.

This page no doubt has wonderful flow and feel on the developer's monitor. The generous white space must be pleasing to the eye. But given

Confirm Order

Please verify your order information, shown below. If the information is correct, click on the "Confirm Order" button at the bottom of the page to place your order. If you need to change some information, use the "Back" button on your browser to return to the previous page.

Description	Manufacturer	Quantity	Price	Subtotal
Short Double Curved Track	Brio	2	$ 12.35	$ 24.70
Double Track	Brio	2	$ 6.80	$ 13.60
Supports	Brio	1	$ 10.20	$ 10.20
Order Subtotal				$ 48.50
Shipping				$ 4.85
Total				$ 53.35

Billing Information:

First Name: Jean
Last Name: Camp
Street: 1 Nowhere St
Apt/Suite#: NO INPUT
City: Anytown
State/Prov: MA
Zipcode: 01234
Country: us
Phone: 123-456-7890

Shipping Preference:

You have selected Domestic UPS Regular Ground.

Payment Preference:

You have selected to pay for your order on-line with a credit card.

If you are ready to submit your order to us, press "Confirm Order."

**It may take a few seconds to process your order.
Please be patient, and don't press "Stop."
If you press "Confirm Order" more than once,
your order will be submitted multiple times.
You will receive an email to confirm that your
order was processed.**

If you need to make changes, use the "Back" button
on your browser to return to the previous page.

If you encounter any problems or difficulty while using our shopping cart,
please notify: **shopcart@a2ztoys.com**

A2Z Toys™ A Division of Timeless Hobbies, Inc.
75 Danada Square East
Wheaton, IL 60187

(630) 690-5542
M-F 10-8; Sat 10-5; Sun 11-5
Email: **info@a2ztoys.com**
http://www.a2ztoys.com

Copyright © A2Z Toys™ & Timeless Hobbies, Inc.

Figure 7.2
Full-page version of A2Z site

the amount of information available about the customer's machine once the customer links to the A2Z site, there is no reason not to tailor the screen presented to the customer's monitor. There is no reason to squander the customer's attention span by requiring her to hit the PAGE DOWN button four times.

My second example of how a lot of information that is collected and analyzed is far less useful than other types of information that is ignored refers to helper functions. As discussed in chapter 1, Disney is a fine example of excessive use of helper functions. Disney has the most time-constrained set of surfers on the net: young children. Children are in a hurry. Yet the site makes no alteration of presentation or content for the at-home browser despite having information about the connection speed. For example, Disney Radio could be offered in multiple formats with the browser automatically choosing the format suitable to the user's browser and connection speed. Instead, the browser is expected to download at least five helper functions, while (this being Disney) a toddler sits expectantly before the machine. (The toddler actually leaves before the first function is installed.) Simple use of the consumer data already available would provide a far better site from the consumer standpoint than the compilation of further data. Which, then, represents the better use of the vendor's resources?

I cannot say that Disney is the finest example of oblivious Web page design I have yet experienced in terms of lack of responsiveness to information about customers' varying connection speeds, because the Star Trek Insurrection site has Disney beat. Perhaps it is reasonable to assume that every person viewing the Insurrection page has a series of tasks surrounding the computer on which to work while the page laboriously downloads. Perhaps Star Trek is unique in the commitment level of its fans. It is likely to have fans with far more patience and longer attention spans than the Disney site. In either case, there are no convincing arguments for collecting even more data when not even the most basic data already being collected—like connection speed, helper functions, and monitor size—are even being used.

The fundamental reason for customers to insist that merchants choose privacy-enhancing systems is the recognition that we are building a global infrastructure for generations to come. It is a time of heady dreams of millions of dollars, but it is also a time of quiet responsibility. Privacy matters because it does. We can choose to build a surveillance system that shames the simple video technology of Orwell's 1984, or we can choose to continue to build a democratic infrastructure that addresses the range of needs of customers as citizens, parents, workers, and consumers.

There is a fundamental conflict in every information system, including electronic commerce systems: privacy versus data availability. This conflict also exists in the law. Currently legal requirements both protect and prohibit privacy. This chapter has identified specific laws and general principles that affect privacy and are likely to affect electronic commerce.

The concept of privacy has a broad philosophical base. On that base are built state laws, federal laws, and constitutional prohibitions. The applications of these laws to information technology, and digital commerce in particular, are as yet undetermined. Information technology enhances the availability of data, making information easier to collect, analyze, and disclose. It will therefore require a new balance between information privacy and information disclosure that is not reflected in current law.

At times, the laws and regulations on privacy appear to be a maze, constructed of varying and potentially conflicting laws for each category of information. Under which category or categories the Internet will fall is far from clear. Thus only the outline of the structure of privacy law has been included in this text. Examples from the most relevant categories have been considered. This chapter began with a with a brief overview of state laws, because on the Internet one can be doing business in any state. The state laws are based on tort law, which is the earliest privacy protection in the American tradition, drawing heavily on common law. After a discussion of state laws, I touched on federal statutory law was touched upon, and finally, constitutional law.

Having discussed privacy in this chapter, I next turn to data availability. Federal law on information technology and financial transactions, as well as federal cryptography policy, will be discussed. Reporting requirements of financial transactions and limitations on strong cryptography, as the regulations that most affect the design of Internet commerce systems, will be given special attention.

8

Data Reporting: Trusting the Government

A conflict exists between protecting consumer privacy and ensuring that information is available to government so that it can perform its legitimate duties. Thus, in addition to laws protecting privacy, there are laws requiring data reporting and disclosure. New technologies for electronic payment present new risks and require new regulatory approaches, but the basic social motivations behind the regulations remain unchanged. Technology changes, but the core roles of government continue to be security, justice, and general welfare. To consider regulatory requirements for electronic commerce, I strip away existing conventions derived from paper models to categorize the underlying social goals and then suggest new regulatory approaches based on the new mix of concerns electronic commerce is raising. The suggested changes are revisited in the discussions of systems in the last chapters, where information availability for governance is considered.

The fundamental choices for reporting economic data remain the same when the data becomes electronic. Financial information is more prone to privacy violations than other information, however, not only because financial information is innately commercially valuable, but also because the Fourth Amendment does not apply to financial information.

I close the chapter with general policy suggestions. I refer to these suggestions as appropriate in the system analyses in later chapters.

Required Information Reporting

Reporting requirements are a tangential and possibly minuscule part of funds transfer and electronic banking laws. (For the purpose of this chapter, reporting requirements are defined as requirements that information about a transaction or a set of transactions be available to either party of a transaction or to government.) Yet the laws requiring information availability for government can have a tremendous impact on the design of electronic commerce systems—not least by unnecessarily prohibiting the provision of consumer privacy in electronic commerce. Current reporting requirements are based on the assumption of a paper currency model, in which transaction information is either documented on paper or potentially unavailable.

Laws requiring information in the private sector and those involving the public sector are of interest here, especially considering the decreasing distance between public sector and private sector data repositories. For example, to track both federal tax debtors and parents delinquent in providing child support, the federal government has weakened the Privacy Act and the Social Security Act by expanding the use of Social Security numbers as universal identifiers. The laws that require the use of Social Security numbers as financial universal identifiers are the Debt Collection Act and Child Support Enforcement Act.

Sometimes the biases against privacy in reporting requirements are implemented on purpose, as with laws that prevent anonymous payments above a certain size. Sometimes, however, there is simply a mismatch between the paper model on which these laws were based and the strengths and weaknesses of electronic currency systems. I illustrate here that within each category of electronic currency system, technical enhancements can alleviate the need for the trade-offs that have been necessary in paper currency systems.

Similarly, every company and consumer has practices for record keeping and risk mitigation in the paper world. The discussion of appropriate updates for record keeping in government might apply to these private sector practices as well. In what ways is the information required appropriate, and in what ways may that information be inadequate for the electronic realm? The previous explanations of security goals can serve in part to answer these questions.

Consider these questions from the perspective of the federal government. Two classes of businesses should be specifically addressed in this section for the purpose of exploring trust in the government with respect to electronic commerce: depository institutions and consumer credit reporting agencies. These two business types maintain most consumer financial records, and reporting requirements are often specific to these institutions. Businesses that currently handle the most cash—credit unions, savings and loans, banks, and thrifts—have specific record-keeping and reporting requirements. These businesses will be discussed together here as depository institutions. (Note that other regulatory changes, especially the loosening of controls on line-of-business and the reduction of marketing restrictions, are allowing these businesses to merge and converge.) The data kept by these institutions are primarily for risk management and dispute resolution.

To consider reporting requirements without the biases created by the assumption of paper currency, I separate the reporting requirements along two dimensions: system requirements and social goals. First considered is the range of system requirements inherent in regulatory requirements; for example, data must be trapped in a transaction; data must be stored and searchable by account number. The second variable considered is the underlying social motivation of the financial reporting requirement. A single unifying principle in regulations on commerce is lacking. Instead there is a set of underlying reasons that together motivate most reporting requirements.

After having categorized reporting requirements according to data availability requirements and underlying social goals, I construct a matrix that spans the range of goals and techniques. The general alternatives for reporting in the electronic realm are considered. Finally, specific suggestions are included for making the techniques used more compatible with the capacities of electronic commerce so that the goals can be better met and unnecessary violations of privacy reduced.

Techniques for Fulfilling Regulatory Information Requirements
Laws that require certain types of record-keeping are manifestations of social goals. Within electronic information systems exists a wide range of techniques for ensuring information availability, including anonymous updates to aggregates[39] and distributed escrow.[40] Within

39. Anonymous updates to aggregates refers to the ability to alter average information without keeping data on every transaction. It is possible to provide updates to averages and compilations without keeping the individual records.

40. Key escrow is as previously described: trusting encryption keys with some other party besides the person who is linked to the key. Distributed escrow would

regulations based on a paper model, however, this same range does not exist; instead, four basic techniques are used to obtain the data necessary for the government to fulfill its legitimate purposes:

• immediate reporting,
• periodic reporting,
• periodic aggregate reporting, and
• data storage requirements for later access.

Digital information is more easily subject to secondary use, and if data are required for storage, it makes economic sense to try to find other uses. Data requirements increase the burden of trust on the subject of the data when information becomes digital. Additional protections of the information are required to recreate the balance of trust that existed when the data storage was on paper.

Immediate reporting means that documentation on a specific transaction or event must be reported immediately. An example of immediate reporting (not further addressed here) is a police report after a burglary. For the insurance company to respond, there must be a record of the crime filed with law enforcement.

Periodic reporting requires that data are compiled and reported. An example of this is the annual report that wage earners make to the IRS, usually with a 1040 form.

Periodic aggregate reporting requires that aggregates—means, distributions, and trends—of data be reported. For example, companies may report aggregate warehouse numbers for insurance purposes without having to report the specifics of a single day.

Data storage requirements are implicit in all of the previous categories; however, sometimes data storage is required without reporting. In particular there are guidelines for information of many types that must be kept on file but need not be reported. One mundane example is the safety and capacity records of an elevator. It may be in the elevator or in the file. No copy need be mailed to any level of government. Yet it is required that such an inspection occur and be documented.

---

mean trusting some number of parties greater than one (usually much greater than one) in such a manner that to get the key out of escrow, all the parties with pieces of the key must cooperate.

Each type of reporting has different system requirements. It is unusual to approach data reporting from this perspective. The standard approach is to consider the goal and then decide on the reporting. The purpose of this examination is to reconsider how the relationship between goals and requirements is altered by electronic rather than paper records. This examination will be based on how trust is required by the regulatory mechanism chosen, how this is altered as information become digital, and how a change may be an enhancement if the regulatory purpose can be met with a reduction of the trust required.

To implement immediate reporting, a commerce system can consider each transaction to see if immediate reporting is required, such as purchase amount or item purchased, and then initiate a reporting action (e.g., email to fcc.gov, printing a form) when the conditions for immediate reporting are met. Alternatively, the commerce system can prohibit transactions of a given type to avoid immediate reporting requirements, or assume that such reporting is the merchant's responsibility.

Periodic reporting requires collection of data to be compiled and reported. The types of data and the circumstances of reporting vary by justification of the reporting requirement. Gun dealers make some report to the FBI or the ATF, while depository institutions provide data to the Federal Reserve. In all cases here I am concerned with federal requirements that data be compiled and stored. (The local reporting requirements above were simply examples.) With periodic data reporting, the data may be disposed of after the required report is submitted or deleted from general-access computers, so that the potential for internal misuse is minimized.

Periodic aggregate reporting in the paper world requires that all records be kept for verification of the information reported. For example, for a page of tax return there may be a shoebox filled with check stubs and receipts. Again, the types of data, the circumstances of reporting, and the particular agency that has the requirements vary. The commonality I am addressing here is the manner in which the digital form of records changes the trust requirements. Because of the paper model, keeping long-term records for verification is followed in the electronic realm as well. However, there are greater options for data reporting in the electronic realm. For example, individual records could be encrypted for auditing, policies against secondary use could be adopted, and close tracking of internal use of data could decrease risks of misuse. Alternatively, electronic escrow is far more simple than escrow with paper documents. Data storage options are also greater in the electronic realm than the paper arena. Data may be stored encrypted or in such a way that subversion of a single depository provides no useful data. In contrast, with paper records the records are either readable, identifiable and whole, or unavailable. With paper records the common risks are that the records are lost, destroyed, or unavailable. Digital records shift the risk from the entity needing the data (that the records are unavailable) toward the subject of the data (that the records are misused).

Note that where an information requirement fits within these categories is sometimes a matter of interpretation. For example, filing taxes is aggregate periodic reporting in that sources of income are aggregated over the year. It is not aggregate, but still periodic, reporting in that each individual or couple provides their own report. With this caveat in mind, consider an example for each of the four reporting categories.

The 1988 Money Laundering Act empowered the Treasury to require that all suspicious transactions be recorded, and extended the provisions of the Bank Secrecy Act. The Treasury interpreted this as an *immediate reporting requirement*, mandating depository institutions to report all cash transactions above $10,000 and all purchases of financial instruments (such as traveler's checks) over $3,000.[41] All transactions greater than $9,999.99 must be reported by all merchants, using the appropriate forms, to the Treasury. The Money Laundering Act of 1994 expanded this requirement to include all money transmitters, such as Western Union, American Express, and currency exchange houses. Given the extension in 1994, it appears that the Money Laundering Act will also apply to transaction processors in electronic commerce systems.

The most common *periodic data reporting requirement* is the annual individual federal tax filing on April 15. Wages, tips, and other forms of income must be reported to the federal, state, and local governments as

41. For every cash transaction over $10,000, banks must file a Currency Transaction Report; for every $10,000 in cash or monetary instruments exported, the exporter must file an International Transportation of Currency or Monetary Instruments Report. Every business must report cash transactions over $10,000 by filing an IRS form 300. This form is made available to federal tax investigators.

necessary for tax purposes. The details of expenditures can be reported according to taxpayer preference. The increased record keeping possible in electronic currency systems allows for greater detail in records of buyers and sellers. Compare auditing the income of a home business conducted over Ebay and a home business conducted over paper advertisements. That such record-keeping would be effective in preventing tax fraud is suggested by the 800,000 "dependents" who disappeared from tax returns as soon as their Social Security numbers were required (Davis 1995).

The Community Reinvestment Act requires *periodic aggregate data reporting*. It requires financial institutions to make credit and depository services available to all neighborhoods in their service area on an equitable basis. Typically this means that loan application aggregates (sorted by ethnicity of the borrower, neighborhood, or loan amount) must be reported. Specific data requirements vary over time, among states, and even among institutions.

The Bank Secrecy Act, despite its name, actually limits consumer privacy by requiring *detailed record keeping*. It was passed to ensure law enforcement access to detailed records of personal financial transactions under subpoena. It requires that financial institutions maintain records of all transactions over $100 for at least five years. The act requires not only that the records not be encrypted, but also that they consist of images of the bank's record of the transactions, such as a copy of checks. Although the act applies only to cash and cashlike instruments and not to wire transfers at this time, it is reasonable to include it in this analysis, given the number of electronic systems that use cash and checks as the basis for their model, as illustrated in later chapters. (Of course, recording an image of an electronic check is nonsense.)

Many of these reporting requirements are based in part on the "Know your customer" regulations, which prohibit anonymous or pseudonymous bank accounts.

Motivation of Regulatory Information Requirements

To determine if a technological alternative, such as escrowed data or pseudonymous reports, can be optimized to fulfill the requirements for reporting data, the motivation for the reporting requirements must be considered.

It is neither reasonable nor necessary to go through every reporting requirement to ensure that certain alternatives in the electronic realm can accomplish the same objectives. Illustrating that changes can be made in certain reporting requirements without loss of effectiveness of the data is sufficient to illustrate that regulatory flexibility can enable satisfactory auditing to take place without surveillance.

Traditionally four basic reasons have been identified for the existence of reporting requirements (Heggestad 1981):

• law enforcement
• tax collection
• optimization of social welfare
• risk management of the financial system

Law enforcement in this case includes the Federal Bureau of Investigation, the Internal Revenue Service, the Drug Enforcement Administration, and the Customs Service. Data obtained by law enforcement through periodic reporting is made available through FinCEN[42] to other agencies, including Interpol, the Postal Inspection Service, and the Immigration Service (Office of Technology Assessment 1995).

There is some correlation between the reason a reporting requirement exists and the technique selected for compliance, in that law enforcement cannot require periodic individual or aggregate reporting. This is partially a result of the Fourth Amendment: Absent a warrant, the government cannot require that individuals report private activities periodically to law enforcement. Data for use in criminal investigations must be obtained with a warrant. Therefore the following examples of motivation and technique do not include examples of law enforcement in the periodic reporting categories.

Reporting Examples

In this section I construct a conceptual matrix by providing examples for each of the sixteen possible combinations of motivations and techniques

42. The Financial Crimes Enforcement Network (FinCEN) is part of the Department of Treasury and maintains databases used to track financial crimes, including fraud and money laundering.

previously delineated of how reporting requirements could be modified for the electronic realm without compromising the purpose for which the data are required. Only statutory reporting examples are considered, not the regulations written to implement these laws. Regulations are more fluid than statutes, and thus less of a long-term concern. Regulation E, which mandates specific requirements for the implementation of the Electronic Funds Transfer Act, provides an excellent example of this fluidity. It can be and has been revised not infrequently, most recently to better suit the capabilities of stored-value cards[43] (Federal Reserve Bank of New York 1996). The focus here is therefore on the less tractable and more stable statutory requirements.

Immediate Reporting

Consider an immediate reporting requirement for each of these categories: tax collection, optimization of social welfare, and risk management of the financial system. In the case of paper-based information systems, immediate reporting implies reporting within hours or days of when the transaction takes place—immediacy being an increasing shorter window of response. (Immediate reporting for the purposes of law enforcement as created in the Money Laundering Act was discussed previously.)

One immediate reporting requirement designed at least partially for the purpose of tax collection is the requirement that exchanges of title to a house be immediately reported. This allows property tax, liens, and other appropriate fines and taxes to be levied. One cannot own a house legally until the title has changed hands in the public record; thus in this case the reporting finalizes the transaction. In Internet transactions the reporting would be the end of the entire transaction, that is, the global commitment. The same message that confirmed the commitment of all parties to complete the transaction (the global commit) can include the necessary reporting when electronic reporting is supported.

43. A stored value card can be a card with an identifier that is linked to payment in a database. For example, phone cards have an identifier that identifies the card issuer as the entity to be billed for a call. Alternatively a stored value card can be a credit card–sized computer with the memory required to store digital money, the processing ability required to enact transaction, and the communications ability needed to interact with terminals or even other cards.

An example of an immediate reporting requirement for the optimization of social welfare is the requirement that any officer of a company selling or buying stock in that company must report the transaction. This regulation, combined with enforcement of insider trading laws, prevents officers from taking advantage of information about their own companies before it is released, thereby preventing manipulation of the stock market.

Immediate reporting requirements in risk management of financial systems do not exist per se, because the parameters of acceptable risk are set forth in general in bank regulation, and actions defined by these parameters as risk seeking require approval in advance. However, a close approximation to an immediate reporting requirement exists in the requirement under the Truth in Lending Act that any changes in interests rates paid by customers be public and that banks not offer discriminatory rates. Not only does this limit discriminatory pricing (for social good), it also limits banks' ability to use discriminatory pricing to compete for the same few high-return, frequently high-risk customers. Most banks fulfill this requirement by mailing interest rate information to customers in their monthly statements.

Periodic Reporting
Now consider periodic reporting requirements for the purpose of tax collection, optimization of social welfare, and risk management of the financial system. (A periodic requirement for tax enforcement purposes—that is, filing for tax payments or refunds—was previously discussed.) An example of a periodic reporting requirement to assure the stability of the financial system (i.e., risk management) is the requirement that all stock trades be reported to the Securities and Exchange Commission (SEC). The SEC cannot prevent actions such as insider trading and speculation that could weaken the market. Full data on trades are necessary to detect insider trading, so that the criminal penalties can serve as a meaningful deterrent (Ziegler, Brodsky, and Sanchez 1993; Zuckerman 1994). Furthermore, SEC regulations and detection of insider trading require not only the identities of those trading stock but also some attributes—for example, employer and position in the organization—to ensure that senior executives are not taking advantage of privileged information.

An example of periodic reporting requirements for optimizing social welfare are contained in the Home Mortgage Act (HMA), which requires that depository institutions make available to the federal government data on the specific mortgage requests they accept and reject. This provides the government with an opportunity to identify, and therefore rectify, discriminatory practices. The HMA requires that the lending institution keep records of the applicant's age, gender, and race along with his or her application. It does not then prevent the institution from keeping these records stored and linked to the applicant for future interactions, although the Equal Credit Opportunity Act forbids considering any of these factors in decisions about awarding credit. This illustrates a potential opportunity for advanced techniques in information technology to remove this apparent conflict, perhaps by requiring encrypted storage of or highly limited access to HMA records.

Aside from tax collection, there is no periodic aggregate reporting for the purposes of law enforcement, as noted earlier. Reporting aggregate financial information to law enforcement would mean that groups that law enforcement has no reason to suspect and that have acted in no suspicious manner must periodically report to the police, which would violate the Fourth Amendment.

Periodic Aggregate Reporting

An example of periodic aggregate reporting for social equity, as created in the Community Reinvestment Act, was previously discussed.

Periodic aggregate reporting would appear to offer the least threat of data intrusion to the subjects of the data compilation. The periodic aggregate reporting requirements that create a threat to privacy do so by virtue of the data storage required for supporting documentation; that is, the detailed data requirements necessary to make across-the-board reports can be intrusive. An example is the HMA requirement that ethnicity and gender be reported for each issuance of mortgage credit. Ensuring that aggregate reporting does not become intrusive would appear only to require a limitation on secondary use, including resale and data analysis for unrelated internal use. Thus without further consideration, I move on to data storage requirements.

Data Storage

Consider an example of record-keeping requirements for each motivation: law enforcement, tax collection, optimization of social welfare, and risk management of the financial system. (A requirement for maintaining data on certain transactions for five years as part of the Bank Secrecy Act is an example of data storage requirements for law enforcement purposes, as was discussed previously.)

As an example of record-keeping requirements for the purposes of tax collection, storage of all data relevant for purposes of taxation is required for any item or deduction that appears on a tax return until the period of limitation is over. For reported income or deductions, this is three years after filing or two years after paying, whichever is later. The period of limitation for unreported income is six years. If no return is filed, the Internal Revenue Service can demand documentation at any time. Thus the granularity of data storage requirements are controlled by the consumer's willingness to itemize.

The Truth in Lending Act was designed to prevent discriminatory and unsafe lending practices by depository institutions. It requires that issuers of credit include in their reports to consumers the name of the merchant and the date and location of purchase for any purchase for which the consumer is charged. Furthermore, if there is some relationship between merchant and creditor, such as a common parent or shared ownership of a subsidiary, then the item purchased must be reported as well.

To limit the exposure of the banking system, banks are required to keep track of all outstanding loans. Banks are not allowed to delete data concerning loans that fail. Interactions with directors and companies that have seats on a bank's board can be traced with this data. Also, individual votes by directors are required to be recorded to enable regulators to detect, and hopefully avoid, conflicts of interests. This helps investigators act to prevent a bank failure, or in the worst case, trace the cause after a failure.[44]

---

44. Directors of a bank can use influence to provide unsecured loans to themselves. This leaves the directors with the money spent, and the bank with no way to secure the loan. This scenario is familiar to Americans from the savings and loan scandal, where much of the money lost was in fact drained from the banks by the directors, and to Mexicans from the country's recent banking collapse.

These examples illustrate that a myriad of disclosure and reporting requirements serve a wide variety of purposes using the same set of technical requirements. Keeping this set of purposes and techniques in mind, consider the options in an electronic system.

Reconsidering Requirements

The previous set of alternative electronic approaches to obtaining necessary information suggests interesting possibilities. Now we will revisit the set of examples and consider ways that the adoption of technical solutions can be encouraged. Note that as electronic currency evolves, not only are the possible methods of data reporting and compilation different, but the market's capabilities and desires may differ as well. Governance requires data reporting and compilations under the following circumstance:

• The government needs the data to perform legitimate functions.
• The market has been unable to provide the required data adequately without regulation.
• There is no less intrusive reporting requirement under which the market could provide the data.
• The need for data is sufficient to justify the costs.

The costs to meet the need referred to in the last bulleted point include the risks of decreased personal privacy, the monetary cost to those required to report, and the administrative costs to the government in collecting the data and regulating and enforcing its collection. With this in mind, consider those cases where immediate reporting has been deemed necessary.

Immediate Reporting
Of the types of reporting required, immediate reporting may be the least changed by electronic capabilities, with data transmission simply replacing the U.S. Postal Service. Yet the quantity of data reported may be reduced, since electronically reported data can be analyzed at the time of the report. More efficient use of information may require less information to obtain the same result. Reporting data via electronic transmission offers certain options not available in a paper-based reporting, including

masking the identity of participants except as necessary for an investigation and using specialized software to analyze the data for suspicious activities. Immediate data reported on individuals are not usually interesting to the market or to government. Only when a particular case out of multiple data records is identified as worthy of investigation does the information becomes valuable. This suggests that constant pseudonyms could be provided for reporting on the activities of individuals—thus the activities of those who are not acting in a suspicious manner are not recorded in an easily searched way, while those whose actions suggest prohibited activity can be identified after the actions of their pseudonyms have been identified as suspicious.

Immediate reporting requires data compilation. Reports are not sent in and discarded; the data in the reports are kept. The data becomes valuable compilations to be used for direct marketing, business siting, and a myriad of other secondary purposes. Thus the major issue of immediate reporting is the major issue of all four categories of required reporting: secondary use of data. In the next paragraphs I discuss alternatives that would allow use of the aggregate data compilations that result from immediate reporting requirements while maintaining personal privacy.

Consider the promise of pseudonyms in the cases discussed previously. Immediate reporting of title exchange is required when a home is purchased, allowing the local government to levy taxes and identify the correct individuals to pursue when violations of building codes are discovered. What information needs to be accessible on-line to provide those with legitimate needs with easy access while not providing equally easy access to the price of your home and the sum of your holdings? That is, there are degrees of availability. One can make information available in parts and pieces as opposed to selling entire databases. This is a case where limits to disclosure or conditional pseudonymity should apply. If a homeowner pays the bills and maintains his building up to code, then there is no reason for anyone to easily access information about the owners of the property for purely business purposes. For example, to decide how to value my property, it is not necessary to know my identity. Secondary uses of aggregate information would still be allowed, with privacy protected by pseudonyms. In the cases of community need for individual information—for example, when a building is a neighborhood hazard—concerned individuals (e.g., the neighbors or community groups) could request identity information. For example, listings of buildings that owners do not maintain at code would allow community groups and others with an interest in contacting the owner of a specific property to identify that person. Similar arguments hold for making available automobile ownership records.

Conversely, the identity of the individual and the data on the property he owns could be stored with separate agencies so that the agencies must cooperate to link an identity with a purchase. This would allow identities to be made available under special circumstances while preventing the widespread dissemination of information for further analysis, which as shown in the examples in chapter 6 are not always in the interest of the government or the governed.

As discussed earlier, the only immediate reporting requirements currently in place for financial transactions are based on a threshold—for example, the size of the transaction. The techniques for reporting such transactions can be made less intrusive through electronic transmission, as electronically reported data can be immediately analyzed for suspicious activity. Thus, while the same information would be reported, the compilation of stored data resulting from the reports would be more limited and therefor have less potential to violate privacy. Information transmitted that reveals no suspicious activity can then be deleted almost immediately by the receiving agency. Thus it is possible that while less information is compiled, more suspicious activity may actually be identified.

The purchase of stock in a company by one of its directors is a rare case where reporting the identity of the person making a transaction is important because the position of the person must also be identified to establish the transaction's significance. A stock purchase by an individual in charge of mergers and acquisitions in any of the companies involved would be of interest to regulators, as would be a sale by counsel of stock in a company she represents when litigation is pending. Here individuals limit their privacy by choosing a position of responsibility that subjects them to a higher level of scrutiny. A similar argument could be made in the case of examination of financial decisions made by high-level officials in government. In summary, there are cases where the identify of the participant is a critical reason for the reporting requirement. In these cases advanced electronic techniques for protecting privacy may not be useful, as the identity information is a core element of the information.

The reporting required in the Truth in Lending Act is an excellent model for data for institutional oversight without privacy violation. Under that act, banks are not required to report the identity of their customers to the state to prove that all customers have been notified of changes in rates. The banks need only show that a policy exists for such notification and that the institution has followed the procedures established in the policy.

Periodic Reporting

Consider the cases of periodic reporting previously discussed. The HMA is intended to ensure that individuals are not discriminated against on the basis of race or gender. The Community Reinvestment Act (CRA) is similar in that it is intended to ensure that communities, rather than individuals, are not subject to discrimination in lending policies. The reporting requirements in the CRA and the HMA can be unified using the capabilities of electronic data reporting, with loans approved and denied being identified by ethnic origin of requester, ZIP code, minimal financial data, and gender. Financial institutions are thus required to avoid the statistical appearance of discrimination. To avoid fraud in reporting, the agencies could use a cut-and-choose[45] technique to identify fraud statistically. The number of records checked would increase the certainty that no fraud has been committed and would remove the veil of privacy only from those individuals whose records are chosen. Records for verification would be chosen randomly; the point would be detect fraud on the part of the lending institution, not the individual requesting a loan. Mortgage information is already maintained on-line, and is in fact sorted so that information can be sold to other providers of financial services (Fenner 1993). Thus, using a cut-and-choose technique is not as costly a proposal as it might initially appear.

45. In a cut-and-choose technique, selected records are chosen (or challenged) and the information necessary for further verification for the chosen records is demanded.

Periodic Aggregate Reporting

Periodic aggregate reporting is problematic in that it implies storage of individual consumer data to obtain the aggregate data required for reporting. Thus, while periodic aggregate reporting may appear much less of a risk than immediate reporting, in fact the risk in both cases results more from the supporting compilation of data than the reporting itself.

If consumers had smart cards,[46] periodic reporting without identity information could be possible with anonymous updates of aggregate information (Camp and Tygar 1994). The creation of smart cards offers one solution to the need to keep specific data to support aggregate reporting; however, some individuals will inevitably lose such cards. This implies that those with data they might wish the bank would forget could simply lose the information. Mandatory back-ups at a trusted facility could mitigate this problem, but selecting widely trusted machines for back-up, and solving disputes about transactions that have not been backed up is no minor matter in technical or political terms. (In technical terms, it may not be simple to correlate the data across the databases in different institutions. In political terms, deciding who is at risk for losing money is rarely easy.)

Data Storage

A fundamental problem with reporting data is that it requires that these data be captured. Once data have been captured with internal disclosure, external disclosure and the resulting creation of privacy-threatening compilations present further complications. Thus the techniques to mitigate the risk to privacy for those data compilations required to support various types of reporting will also apply here. Because no reporting is required for data compilations, however, it is possible that regulatory—as opposed to technical—mechanisms may be more feasible. This is because private institutions need not be concerned about forced judicial release of information under sunshine laws, so hiding identity information is less critical. Misuse of the data, however, remains an important issue.

---

46. The stored-value cards with processing power, memory, and connectivity mentioned in footnote 36 are sometimes referred to as "smart cards" to distinguish them from the "dumb cards" that passively link to a database.

Current limitations on and requirements for disclosure apply only to the government, not to the institutions required by the federal government to store information. Furthermore, financial data have only limited protection under the Fourth Amendment. Thus only weak limits exists on disclosure of information to government.

Internal disclosure refers to the use of required data compilations within the financial services institution for purposes other than those for which they were collected. When financial regulation requires investment in data compilation, allowing institutions to use the data collected internally can soften the financial blow.

When concentration or monopolistic powers are involved, however, the use of such data can become more problematic. As the type of transactional information collected becomes more detailed, the use of this information in decisions about internal hiring, promotion, and consumer credit provision becomes an increasingly important issue. For example, can a bank look through consumer records to evaluate applicants for positions within the bank? Currently the bank has the right to do so, since this is considered valid internal use under current law.

What of internal disclosure for purposes of prosecution? A hypothetical example that that not too far-fetched is the possibility that Microsoft could use information obtained through its network services to identify possible violators of electronic copyright. There is currently no prohibition against Microsoft using its own internal data to assist law enforcement in identifying possible thefts of software. Legally, it does not matter that data used in this way were obtained without the consumer's knowledge. An example of this use of Microsoft's data compilations can be found with the Melissa virus. Melissa used the MicrosoftWord macros to subvert Microsoft mail programs and servers. Microsoft used registration information that linked the identity of the user to the copy of MSWord used to create the macro. This was secondary use of data in order to cooperate with government prosecution and investigation. (A difficult and expensive alternative to cooperating with detecting misuse of badly designed features would be for Microsoft to build secure, reliable software.)

Consider now external disclosure. Any data collected that can be used for internal decisions may be sold under current law to other organizations for similar decision-making purposes. Data sold include house purchase records, medical records, records of grocery store purchases, and records of on-line buying habits. There are currently no constraints on the commercial trade of such data. In fact, for most data the government requires that once the government has obtained the data, it must release it to organizations who request it, regardless of their motivation. Two examples of this were include in the previous discussion of privacy with respect to billing information for women's health services and worker's compensation.

In light of the motivations and the options that electronic information systems and information storage create, existing requirements seem unnecessarily intrusive. The Truth in Lending Act storage requirement for documentation of each consumer's transactions could be changed so that the customer need have only a valid signed agreement for every transaction, and upon presenting that receipt can obtain a full refund from either the merchant or the financial intermediary. Current electronic commerce protocols can be designed so that the credit grantor need not store records of items bought in order to provide receipts—encrypted signed receipts or transfer of purchase orders provide nonrepudiation. (Recall the discussion of public key cryptography and the capacity of digital signature techniques to provide nonrepudiation.) The practical requirement that information about purchases be recorded in a format that can easily be searched, correlated, and reproduced exacerbates the threat of data surveillance. Reporting requirements, implicit data storage requirements, and explicit data storage requirements should be evaluated in part on the basis of this risk to privacy.

Before requirements for reporting of transactional data are created, the threat of possible surveillance should be balanced against the wrong being addressed by the requirement being imposed. This suggests that any consumer whose data is compiled in fulfillment of a government requirement should have her privacy protected by law.

Cryptography Policy

Although information technology has increased threats to and breaches of privacy by increasing data availability, it has also increased the power of individuals to maintain their privacy—particularly through cryptography. However, the federal prohibition of the export of cryptographic technology (discussed in the following section) has effectively prevented the widespread implementation of strong cryptography[47] in operating systems and communications packages intended for the global market (Froomkin 1996). This prohibition has affected the design of electronic commerce systems intended for export (including the Secure Electronic Transactions and the Secure Sockets Layer systems described in detail later in this text).

Cryptographic technology has historically been the purview of governments. In the United States the now defunct Coordinating Committee for Multilateral Export Controls explicitly classified cryptographic technologies as exclusively military technologies shortly after the committee's creation in 1949. Control of exports of cryptographic technology falls under the Export Administration Act, the Arms Control Act, and the International Traffic in Arms Regulations (ITAR). The view of cryptography as war technology is expressed in the Export Administration Act, which prohibits "the export of goods and technology which would make a significant contribution to the military potential of any other country." Thus cryptography has been controlled as Auxiliary Military Equipment under ITAR. Note that any cryptographic technology that can be used by civilians can be used by the military. There is, as explained earlier, no such thing as military-grade cryptography.

Under ITAR, cryptographic technology can be exported if restricted to the following purposes: copy protection, authentication, financial information, integrity without confidentiality, compression, or prevention of theft of information services (such as pay television). Thus without a specific license to do so, the export of any device that provides strong cryptography for protecting privacy in an electronic system is prohibited because it falls outside of the categories listed above (and such licenses are rarely forthcoming).

Note that the recommended key lengths for encryption recommended in the previous chapter would be allowed specifically for the encryption

47. Recall that in some cryptography systems, the keys can be broken or retrieved through escrow. Systems in which there is no key escrow and the key cannot be obtained through cryptographic analysis are considered "strong," in contrast to "weak" escrowed or breakable systems.

of payment information in systems intended for international use. However, a general use system, such as the Secure Sockets Layer, cannot incorporate strong encryption technology (for export) because that encryption technology could also be used to provide general communications privacy.

Current national cryptographic standards are not adequate for protection of privacy and security in Internet commerce (National Research Council 1996; Schneier 1995). In 1988, the National Institute of Standards and Technology (NIST) determined that the Federal Information Processing Standards (FIPS) on encryption needed to be replaced, and that any replacement should be "public, unclassified, implementable in both hardware and software, usable by Federal agencies and U.S. based multinationals." The criteria developed by NIST with public input reflected the needs of Internet commerce: portability across operating systems, exportability across national borders, the need to provide privacy as well as financial security, and the capacity to optimize for specialized applications.

The standards NIST actually adopted fell short of accomplishing these goals, as have the subsequent proposals. The first proposal, which included a requirement for a flawed escrow system, as defined in the Escrowed Encryption Standard (National Institute of Standards and Technology 1994), was classified (not public) and could therefore be implemented only in hardware. Because of strong objections,[48] the requirement that the Federal government maintain databases for key escrow has since been removed. The algorithm has been declassified. This Escrowed Encryption Standard has been followed by multiple additional proposals for escrowed systems, and governmental implementation of escrow systems plods determinedly along.

The analysis and evaluation of cryptography policy was subjected to a complete review by the National Research Council. The resulting report, *Cryptography's Role in Securing the Information Society* (National Research Council 1996), recommended a new approach to cryptography. The report's recommendations most relevant to electronic commerce are:

48. In the NIST comments period on the Clipper proposal, NIST received 320 comments. Of 22 government, 22 industry, and 2 individual comments, 2 were positive, 4 were neutral, and the remainder covered the range of negative, from those expressing specific misgivings to condemnations of the entire proposal.

• National cryptography policy should be developed by the executive and legislative branches on the basis of open public discussion and should be governed by the rule of law.
• National cryptography policy affecting the development of commercial cryptography should be more closely aligned with market forces.
• Export controls on cryptography should be progressively relaxed but not eliminated.
• The U.S. government should take steps to assist law enforcement and national security to adjust to new technical realities of the information age.

Cryptography policy has managed to appear to be constantly in flux for several years, without many significant changes actually occurring. Even with the possibility that this book may be in print for a number of years, it is nevertheless safe to write with the assumption that the following will be true at any point in the near future when a reader might pick up this book: "Currently the Senate is considering a bill to lift controls on export of cryptography, and there is a case under the First Amendment. The current Administration has offered a new key escrow proposal." In 1992 it was widely assumed that any White House containing now-Vice President Al Gore would be an advocate for freedom to export cryptography, yet export controls remain in place today. Thus although it may appear from the foregoing discussion that this problem will be addressed shortly, there is historical basis for believing that this will not be the case.

Cryptography policy is a case of conflict, with data availability on one side and privacy and security on the other. On the one hand, cryptography is currently restricted for the purposes of law enforcement and national security. On the other hand, removing constraints on cryptography would serve commercial, security, and privacy interests. Controls on cryptography forcefully illustrate that there are reasons other than reliability for providing identity information.

Disclosure Summary

In this chapter I have illustrated that current policies, including cryptography policy, immediate reporting requirements, and data requirement, reflect an awareness of the utility of electronic information, in exclusion of an understanding of the threats posed by emerging technology. The juxtaposition of limited availability of true anonymity and a legal regime that arguably promotes privacy violations hinders the development of secure, reliable, and private commerce systems.

One clear conclusion from this examination is that laws written for rapidly changing areas, such as funds transfer and consumer lending, should be written in the least technologically restrictive language possible, so regulators may allow or require innovative solutions without waiting for an act of Congress.

The response by the legal and regulatory communities to privacy-threatening innovations, and to new technologies in general, has been the development of technology-specific rulings after these technologies have been dispersed through the marketplace. This approach is becoming progressively less successful as the rate of technical change increases. It may not be possible to respond to information technologies after they have reached some critical mass; privacy protections may need to be included in the hardware (Morgan 1992). Arguably, in this information age, there needs to exist a system of laws recognizing that the right to privacy is technology independent.

In the conflict between privacy rights and data reporting, many problems associated with paper currency remain with electronic currency: law enforcement concerns, tax collection, auditing and fraud detection, prevention of discrimination in the provision of financial services, financial privacy, the assurance of funds for socially desirable goals, and the balance between risk-reducing regulation and productive but risk-seeking free market behavior, just to name a few. There is no reason to abandon the goal of solving these problems as currency becomes increasingly electronic. But as the nature of currency and commerce change, previously chosen methods of advancing regulatory interests are increasingly ill-suited to the progressively more electronic environment in which they operate. Just as different regulatory techniques are appropriate for different forms of paper currency, different regulatory techniques are appropriate for different electronic applications. This presents a particularly difficult problem in the case of transactional data. From the perspective of customers, information about their purchases is clearly personal. For merchants and electronic commerce providers, it is critical business information about consumer preference, as well as a product in its own right.

The current debate over customer information in the increasingly competitive voice telephony market may provide a glimpse of the conflicts to come. Data about whom a customer calls, and when, are Customer Proprietary Information (CPI). The collection and use of this information has tremendous privacy implications. It also has increasing market value, especially as local telephone markets become competitive. Knowledge of the calling patterns of a region, a neighborhood, or an individual is a powerful weapon in the competitive marketplace because such information can inform infrastructure development, pricing, and marketing decisions. To provide a level playing field for the incumbent local telephone service provider (the regional Bell operating company) and any new entrants into the local telephone business, all possible entrants into the local communications market should have the same information. However, this implies that all information about the location and duration of every phone call a consumer makes should be available to anyone who can claim a possible competitive interest.

CPI is both important commercial and private personal information. Customers expect privacy concerning the recipients and the contents of their phone calls, and there is a tradition of providing such privacy in the Bell system. Yet there is also a public interest in fair competition that would compel the release of such information. This type of conflict will become increasingly common as information technology proliferates. The likely solution to the CPI debate—widespread information availability— is not entirely promising as a model for resolving the conflict. The intelligence in the hardware at the endpoints of Internet commerce, however, offers a broader range of possibilities for resolution than are available in telephony.

Now the discussions of privacy and security are complete. The next chapter addresses transactional reliability. Specific systems are then examined before the book concludes with some basic risk-avoidance practices.

9

Transactions

The relationship between reliability and anonymity is this: with high levels of reliability, anonymity is a not a threat to accountability. With no reliability, anonymity is a license to steal for one party or another, as an anonymous party can neither demand compensation nor be found to be subject to the demands of others. Identity is often part of the information about transaction participants that is exchanged during a transaction (or dispute resolution, in the case that a transaction fails).

Transactions with transactional reliability have atomicity. Transactional reliability originated in the study of fault tolerance. A system's fault tolerance is its ability to provide reliable service despite some classes of failures. For example, one would not want a computer to fail because a single transistor fails. Therefore computer hardware design includes fault tolerance to ensure functionality in the event of such small failures. Similarly, if a single message is lost, a transaction should not fail; for example, there should be no confusion between the parties as to the status of the transaction. A transaction should be reliable despite certain network failures. Some systems have limited transactional reliability, which provides sufficient information for governance (as defined by the information requirements enumerated in the previous chapter) regulations—for example, First Virtual. Additionally, some systems with transactional reliability would nevertheless not meet consumer protection or law enforcement requirements for transactional information. In this chapter I explain how this is possible, how to evaluate the technical reliability of a system, how to recognize when dispute resolution is based exclusively on policy frameworks, and when such resolution is supported by reliable design.

Reliability

Reliability is the ability to recover from failures to a consistent, isolated, and durable state. Reliable electronic commerce protocols provide certainty in the face of network failures, memory losses, and attackers in that the more reliable a transaction, the less the uncertainty that comes with extensions of trust. An unreliable electronic commerce system cannot distinguish a communications failure from an attack on the system. If a failure can be used effectively to commit theft, then such attacks will certainly occur.

Reliability and security are interdependent. Reliability is not security. Reliable protocols on servers that are not secure will provide reliable services to attackers as well as authentic users. As noted above, attackers can exploit a lack of reliability in an electronic commerce system to commit theft.

Reliability in electronic commerce requires security to provide authentication, integrity, and irrefutability. Reliable electronic commerce provide fail-proof transactions. This fundamental requirement implies other technical requirements. It is widely agreed that providing fail-proof transactions in an electronic currency system requires divisibility, scalability in number of users, conservation of money, exchangeability or interoperability, and availability (Cross Industry Working Group 1995; Okamoto and Ohta 1991; Medvinski and Nueman 1993; Low, Maxemchuck, and Paul 1993; Brands 1993). The properties that characterize a fail proof transaction are described in this section.

ACID *Properties*

The acronym ACID refers to transactions that are atomic, consistent, isolated, and durable, as defined in chapter 2 and explained further below. (Recall the concepts introduced in the discussion of cash transactions.) ACID transactions are robust, meaning that they can prevail in the face of network outages, replay attacks, failures of local hardware, and errors of human users (Gray and Reuter 1993).

Atomic with respect to transactions has a Newtonian sense. That is, atomic transactions cannot be split into discrete parts: customer's payment, merchant's receipt of payment, and merchant's delivery of receipt or goods. An atomic transaction either fails completely or succeeds completely. An atomic transaction conserves funds—money is neither created nor destroyed during the transaction. For example, consider what happens when a customer transfers funds from a savings account to a checking account. Either the checking account is credited and the savings account is debited, or neither account balance changes. In atomic transactions, there is no case where money either disappears from both accounts or is credited to both accounts.

A transaction is said to be *consistent* if all parties relevant to the transaction agree on critical facts of the exchange. If a customer makes a $1 purchase from a merchant, then the transaction is consistent if the merchant, the customer, and the bank (if it is involved) all agree that the customer has $1 less and the merchant has $1 more.

Transactions that do not interfere with each other are termed *isolated*. The result of a set of overlapping transactions must be equivalent to some sequence of those transactions executed in a nonconcurrent, serial order. Transactions may be overlapping because they are made at the same time and place, or near the same time by the same parties. If a customer makes two $1 transactions, then the two payments should not be confused by the customer, merchant, or bank. The customer should not end up being charged twice for one item, nor should one of the payments be counted twice to give the customer $2 in total goods for the single (miscounted) $1 payment.

When a transaction can recover to its last consistent state, it is *durable*. A transaction recovers when uncertainty is removed and there is a clear state—that is, everyone knows where they are, what message they are expecting, and the status of the transaction. For example, if a customer physically drops a dollar when making a purchase, that dollar does not disappear. When the customer retrieves the dollar, it is restored to its last consistent state. Similarly, money available in a computer before it crashes should not disappear during the crash, but should still be available when the machine reboots.

Atomicity, consistency, isolation, and durability in a transaction make nonrepudiation possible in electronic commerce. Suppose, for example, that a customer wants to make a purchase from the local software store. The customer must pay, or promise to pay, the purchase price for the item she wishes to purchase. The merchant either gets payment (cash) or proof of intent to pay (a standard purchase order or check). The customer gets a receipt from the merchant indicating that she has paid and expects certain merchandise to be delivered. When it is delivered, the customer signs a receipt for the merchant indicating that delivery has occurred. Each action is linked with some verification of the action so that each party has some proof in case the other party attempts fraud or fails to perform. Linking an action with the proof of the action provides nonrepudiation for that specific action. When all the steps of a transactions are bound together (atomic), consistent, isolated, and durable from other transactions, the nonrepudiation of the steps creates nonrepudiation in the transaction as whole.

Degrees of Atomicity

Electronic commerce systems have widely varying scopes, some covering only payment and others addressing everything from negotiation to delivery. Different electronic commerce systems offer different degrees of atomicity to address the problems of remote purchases: money atomicity, goods atomicity, and certified delivery.

Of course electronic transactions may have no atomicity. No atomicity requires mutual trust among participants. The physical equivalent is sending cash or goods in the mail to a post office box. Sending cash to the post office box is a bad idea because the recipient can claim never to have received the cash. The recipient then provides no receipt and delivers no goods. Among electronic currency systems considered here, Digicash has no atomicity. This means that the merchant can receive payment and claim never to have had it (Yee 1994). It can be easy for a customer or merchant to commit fraud in systems with no atomicity.

Electronic transactions may have money atomicity. The physical equivalent to money atomicity is paying cash in person. Money-atomic systems have no mechanism for certifying that merchandise has been delivered. If used for remote purchase with accepted techniques for the delivery of physical goods, money atomicity is quite adequate. But fraud, through a customer's theft of goods or a merchant's refusal to deliver goods after payment, may be easy when systems with only money atomicity are used for transactions involving goods with on-line delivery, such as software. Among the systems discussed here, the Secure Electronic Transactions system provides money atomicity (Mastercard 1996).

The highest level of atomicity in electronic transactions is goods atomicity. Goods atomicity corresponds (in a physical transaction) to using a certifiable payment mechanism with certified delivery. Goods atomicity provides high reliability and reduces the opportunity for merchant fraud. Goods atomicity is the electronic equivalent of cash on delivery: the merchant is not paid unless the delivery is made. The customer does not pay unless there is a delivery.

The highest level of atomicity possible in an electronic commerce system is certified delivery. With certified delivery the customer pays only if the item delivered matches the description of the item promised. Although this amounts to a semantic matter, it is powerful nonetheless. Cybercash owns many of the relevant patents on certified delivery.

Atomicity depends on design and implementation of the electronic commerce system in use as well as the business assumptions on which the design is based. Atomicity depends on funds-available policies because of rollback. Rollback is a technique in which all steps in a transaction are recorded and then reversed until the most recent consistent state of the transaction is reached. For example, if a customer's attempt to transfer funds from checking to savings fails to occur, funds withdrawn from the customer's checking account are placed back into the customer's checking account, restoring the transaction to the last consistent state.

Rollback becomes more complicated as financial transactions involve transactions in multiple databases. For example, suppose a customer orders, as a frequent flyer award, a free ticket and supplies a credit card number to pay for the courier charge. If the entire fare is mistakenly charged to the card, rollback is obviously possible, but requires coordinating three databases: the airline frequent flyer database, the airline billing database, and the billing database of the credit card company. This is obviously a bit more complex than simply redepositing unused funds at a single institution. As transactions become still more complex and involve even more databases, rollback becomes progressively more complex.

Superficially, electronic transactions are just exchanges of bits, and if such an exchange can be reversed, then the transaction can be made atomic. Yet for Internet commerce to expand, there must be some interoperability not only between different Internet commerce systems but also between Internet currency and traditional forms of money.

Therefore, if the rollback for collecting a fraudulent transaction takes too long, the fraudulent party could abscond with unrecoverable cash prior to rollback, making the later acquisition of bits meaningless. This implies that a transaction that implements atomicity using rollback and that is theoretically atomic may not truly be atomic. Two-phase commit, in which the record or funds involved are locked until all parties commit to the transaction, solves this problem. (The point at which all parties agree that the transaction has been completed is called the *global commit* or *global commitment.*) This implies that for rollback to be possible for long periods after a transaction has been entered into, funds should remained locked until commit, so that the money can not be withdrawn or moved in the interim.

Money atomicity, consistency, isolation, and durability provide conservation of money: money is neither created nor destroyed in a transaction.

Scalability

Scalability sounds exactly like what it is: a system's ability to scale transactions. Transactions can scale in the size of a transaction (very small to very large) or in the number of parties (upward to millions).

Electronic transactions were initially adopted for business-to-business relationships because the amount of the transaction can be scaled upward. Because of the difficulty of securing large amounts of physical cash, paper cash is troublesome for large-scale transactions, such as those over hundreds of thousands of dollars. Electronic fund transfers started with large-scale transactions made through private networks between large institutions. These large-scale transactions are sufficiently valuable that they make the cost of extremely careful management of single-use cryptographic keys an eminently reasonable expenditure. (Of course, these transactions often also occur on a proprietary network, but with careful key management a proprietary network is unnecessary, and without careful key management a proprietary network is inadequate.) Obvious examples of high-value networks include FedWire and CHIPs.[49]

49. FedWire is the largest of the electronic funds transfer systems in that the largest-value transactions pass through FedWire. FedWire links domestic financial institutions with the Federal Reserve System.

Microtransactions are at the far end of the same scale. Microtransactions are valued at fractions of a cent. Microtransactions enable entirely new markets. For example, consider banner ads an inchoate form of microcurrency. There is now a market in single clicks on an ad and sets of eyeballs viewing an ad. An as-yet-undeveloped market is that for temporally valuable or specialized publications. For example, consider the number of people who might have paid to read some number of words in the *Wall Street Journal* on "Black Monday," October 19, 1987, compared to the number who would want to buy the *Journal* on a daily basis. The difference between the daily purchasers and the potential purchasers on October 19 is large enough to be of interest, but not sufficiently large that the cost of building the distribution infrastructure to reach all potential customers on October 19 can be justified. The Internet can serve these tiny temporal information markets by reducing transactions costs, providing instant connectivity, offering and widespread distribution.

Microtransactions on the Internet can be implemented using techniques that are inherently suitable to small transactions (e.g., Millicent) or by spreading the cost of multiple transactions over many transactions (e.g., MicroMint). (Both systems are described in detail in chapter 11.)

Divisibility

Divisibility is essentially the ability to make change, to divide a currency into discrete parts so that any sum might be exchanged. This is not the trivial matter it might seem at first. The ability of instruments like checks to create instructions with exact amounts, such as $435.68, removes the need to make change. But once created, the amount designated on such an instruction cannot be divided. A check for $435.68 cannot simply be torn and used to make two purchases of $217.84. It cannot be divided; it must be converted (through interoperability) to another form that is divisible.

There are two basic types of currency: notational and token. Token currencies are currencies in which the value is bound to the currency, as with commodities, gold, and bills. During transactions, the tokens are exchanged. Notational currency exists as a notation in a ledger, and during transactions instructions to alter those notations are exchanged. (This distinction is explained further in chapter 11.)

Notational currencies address divisibility by requiring an exact transactional amount for each purchase. Notational currencies require that notes be validated (deposited, in the case of checks, and authorized, with credit cards) for each transaction.

Some token currencies for microtransactions do concern themselves with making change, by effectively making every payment in pennies. So that the division of 43,568 pennies into two equal amounts is not difficult. Thus divisibility is not an issue in token systems for microtransactions.

Note that availability is a security issue as well as a reliability issue, as described in chapter 4. Systems where the money cannot be accessed or spent do not provide reliability in that money is effectively destroyed.

Interoperability

A rainy day. A check. A wallet full of credit cards. No cash. No taxi. The taxi takes only cash. The potential passenger is wet and the driver has lost a sale because of the lack of interoperability. As illustrated by this example, interoperability is the ability to exchange money in one form for money of another form. Cash and credit cards do not have real-time interoperability, so the potential passenger is all wet. While credit cards can be used for cash advances, and checks turned into demand deposits, cash and credit cards are not perfectly interoperable. Yet for money to be a standard of value does require interoperability. As the wet traveler example illustrates, interoperability is not absolute; there are degrees of interoperability.

The ideal market goal of every purveyor of an electronic commerce system is its offering become the sole standard. The ideal of all customers and merchants is that they get to choose among a suite of commerce mechanisms that are widely accepted and can interact.

The best way to prevent competition among systems is to establish a system that is not interoperable. The best way to assure competition among systems is to require that all systems be interoperable. Thus it is in the interest of those searching for a monopoly to create commerce systems that lack interoperability. The vendor of such a commerce system can then extract payment for every transaction.

In the electronic environment, interoperability of a protocol in terms of wide use also means that it can be implemented on many and diverse platforms. Open standards encourage this type of interoperability. Low requirements (e.g., have good credit, have a bank account) for participation in electronic commerce also encourage interoperability through wide use, by expanding the base of possible customers. Restrictions on participation have the reverse effect. For example, an electronic commerce system that requires that customers have a credit card (Mastercard 1996) prohibits the participation of anyone without a credit history and significant income, as well as anyone who simply chooses not to possess a credit card. Credit card requirements may exclude some of the heaviest Internet users: students.

Interoperability of a protocol in terms of convertibility means that different vendors' software can exchange data; in electronic commerce, converting money requires the ability to exchange data. Agreements to exchange funds can be handled within the business community, as shown by the evolution of the check-clearing system, without regulatory requirements for interoperability, but this requires informed consumers. Interoperability is important for the expansion of Internet commerce; without it the number of customers who can be reached may be dramatically decreased.

Interoperability is not a critical research issue in the theoretical study of secure electronic commerce protocols, because even systems that are not secure (First Virtual 1995a) can provide interoperability. However, understanding the details of interoperability means understanding some of the risks involved. In particular, if two systems are interoperable, a failure of one system can cause problems with the other system. A cynical definition of a distributed system—"one in which a computer that you have never seen, that is not part of your organization, and that is miles away can prevent you from getting your work done"—echoes this problem. When a system failure causes a failure in a connected but not necessarily related system, the effect is called *cascading*. Interoperability can create the possibility for financial cascading. Conversely, a lack of interoperability means that one system must eventually emerge as dominant, and then the discovery of one weakness will infect the entire system. That is, just like biological communities, information networks resist viruses more effectively if there is heterogeneity. Heterogeneity requires interoperability.

Fully interoperable systems can interact seamlessly. Systems can also have limited interoperability. Examples of limited interoperability today can be found with cash, credit cards, and checks. That all merchants who accept cash cannot accept credit cards illustrates the limits to interoperability (recall the empty taxi). A credit card bill may be paid with a check. Cash can be obtained using a credit card. A check can be exchanged for cash at a bank, and cash can be deposited into a checking account. Another example of limited interoperability is the credit approval system: although a merchant must have a relationship with Visa and American Express to take both cards, the same hardware can be used to check multiple credit cards. The acceptance of one card does not enable the acceptance of the other. However, there is a shared interoperable standard that means that the merchant need not purchase new hardware to handle transactions involving one card if he already has the hardware to handle another.

Let's return for a moment to the example of the taxi. The driver of the taxi does not accept other mechanisms of payment for three reasons: specialized equipment, trust, and overhead. Consider the specialized equipment required to accept payment mechanisms other than cash. In the case of the credit card, the driver needs to have at least one piece of unconnected hardware that he can use to record the information on the credit card. Ideally the driver would also have a telephone-based link to the credit card provider to verify that the card is valid. Though a wireless phone does not qualify as specialized equipment, the hardware to read the magnetic strip on the card and communicate with the card issuer certainly falls into that category. For owner-operated cabs, each driver would also have to have a merchant account with the company that issued the credit card the customer is presenting.

The second issue precluding the driver from accepting payments other than cash is trust. To accept a check, the taxi driver would have to extend trust to passengers with respect to their creditworthiness. To accept currency, on the other hand, the driver needs only trust his ability to detect counterfeit bills and the stability of the coin of the United States.

Overhead is a function of trust and specialized equipment, yet it deserves consideration on its own as an obstacle to the driver's accepting means of payment other than cash. In the case of credit cards and checks, a significant part of the overhead costs involved is incurred in establishing a relationship with the purveyor of the commerce mechanism. Note that one does not have to have a relationship with the U.S. government to use its currency. In fact, many users of U.S. currency—drug dealers for example—would like to prevent any type of relationship with the federal government. Yet to accept credit cards or a check, it is necessary for the merchant to have an established relation with a depository institution approved by the Federal Deposit Insurance Corporation. (Of course many of the aforementioned government-avoiding drug dealers manage to have an arms' length relationship with the FDIC by using approved banks, despite the best efforts of law enforcement.) Given a bank account, there is also the issue that the check must be deposited. In both the check and credit card cases, there is the cost of money over time. That is, the funds are not available immediately after the transaction. These same constraints can exist in Internet commerce, as discussed in chapter 2, although there the concern is the ability to reach all users.

Because conducting transactions in hard cash is all but impossible, Internet commerce faces the same three issues: need for specialized equipment, trust, and overhead. In the case the of Internet commerce, the equipment required is specialized software, usually free to the consumer but at some cost to the merchant. Trust is a ubiquitous issue, as discussed throughout this text. Overhead is a function of network bandwidth required and processing on the consumer's computer.

Open Systems, Standards, and Protocols

A relevant example of electronic interoperability is Web clients (browsers) and servers—any browser can be used with any server. A contrast is the use of a proprietary system, such as LotusNotes or Microsoft groupware. If a company chooses a Microsoft groupware product, then its ability to offered controlled but seamless access to the Web is limited. An example of limited interoperability is Macintosh and Microsoft operating systems. A program written for Windows will operate on a Macintosh (using

SoftWindows), but the reverse is not true. A Macintosh can read an IBM-compatible disk, but a IBM compatible is just that, and an IBM machine cannot access information on a Macintosh-formatted disk. Yet none of the operating systems—MacOS or any member of the Windows family—is open. So any interoperability that exists can be removed as soon as the market is considered sufficiently captured (not likely with MacOS).

In chapter 1 I noted that the Internet is built on open standards. Increasingly today there is a buzz over open systems and open source. Standards are documents that define protocols. Protocols are communications standards that define a series of messages and the syntax for those messages. Code is the implementation of the protocol (which should be compatible with the standard). Code is the actual software, the detailed language description of how the standard actually works in practice. Standards are the ideals of how the code should work. Open standards enable interoperability. Open source code ensures that interoperability is possible. Interoperability does not require open code. Open source code is open to review and reuse. This has fundamental trust implications, but first, let us address the issue of interoperability. Because the code is open, it can be wrapped—that is, other code can be added so that the input to and output from the code can be altered to any format. Since the code can be altered, it can be made compatible with any system.

Consider the drivers for vendor, merchants, and customers. Many vendors selling electronic commerce solutions offer open standards. This means that the stated trust relationships between the parties can be understood with a close analysis of the protocol. Standards that are not open (for example, Mondex) ask all users to take on faith that Mondex has the judgment to set correct trust relationships. Since the proliferation of physical monetary mechanisms suggests that different trust relationships are appropriate in different transactions, it is unlikely (bordering on impossible) that Mondex can make such judgments correctly for all parties. In fact, it is extremely unlikely if not impossible for any vendor to make such judgments.

Open standards require less trust in the vendor than closed standards. There are no security advantages to closed standards, as explained in chapters 3 and 4. Open standards are more likely to offer interoperability, and they allow the trust implications of interactions with other systems to be examined.

Open source code, also known as open code, requires the least trust in the vendor. With open code there is no lock-in. Customers and merchants can move between code suppliers, service suppliers, and thus probably between Internet commerce mechanisms as they evolve. Open source can be viewed and examined. After open source is purchased and installed, any competent programmer can alter the programs to add interoperability. Notice that this does not imply a lack of security. Linux, the open source operating system, is more stable, more powerful, and has fewer documented security flaws than Windows NT. (In addition, there is no version of MSWord for Linux, so the MSWord macro viruses that exploded onto the Internet in 1999 cannot effect Linux.)

If the code for a commerce protocol is open, that code can be examined. Any shortcuts that have trust implications—for example, shortcuts in key generation—or deviations from the open standard implemented in the code can be seen.

Selecting a proprietary standard is an extreme extension of trust: trust that there will be support for critical functions in future upgrades, trust that security failures will be addressed quickly, trust that the level of security selected by the vendor will remain appropriate for the merchant and the customer, trust in the efficiency and efficacy of the vendor, trust that the vendor is solvent and will remain solvent and available to provide services indefinitely.

This trust can go badly wrong. Trust in proprietary code has already gone badly wrong. The Y2K problem would be a minor concern with open source. The source could be examined, improved, and reinstalled. As it is, problems are myriad. The source for code is not available. It cannot be upgraded without reverse engineering. Vendors have gone out of business, or no longer offer support for an old package (which may remain the core of a business built upon it).

Open code supports much of the Internet. Building a business on proprietary code is clearly not insane or else why would it remain so popular? It is simply a great leap of faith, an extension of long-term trust, and an acceptance of long-term risk.

10

Examination of Internet Commerce Systems

Reliability, security, and privacy are critical in commerce systems. Current commerce systems include examples as diverse as paper cash, Internet commerce, and hardware-based commerce. Credit card verification systems, point-of-sale transfers, lines of credit, billing servers, secure coprocessors, and systems based entirely on software all coexist, competing for consumer and market interest. There are also special-purpose systems such as electronic postal metering systems and copyright collection services.

Electronic currency systems are as widespread as they are diverse. In the 1970s electronic currency systems such as electronic funds transfer (EFT) began to be widely used (Reid and Madam 1989). In 1990 more than 40 percent of the $500 billion in federal benefits and state-administered programs were paid using some form of electronic funds transfer (Wood and Smith 1991). In 1988 physical rather than electronic currency, including cash, credit cards, or financial instruments, accounted for more than 99 percent of all transactions (Newberg 1989). The same statistics reflect transaction patterns today; but the total value of all electronic transactions nevertheless dominates the total value of the vastly more numerous cash transactions. The net value of all electronic transfers exceeds the total value of all cash used, has for many years, and will continue to increase its domination.

In addition to the widely used ATM systems and the FedWire, private networks and products provide automatic budgeting, check writing, and invoice creation. The sheer number of electronic currency and invoice systems available for private institutions overwhelms the possibility of an exhaustive report. Furthermore, most of those systems are proprietary, and therefore examination of trust assumptions is extremely difficult.

Given that an exhaustive report is not feasible, which systems should be considered here? First, only systems based on open standards can be properly evaluated. Separating systems into categories removes the need for detailed analysis of every system without unreasonably limiting the scope of this work. Recall that the only concern here is with systems for general Internet commerce. These systems require that the user have no specialized hardware.

Distinctions among Commerce Systems

Electronic commerce systems are separated into *token* and *notational* systems. In token currency the strings of bits transferred in a transaction are themselves legitimately valuable. For example, a dollar has value in and of itself, and is not a promissory note for a particular transaction from a specific account, as is a credit card purchase slip.

The implementation of anonymity in token systems underlies trust requirements. Thus token systems differ from one another with respect to the existence of anonymity. This is because of the relationship between anonymity and accountability: an anonymous party cannot be subject to penalties. Anonymity in token systems determines who is able to take untraceable, and therefore potentially deniable, financial action. Note that untraceable steps implies that the steps are not linked to identity, not that the steps are immune to rollback.

In a notational currency system the information transferred is an instruction to change notations in a ledger, such as a bank's records. In notational currency the value is held in the records, not the instruction. Notational systems are further subdivided by the business model on which they are based. The business model encompasses the underlying commerce model, the distribution of risk among the parties to the transaction, the distribution of liability among those parties, and therefore the distribution of trust as well.

Notational money exists as notations in the ledgers of an institution. Electronic commerce systems based on notational currency differ from one another in the role of the institution that holds these ledgers. Notational currency systems require customers and merchants to trust, to some degree, the holder of the ledgers. However, the degree of trust required and the concentration of trust vary widely from system to system.

Notational systems are based on three different models, in which customer and merchants pay different fees and take different risks: the checking model, debit card model, and the credit card model. The checking model places the most risk on the merchant, and requires that the merchant trust the customer. The debit card model places risk on the customer and requires that the customer trust the merchant to deliver the goods—the merchant is certain to be paid. The credit card model distributes trust, as described in the analyses in this chapter. Some systems involve additional financial intermediaries that alter the traditional assumptions of interaction among merchants, customers, and their respective financial institutions. The existence and roles of these intermediaries may change the distribution of liability, and therefore trust, in financial transactions that the systems require. I select systems based on their distribution of risk, rather than the designer's intellectual model.

Other characteristics may be incidental to a system (either token or notational) and can differ in a given implementation. This fact enables me to collapse the systems into classes for the purposes of discussion and analysis. Then within each class I select one system as an example for more detailed analysis.

The token systems analyzed here and their respective levels of anonymity are:

• Digicash: token, complete anonymity
• MicroMint: token, both anonymous and identifiable implementations
• Millicent: no anonymity

The notational systems analyzed, and the banking models, are:

• First Virtual: transactions without security, merchant trusts customer (checks)
• Secure Sockets Layer: secure transactions, merchant/customer trust (credit cards)
• Secure Electronic Transactions Specifications: multiple acquirers with on-line presence and mutually respected certificates, customer trusts merchant (debit cards)

Analyses of Various Systems

Having selected examples from each trust category, I analyze these systems along legal, market, and technological axes. The discussion focuses on the system's ability to meet market and legal constraints.

Transactional Reliability

Each analysis begins with an overview of the vendor's business model. Both the reliability and security of a system depend on the business plan on which it is based. If the business plan is flawed, a lucrative security hole may exist as a result. Thus security is not as straightforward as algorithm choice and key management (not that those are particularly simple), but also involves an understanding of the business implications of any system failures. Similarly, a system's atomicity also depends on design, implementation, and business policy. Atomicity depends on funds-available policies because of rollback.

The second step in the analysis is a detailed description of a transaction. It is in this description that it becomes clear which parties are considered trustworthy and for what, and thereby reflects the trust model of the system. The bank, for example, may be trusted based on how much documentation is necessary for the bank to take durable action. The business perspective may explain how a technical failure is not unacceptable, since the realization that such failures occur is addressed explicitly in the business plan.

Three encryption functions are commonly used in electronic commerce protocols: a one-way secure hash algorithm, asymmetric encryption, and symmetric encryption. (Recall the definitions in chapter 3.)The following notation is used when the variable or message being encrypted or hashed is x:

$h(x)$ the hash of x
$E_k(x)$ x, encrypted with symmetric key k
$(x)_i$ x, encrypted with the secret key of i's asymmetric keys
$(x)_I$ x, encrypted with the public key of i's asymmetric keys

The public and private halves of a public key pair are identified as I and i, where i is the first initial of the party or item to which a key corresponds. For example, values of *I* might include *B*, *C*, and *M*; these correspond, respectively, to the bank, the customer, and the merchant.

Each transaction in the analysis is taken apart and considered step by step. The analysis focuses on determining the reliability of a transaction. A step-by-step review allows me to illustrate how the failure of a single message might put the system in an inconsistent state. Each protocol considered is classified as providing no atomicity, money atomicity, goods atomicity, or certified delivery. As part of such a classification, the specific messages that provide or fail to provide atomicity are identified.

Security
Every system makes certain security assumptions, whether about the existence of separate communications channels or that secret keys are indeed secure. For each system analyzed, the worst-case results of the failure of each security assumption are enumerated. Of course not every possible combination of security failures is considered. If the simultaneous failure of two security assumptions creates a different possible outcome than the separate failure of the two assumptions, then that is assessed as well. For example, if both a secret key and an account number would enable an attacker to make unauthorized changes in an account, but access to either instrument alone would not enable such an attack, this combination of security failures is noted.

Certain fundamental, widely accepted cryptographic assumptions are assumed to hold throughout the discussion. For example, though it has not been proven that there is no way to factor numbers in polynomial time, I will make the standard cryptographic assumption that this is the case (Baker 1984; Schneier 1995). (Recall the discussion of one-way functions in chapter 3. The assumption that factoring is difficult—more difficult than multiplication—is a way of saying that I assume cryptography works and no stunning mathematical advances will be made that change this fact.)

Privacy
The next step in my analysis is to evaluate the level of privacy offered in each system, which allows the information available to each party during

Table 10.1
Information available to various parties in a checking transaction

Party	Information				
	Seller	Buyer	Date	Amount	Item
Seller	Full	Full	Full	Full	Full
Buyer	Full	Full	Full	Full	Full
Law enforcement with warrant	Full	Full	Full	*Full*	None
Bank	Full	Full	Full	Full	None
Observer	Full	Full	Full	Full	Full

each transaction to be listed. This allows for simple comparison of different systems without trying to place a qualitative measure on the intrinsically quantitative issue of privacy.

There is broad agreement that privacy is a question of what information is exposed. To consider the efficacy of the method used here to evaluate privacy offered by various systems, consider the specific methodology for evaluating system security recommended by National Computer Security Center 1990 and a subsequent related series of publications (the rainbow series). There elements of this methodology applicable to the analysis of privacy levels in a system are: a general description of all information to be transmitted through and stored in the system; a summary of the expectation of the security of data contained in each subsystem and system; the assignment of final responsibility to a single individual to ensure that security is maintained; the use of mechanisms to ensure security; a description of the entire user community, including those with the lowest level of access; and the types of access permitted provided in each subsystem and system. The simple matrix technique used for assessing privacy in the following system analyses includes many of these elements.

An example matrix, which shows the information available to various parties in a checking transaction, is shown in table 10.1. Each row shows the information available to the party named in the leftmost column. Each column lists a datum of interest: the identities of the parties, the date of the transaction, the amount of the purchase, and the item purchased.

Any party can have "full," "partial," or "no" information about a particular datum.

The row labeled "Law enforcement with warrant" identifies the information that would be available to the government. This row provides a basis on which to compare each system's ability to provide information desirable for social welfare. These entries are derived from reporting requirements, as discussed in chapter 8. Law enforcement can obtain records from banks and merchants. In the case of a specific purchase, however, the merchant may not keep detailed records. In this and later tables, if law enforcement depends on merchant records to obtain item information, this is denoted as *"Full"* in italic type.

For the privacy analysis, we consider an observer who is electronically well placed, that is, the observer can monitor transmissions between the customer and merchant. The observer cannot read encrypted information, but can read all other information transmitted in making the transaction. Using an information matrix as described above as a basis for comparison, each system is roughly classified as providing high, low, or medium levels of privacy.

How does one determine the information made available in a particular protocol? One necessary assumption for comparison (of both privacy and atomicity) is that all transactions have the same scope: that is, all transactions begin at discovery and end at merchandise delivery. This ensures consistency in the comparison of the protocols. Information transmitted during the discovery process is available with every purchase. Thus those protocols that claim that no identity information is transmitted in a transaction assume a communications exchange or remailer. Removing all identity information during communication is not easy. For two-way communications it requires a series of remailers capable of encryption. Even then, partial identity information can be reconstructed with the cooperation of all involved parties; however, such a reconstruction has such a high work factor that it is reasonable to say such services provide privacy.

Keep in mind while reading the privacy analysis of each system that partial or full identity information can sometimes be obtained from IP addresses and commonly available network services, as described in chapter 7.

Governance

Finally, I consider the ability of the system to fulfill governmental needs for data. I consider only the information provided to the government about a transaction itself. Most transfers of value today use auditable channels, meaning channels where the regulatory oversight of transactions is both well established in law and physically possible. For example, any depository institution is auditable, while cash under the mattress is not.

Both reporting requirements and possible improvements in terms of data compilation were suggested in chapter 8. These suggestions are revisited in the governance section of the protocol analyses presented here and in chapter 11. In each case the trade-offs created by the current requirement and the way that the suggested solution would alleviate these trade-offs are identified. Technical suggestions are made as to how each system could be enhanced to resolve or eliminate trade-offs for merchants, financial services providers, and customers. Techniques used in this section are described or referenced in the earlier description of security. The general implication of the governance analyses presented is that current constraints on anonymity of data provided for governance should be relaxed.

Example Analyses

The two example analyses presented in this chapter, those for credit card and cash transactions, are meant to clarify the subsequent discussion of specific Internet commerce systems in chapter 11. Rather than launching immediately into analyses of potentially unfamiliar systems, I begin with these two common examples: credit cards (a familiar notational system) and cash (a familiar token system). Both examples illustrate concepts of atomicity, security failures, and the use of data availability to value a system according to privacy considerations.

Credit Cards: A Notational System

With credit (and debit) cards, the instruction to debit or increment an account is made electronically, as opposed to checks, where the instruction is written on paper When a purchase is made over the telephone, for example, the information printed on the card is sufficient to authorize a charge. This differs from point of sale (POS) systems, in that the physical presence of the card is not necessary in a telephone order. Thus credit card orders can be authorized using *information only.*

Remote credit card transactions are a form of electronic commerce; the critical transaction information is delivered electronically by voice, from one human to another. Orders are entered into billing computers, processed electronically, and delivered physically.

The credit card market developed because checks have limits of interoperability (Rubin and Cooter 1994): merchants who accept checks are at risk for having a check returned for insufficient funds, and therefore accepting a check requires an extension of trust to the consumer. Previously customers who used checks to pay merchants were limited in accessing funds because merchants had to extend trust to each customer who wrote a check. The creators of credit cards, or "entertainment cards" as they were originally called, addressed that weakness by assuming the risk involved if customers turned out not to be creditworthy.

Today automatic teller machines offer international interoperability for checking accounts by providing customers with immediate access to deposits in the form of cash. That the original impetus for the creation of credit cards is gone does not imply that the credit card market will decrease, since the original entertainment cards have evolved far beyond the original market niche.

Although the settlement process for credit cards depicted in this discussion (and in figure 10.1) specifically considers Visa, it is meant to be representative. Visa was chosen for the discussion (and the figure) by virtue of its wonderfully brief name.

The credit settlement system is similar to the check settlement system. However, credit cards developed in a more orderly fashion than checks, and have evolved a clearance system with less need for governmental support. (The Federal Reserve Board handles regional and national settlements of checks. Check law has been built upon tort law, while credit card clearing was developed through private contracts.)

Notice that the clearing system for credit cards is based on regional hierarchies. Each region has a clearing bank. If the customer and the merchant share the same bank, Visa does not process the charge. This means that the national Visa office does not have to process every charge.

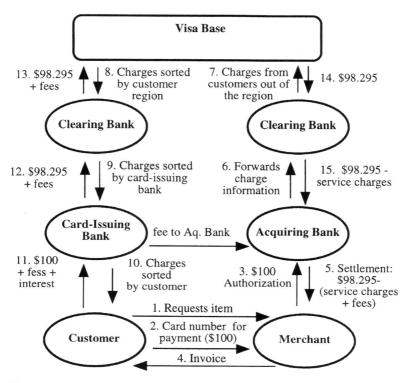

Figure 10.1
A credit card transaction

Each clearing bank has a network of local banks that recruit merchants. Card-issuing banks may further subcontract credit checks for individual transactions to third parties.

When a bank recruits a merchant as a credit-accepting account, the bank accepts some risk. If a merchant defrauds a customer, or a customer stops payment on the basis of fraud, the bank that recruited the merchant may be liable for the fraudulent costs the customer is not required to pay (based on the merchant's contract with the merchant's issuer bank). The merchant may be guaranteed payment from the merchant bank regardless of the claims, and the substance of such claims, of fraud made by the customer. This liability on the bank that recruits a merchant to accept credit card transactions is the control mechanism Visa uses to prevent unethical merchants from entering the system and taking advantage of the assured payment mechanism. Although banks penalized under these payment guarantees may pass this penalty onto the merchants, even doing this will control the entry of untrustworthy merchants into the clearance system.

Payment on a credit card transaction is assured by distributing the losses (accrued when customers refuse payment) across all purchases in the form of fees. The fees are assessed by various entities as customer's payments make their way along the chain from customer to merchant. Each entity receives a percentage of each purchase as the payment fee. This is illustrated by the decrements of funds shown returning to the merchant in the outer loop in figure 10.1.

When a customer is defrauded in a credit card transaction, she can refuse charges. Whether the fraud is a result of physical theft or electronic attack, the customer's losses are limited by law to $50 per card. Customers have sixty days to refuse to pay a charge, much longer than they have to challenge the authenticity of a check presented for payment on their account. Therefore customers do not feel the need to trust merchants as much as in the case of checks, and they expect less documentation in a credit card transaction. This allows the processing of credit charge slips to be radically truncated[50]; that is, the merchant sends the data from the slip, not the slip itself, to the bank. (Although it is legal for check processing to be radically truncated, customers have generally demanded that their checks be returned.)

A Transaction

The following discussion delineates the steps in a credit card transaction as depicted in figure 10.1. The steps in the transaction form two concen-

50. Radical truncation means that the documentation is not sent to the consumer. Instead the information on the documents are compiled and this information is send to the consumer. It is legal for checks to be radically truncated as well; however, consumers have rejected this option. This rejection would have been obvious to decision-makers in the banks if they had considered radical truncation from the risk and trust perspective of the customers. Losses from checking accounts can be far greater for an individual customer than credit card losses. Thus in attempting to truncate the checking cycles, banks were redistributing risk and assuming that consumers had a far greater trust in the banks than actually existed.

tric semicircles: the billing records for the customer travel counterclock-wise in the inner circle, and payment to the merchant moves clockwise along the outer circle. The inner circle depicts the movement of the order information; the outer circle shows the movement of payment in return. The merchant pays a percentage of the amount the customer charges to the merchant bank on every charge. As noted above, depending on the specific authorization and the contract with the merchant bank, the merchant may be guaranteed payment on a credit card transaction even if the customer does not pay the charge. However, in remote credit card orders the merchant usually is not paid if the customer denies the charge.

The difference between the amount paid by the customer for the purchase ($100 in the figure) and the amount received by the merchant ($98.295 minus the fee charged by the merchant's bank) goes Visa's and the associated bank's profit, overhead, and risk management.

Because a customer may receive goods and deny payment, or a merchant may receive payment and deny goods, the system lacks atomicity. The lack of atomicity in credit card purchases is managed through this systemic debiting as the payment instructions move through the system.

A credit card transaction is not money atomic, although it can appear atomic to the merchant if the merchant is guaranteed payment. From the customer's perspective, credit card purchases have a period in which payment can be canceled, either by explicit cancellation request or by a refusal to pay for an item when billed. Thus customers have the ability to generate rollback.

Credit card transactions are consistent in that the customer and merchant agree on the amount paid and whether there has been a reversal of payment, in the case that the merchant is not guaranteed payment.

Credit card transactions are not isolated. In some cases in which a merchant obtains a block on user credit, that is not always promptly erased. These blocks can in some cases lead to failure of isolation. For example, a hotel may block enough on a customer's credit card to cover possible damage done during the customer's stay at the hotel, thus preventing the customer from accessing that portion of her credit line to make a later, unrelated purchase. The practice of obtaining authorization (blocking) for more than the final charge (settlement) is common among hotels and car rental agencies.

Credit card transactions are durable. However, it may take weeks for a credit transaction to become final. The size of a credit card transaction is limited only by the customer's credit limit. ATM machines, in contrast, impose a size limit for an individual transaction regardless of the total available balance in a depository accounts. This limits risk, just as the limit on currency denominations (there are no $5,000 bills) limits risk by increasing the difficulty of counterfeiting money—in both cases the limits increase the number of false payment instruments needed for large-scale fraud. However, even these efforts to limit risk sometimes fail, as the theft of over $300,000 with a single card and access code illustrates (New York Times 1995a, 1995b). Since credit card transactions cost the merchant (in terms of the fees deducted by Visa and various banks in the Visa network), there is a limit to size on the lower end of the scale. Few merchants will accept a credit card for a $.0.25 purchase. Like checks, credit cards are scalable in terms of number of users.

There are limits to interoperability between credit and debit card systems. A consumer cannot pay her American Express card bill with her Visa credit card except by first obtaining cash.

Security

Opportunities for credit card fraud vary depending on the payment policies. With remote credit card purchases, there are two options for dealing with potential fraud: the acquiring bank guarantees payment or the merchant accepts risk.

If the bank guarantees payment, regulating merchant fraud is a straightforward task. Merchants can fail to deliver goods and still demand payment, but banks can limit this type of fraud by tracking complaints against merchants and revoking accounts of merchants who abuse guaranteed payment. Merchants can, however, incorporate in a new guise and request new accounts with these new identities. And because merchants allow other disbarred merchants to use their accounts, this system has weaknesses (Van Natta 1995).

Whichever system is chosen for dealing with fraud risk, it is not difficult for a customer in a remote transaction to commit fraud to obtain goods. Customers may simply claim not to have received goods. The lack of a verifiable physical delivery system constrains security for all remote

purchases of physical goods. Banks address this in the same way that they
address merchant fraud: customers are tracked and rated, and those
found to engage in this type of fraud are subject to the removal of credit
privileges.

If the merchant has a physical presence—that is, an imprint of the card
used in the transaction—the merchant is guaranteed payment by Visa or
the other credit card companies involved. If the merchant is offering
telephone purchases, the certainty of receiving payment for a credit card
transaction depends on the type of merchant (i.e., the business area of the
merchant), merchant characteristics (e.g., business size history), and
transactional characteristics, including merchant credit history, the market served by the merchant, the item(s) purchased, and the amount of the
transaction.

Arguably the greatest weakness in the telephone order protocol is its
vulnerability to replay attacks. Only credit card number, expiration date,
and sometimes billing address are needed to authorize a purchase. Thus
any person who obtains a complete receipt from a credit card purchase
can authorize telephone purchases using the number on that credit card
receipt.

In the next paragraphs I compare the risk of the two transmission
systems. Consider that with telephone purchases, critical authorization
order information must be transmitted over the public telephone networks. In comparison, on the Internet purchases are transmitted over the
networks that together form the Internet (sometimes including the phone
wires). Transmissions over the Internet are encrypted—never transmit
credit card information in the clear. Public phone networks are more
difficult to monitor than Internet transactions, for several reasons. First,
the telephone networks transmit voice data for a telephone-order credit
card purchase. Filtering and searching voice data after it has been trapped
requires decoding the data as transmitted over the phone network and
then using voice recognition technology to obtain the actual content of
the conversation, and thus the credit card number. (Alternatively one
could listen endlessly and hope to eavesdrop on an order, but this does
not seem efficient or likely to be successful given the volume of information on the phones wires not related to credit card purchases.) Voice

recognition is orders of magnitude more difficult than identifying information already optimized for digital content-based manipulation. (Internet content is digital.) After the data is analyzed to determine the content using voice recognition, it must be searched, just as in the case with data on the Internet. Conversely, information on the Internet is typically in a form that is simple to intercept and filter. Finally, the sheer scale of telephony makes monitoring phone calls harder. There are 28 million (Hoffman, Kalsbeek, and Novak 1996) to 37 million (CommerceNet 1995) Internet users in the United States, while there were 172.8 million households[51] (Bureau of Census 1995) subscribing to telephony services in 1995. Telephone service is common to almost all households, with 96 percent of households having telephone service in 1994 (Federal Communications Commission 1995). Computers will not reach this penetration rate for some time.

Privacy

Credit card transactions create machine-readable records. Identities of the parties to a transaction, the amount involved, the date, and some content information (such as the items purchased) may also be recorded with credit card purchases. The ease with which this information is analyzed and distributed compromises consumer privacy.

Credit card purchases provide detailed information about the transaction to merchants and associated financial institutions. Such transactions can also leak information through electronic surveillance by an observer. Because the processing banks obtain information about a transaction, it can be available to law enforcement. The merchant may record detailed content information, and content information in machine- readable format may be obtained by the bank as part of billing. Information distribution in a remote credit card transaction is delineated in table 10.2.

In this discussion of privacy, the banks involved in the billing and payment process have been combined, for two reasons. First, the information about the purchase is passed through the billing system. Second, there is widespread marketing and sharing of data between banks. For the case of examining privacy, these banks have been collapsed into one.

---

51. This includes both access lines and cellular subscribers.

Table 10.2
Information available to various parties in a credit card transaction

Party	Information				
	Merchant	Customer	Date	Amount	Item
Merchant	Full	Full	Full	Full	Full
Customer	Full	Full	Full	Full	Full
Law enforcement with warrant	Full	Full	Full	Full	*Full*
Bank	Full	Full	Full	Full	None
Observer	None	None	Full	None	None

Credit card companies policies vary widely with respect to privacy. American Express offers consumers options on the use of personal information. Mastercard and Visa allow card-issuing banks to set policies on consumer privacy. That one company offers a privacy-protecting option suggests that the market can serve the privacy interests of those with financial resources. Thus secondary use of data by the participant banks depends on the policies of the card-issuing association (e.g., Visa, American Express) and the banks involved.

Governance
Since credit cards have by now become widespread, many of the regulatory issues involved in their use have already been considered. In fact, two specific regulations of interest were enacted at least partially with consideration of credit cards: the Electronic Funds Transfer Act and the financial information provision of the Computer Fraud and Abuse Act. Thus a short consideration of lessons learned with credit cards may be fruitful for later discussions.

The Electronic Funds Transfer Act was passed because of the government's recognition that a customer has neither the ability to manage the risks of the payment system as a whole nor the ability to prevent use of a financial instrument if it is stolen. The initial assumption that a customer would bear the cost of charges made in the event a card is lost or stolen is reflected in the assumption by many electronic commerce systems that the customer will simply bear the cost of charges if a cryptographic key is lost or stolen. In fact, under the Digital Signature Law as originally passed in Utah, if an attacker obtained a consumer's secret key, the attacker could enter into contracts requiring the customer to continue to pay for many years. This results from the law's failure to consider key loss—the law treats keys if they were unalterably linked to an individual, like the signature on which keys are modeled. (Proposal to use biometrics for identification are potentially even more hazardous to consumers. If the data describing biometrics—for example, fingerprint or retina print—is stolen from a database, the consumer will have difficulty stopping any resulting fraud. And of course, it is simply not possible to replace a fingerprint when data are stolen.)

Cash: A Token System

Cash is token currency, as defined earlier in this chapter. The examination of legal tender provides a model and basis for later comparison with electronic token currency. In the United States, federal law ensures the interoperability of cash. It is "legal tender for all debts public and private." The business model of cash is interoperability and availability assured by government action to enable and encourage commerce. Cash is interoperable because it is legal tender. The lack of interoperability of bank and state currencies was a driving force behind the creation of a national currency. Internationally, interoperability is provided by currency exchange services that convert one currency to another (and charge a price for doing so). The ability of American legal tender to serve as a store of a value and a standard of exchange has resulted in its having global interoperability.

The subsequent section analyzing a cash transaction discusses the importance of the various attributes of cash, as well as the problems that arise in trying to use cash to make remote purchases. One fundamental problems remains with electronic cash: how can a customer prove payment for a remote anonymous purchase? The privacy and security sections below illustrate the strengths and weakness of physical cash along those dimensions.

There are no limits to scale in the number of users of cash, except those imposed by limits on the number of bills printed and/or available. Not only are individual transactions isolated, but the system is also free from bottlenecks.

The availability of cash has proven critically important for economic and social reasons. Some scholars argue that the oppression of sharecropping for blacks in the American South was very much predicated by the return to the gold standard and resulting currency shortage.[52] This dramatic example illustrates that should a single standard for Internet commerce emerge, the private control of the currency, the potential lack of availability, and any lack of interoperability may have unforeseen implications.

Cash is divisible in that it comes in many denominations; a single high-value token can be exchanged for many low-value tokens, and many smaller tokens can be exchanged for a single high-denomination token.

A Transaction

Consider a remote cash purchase—sending a dollar through the mail to a merchant to purchase a particular good or product. Assume that delivery of the goods is to a post office box, so that the customer need not offer the merchant any identity information.

First, the customer requests a dollar from the bank, as shown in figure 10.2. The bank decrements the customer's account the appropriate amount and provides the dollar to the customer. The customer then sends the dollar in the mail to the merchant, requesting an item in return. The merchant verifies the dollar through visual examination—this is analogous to off-line verification. The merchant can prove that he has the right to spend that dollar by virtue of having the dollar. Thus the merchant has no need to provide authentication to spend the dollar. The merchant then sends the goods requested to the customer.

When the merchant deposits the dollar in the bank, the bank does not link that dollar to the one given previously. In theory the bank could keep track of the serial numbers of all the dollars it gives out and to whom it gives these dollars, but this would be an extremely costly method of

52. As there was no ready currency (because the supply of currency was limited by the gold standard), towns developed notational currencies. Because the notational currencies, the land, and agricultural supplies were controlled by the same few people, there was no way for others to work their way out of debt. If the crops were good, prices could simply go up. Since the notational currencies in

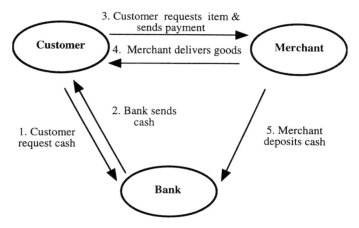

Figure 10.2
A cash transaction

surveillance. This type of surveillance also requires that customer and merchant use the same bank, further decreasing the likelihood of any attempt at surveillance along these lines.

In a cash transaction the customer cannot prove that the merchant received payment; this is not an atomic transaction. If the customer uses registered mail, there is still no proof of the contents of the envelopes; however, this would give the customer some claim. The merchant can simply take the money to the bank for deposit. The customer cannot prove previous ownership of the dollar or that the merchant has made a commitment to deliver merchandise in exchange for the dollar.

What would happen if banks kept records of the identities of all those who withdraw dollars linked to the serial number of the dollars that were withdrawn, and dollars could be spent only once before being returned to a bank? (Notice the electronic analog is not so unlikely when money is on-line, digitally signed, and bank-specific.) The customer could then sacrifice anonymity (because her name would be linked to the serial number), but could verify her claim to have paid the merchant (whose identity would also be linked to the serial number through the deposit).

---

the shopkeepers' ledgers were not interoperable, the sharecroppers could not purchase materials for better prices elsewhere.

This example illustrates one type of conflict between anonymity and atomicity present in the electronic systems examined in this text.

Back now to the cash example: this transaction is isolated. Regardless of what occurs in any other transactions, the merchant can deposit the dollar. The transaction may or may not be consistent. If the dollar is lost in the mail, then the customer may believe that she has been defrauded and the merchant will not know a transaction has been attempted. The dollar may simply disappear. Finally, the transaction is durable. The merchant will have the dollar; the customer will not. The customer cannot arbitrarily reverse the transaction.

Security
Cash does not require trust between users. If a bill is determined to be counterfeit, the holder of the bill is not compensated. Accepting a bill, however, requires only trust in one's own abilities to evaluate it as authentic. Compare this with the impossibility of verifying a check, which would require knowledge of the account status and intentions of the check writer. The validity of a bill can be verified during the transaction by visual inspection. By accepting cash, merchants imply that they trust only their own ability to detect counterfeit, as opposed to a credit card association or a customer's creditworthiness.

Clearly there are security failures in the form of counterfeit notes, but security in cash transactions is generally maintained by a time-tested work factor. The design of the bills is periodically updated to discourage counterfeiting. Systems-level failures in the paper currency system are prevented by risk-limiting regulation, federal depository insurance, limits on denominations, and the huge effort ivolved in passing enough counterfeit currency to upset the entire system. Once the hurdle of printing a single counterfeit bill is overcome, however, the marginal cost of printing each additional dollar approaches zero.

The dollar in the example could be taken from the U.S. Postal Service, which is unprotected—except of course by law. In 1994, roughly 20,976,000,000 pieces of mail were delivered (Bureau of Census 1995). Thus the sheer magnitude of the task of searching the mail, combined with the relative rarity of finding cash in such an endeavor, provides a high work factor that essentially prevents theft by observers. There is no

Table 10.3
Information available to various parties in a cash transaction

Party	Information				
	Merchant	Customer	Date	Amount	Item
Merchant	Full	Partial	Full	Full	Full
Customer	Full	Full	Full	Full	Full
Law enforcement with warrant	None	None	None	Partial	None
Bank	None	None	None	Partial	None
Observer	Full	Full	Full	None	None

advantage to scale in this sort of theft: searching for the nth dollar will be as hard as searching for the first. Of course, if sending money through the mail was common, so that half of all envelopes contained money, then the search would prove worthwhile.

Privacy
Cash offers both privacy and anonymity because a dollar contains no information that can be used to determine its transaction history. Nor does the exchange of cash necessarily create a record that includes the identities of those involved. Cash transactions usually provide anonymity to the customer, but not the merchant. The privacy afforded by a cash transaction is limited by the potential for physical observation of the customer by the merchant. Yet it would be unlikely that the merchant kept records of customer attributes. The information available to different parties in a cash transaction is shown in table 10.3.

A cash transaction produces no bank or law enforcement records. It is reasonable to assume that no bank employee or law enforcement officer observes most cash transactions. Therefore the information available to a bank or to law enforcement is limited by what it can obtain from written records of the transaction. The law requires reporting of some transactions, but these reports depend on the active cooperation of the parties involved. Use of a bank imposes an upper limit on the size of any transaction, since the bank knows the amount of any deposit and must comply with government reporting requirements.

In a remote transaction the customer can choose to have materials delivered to a post office box, so only the customer's region of residence is known to the merchant. With a warrant, law enforcement could obtain the identity of the box holder if given access to the merchant's records and if the P.O. box was not rented under a pseudonym.

A well-placed observer—for example, one beside the customer in the post office when the customer places the envelope containing the dollar bill in the mail—can watch the item be placed in the post, but cannot open the envelope to discern what it contains. Again, the work factor in searching the mail makes it unlikely that any given letter will be intercepted.

Governance

The current regulatory structure has been built over time to deal with issues involved in money transactions. The regulatory structure has as a fundamental goal that risk be placed on the party in the transaction who is more able to prevent loss. For example, if a merchant steals money (receives it but does not send the requested merchandise), the customer absorbs the resulting loss. This is because in this case, the customer is the only person empowered to choose to send cash in the mail. Similarly, merchants and banks lose if they accept counterfeit cash because merchants and banks are in the best position to prevent counterfeiting.

This principle of assigning risk to the party more able to prevent loss has not yet been widely applied to electronic commerce, in part because the ability and responsibility of keeping information secure has not yet been culturally determined, and in part because there has been no market failure thus far to allocate risk in a way that is acceptable to consumers.

Summary

In this chapter I have explained the core differences between token and notational commerce systems. I have also developed a method for examining the placement of risk in electronic commerce transactions. This method of examining the reliability, security, and privacy in a transaction should be applicable to the plethora of commerce systems already on the market, as well as those that are emerging. Every commerce system sounds ideal from the vendor's perspective, and one of the basic tools of this method is to provide a common framing for all commerce systems.

In the next chapter I apply the analytic methods described and used in examples here to Internet commerce systems. The following examples serve not only to examine popular and proposed Internet commerce systems, but also to further illustrate the use of the step-by-step method for evaluating trust in an Internet commerce system.

11

Internet Currencies

I separate the currency systems discussed in this chapter into notational currencies and token currencies, as described in chapter 10.

Notational Currencies

In notational currency, the information transferred consists of instructions for payment. The value in this currency is stored as notations in the ledger of a trusted institution. Transactions made using this currency include instructions that these notations be changed.

The advantage of notational currency is that record keeping is an inherent part of the system. This simplifies recovery from failure. If a single ledger is used, the transaction is certain to be serialized. As a result, implementing ACID transactions is straightforward. That is, if all the steps are recorded in order, in one place, dispute resolution should be simple—all that is necessary is that a central ledger be queried.

Here I analyze three Internet commerce systems that use notational currency—First Virtual, Netscape's Secure Sockets Layer, and Mastercard's Secure Electronic Transactions—using the method described in chapter 10.

First Virtual

First Virtual is a protocol for the first generation of Internet commerce. As do all on-line systems, First Virtual offers automated customer support, promotion, administration, and processing. Some First Virtual transactions are large enough that aggregating them to meet the economic threshold for a credit card transaction is unnecessary; First Virtual can, however, aggregate small transactions and thus can overcome the lower limit to scale in credit card transactions. The goal of First Virtual is not to decrease transaction costs, but rather to provide immediate access to customers on the Internet for medium-priced information goods.

First Virtual is based on the theory that the provision of information goods over the Internet is practically free and that the Internet itself is inherently without security. First Virtual aggregates Internet transactions, filters Internet transactions, provides billing for Internet transactions, and resolves disputes about transactions over the Internet (First Virtual 1995a). First Virtual is an account acquirer from the perspective of consumers and merchants; in contrast, First Virtual is a single merchant from the perspective of the Visa-associated merchant acquiring bank.

First Virtual filters transactions and resolves billing disputes about these transactions by maintaining that the customer is always right. First Virtual limits customers' abuse of this policy by limiting the customer's total number of refusals; after a given number of refusals of payment, a customer's account privileges are terminated.

First Virtual's protection against fraud is based on three business practices:

• no credit card numbers are ever transmitted on the Internet
• no replay attacks are possible
• a merchant who is unpaid for network-delivered information goods suffers negligible losses.

Commerce without security has limited application. The size of a purchase using First Virtual is limited by the tolerance for fraud of the merchants involved. Merchants with high-cost goods for which there is a high demand are unlikely to accept the potentially high levels of fraud possible in First Virtual transactions. First Virtual works well, however, for low-priced goods with a small to medium-sized market, or high-priced goods with a specialized market. The acceptance of First Virtual is also subject to how often attacks on customer account identifiers occur and customer tolerance for the time and effort in addressing these attacks.

First Virtual is a useful means of transacting for information goods delivered over the Internet. The fact that many on-line information goods are widely distributed and often have very low value hampers the market for these goods. Many on-line information merchants are not large enough to find having merchant accounts with credit card companies practical. In addition to the number and small size of many information providers, the market is problematic for current Internet commerce protocols because the value of these merchants' items is low, consumption happens soon after delivery, there is no standard for proof of on-line delivery, and there is no physical presence of merchant or customer at the other's location. Because First Virtual's business model is based on negligible merchant losses, First Virtual is not well suited for orders for physical goods—the losses of a merchant who is unpaid for physical goods are not negligible, unlike those unpaid for a copy of digital goods.

Becoming a First Virtual merchant requires a credit card, email, data storage capacities, and Web access. An Internet user can be a First Virtual merchant with a standard credit card account, while other systems require that merchants have merchant accounts. First Virtual's approach vastly expands the number of possible merchants who could use the system and therefore the probability that there will be goods of interest to a customer.

To obtain a First Virtual account, a customer must have email and a credit card. The prospective customer sends email to First Virtual that includes a customer-selected password. The customer then calls First Virtual and provides credit card information over the telephone. The credit card information itself is never sent over the Internet. Customers use their password and user name (which First Virtual calls an *account identifier* by) to authorize charges against their accounts. First Virtual charges a low initial fee to become a customer.

Presumably, First Virtual also profits from the redistribution of the email addresses of its customers. Customers are allowed to opt out of this program when they sign up for an account; however, if they do not ask to be excluded, the default value is to have their email addresses available for redistribution.

A Transaction

Figure 11.1 shows a First Virtual transaction. The bank involved in the transaction is actually off-line and is contacted by First Virtual after a transaction or a series of transactions have been completed.

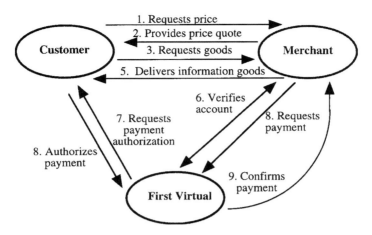

Figure 11.1
A First Virtual transaction

The transaction begins when a customer selects an item and requests a price quote from the merchant. The customer then requests the item with a message to the merchant that includes her First Virtual account identifier and the associated password. The merchant can authenticate the customer's claims to be a valid First Virtual customer at this point, or wait until after the goods are delivered (as shown in the figure). First Virtual verifies the password and account identifier supplied by the customer at the merchant's request. If the customer is a valid First Virtual customer, the merchant is contractually obligated to deliver the requested items.

The merchant sends the goods to the customer. Then the merchant transmits a request for the customer's payment authorization to First Virtual and requests payment, as shown in step 6. If he has not sent the customer's authentication information previously in step 4, he can do so now; in any case, the merchant is required to send the merchandise requested before asking for payment. First Virtual then sends an email message to the customer requesting final authorization of the charge. The customer is charged only if the customer verifies the charges. Finally, First Virtual notifies the merchant of the result. (At some number of amount of charges, First Virtual charges the customer's credit card off-line, as does a traditional merchant as described in chapter 10.)

The merchant may choose to validate the customer at the price request, or before or after delivering the goods. Validation at the price request means that the merchant never serves a request with an invalid password. There is a trade-off in this choice: a merchant saves one message on every valid transaction or saves processing invalid requests. The appropriate choice depends on the ratio of valid purchases to fraudulent requests as well as the relative costs of communications and processing.

Regardless of the merchant's timing of verification, the customer has the right to refuse to pay for an item after having received it. This prevents conflicts based on quality and deceptive advertising. First Virtual reserves the right to limit the number of times a consumer may choose not to pay for an item received; but a merchant cannot choose to refuse to send an item to a valid First Virtual customer. This means the merchant must accept First Virtual's definition of acceptable risk.

First Virtual's email to the customer in step 7 and the request in step 1 travel to their destinations through different parts of the Internet, like a telephone call to Tokyo and a fax to New York travel from Boston to their destinations through different parts of the telephone network. Therefore First Virtual considers these independent channels. Although it is simple to obtain a packet containing ordering information from First Virtual, intercepting the authorization request message to the customer is more difficult. It would require either filtering every message received by the customer or sent by First Virtual, or alternatively breaking into the customer's home email account to respond. In contrast, there are locations where the majority of the traffic consists of First Virtual identifiers or purchased goods, so fishing for a First Virtual identifier there would be profitable and require searching through fewer email messages. More important, there would be no gain in completing the second, more difficult, part of the process because any attacker has already obtained the goods. So it is likely that the email sent to the customer results in a valid reply in step 8.

First Virtual transactions use off-line billing. First Virtual does not provide money atomicity. The actual transfer of funds in the First Virtual system is implemented off-line using standard payment mechanisms (like any merchant who accepts credit cards unrelated to the Internet). While First Virtual looks like a bank to the on-line consumer, First Virtual is a single merchant from the perspective of the financial infrastructure. Like a card-issuing bank, First Virtual can cancel a customer's account if First Virtual makes a payment to a merchant on the customer's behalf and then the customer refuses payment to First Virtual using his card-issuing bank's dispute resolution mechanisms. However, canceling this customer's account will not make the previous transactions money-atomic.

First Virtual does not provide goods atomicity or certified delivery. The customer can receive goods and refuse payment.

Successful First Virtual transactions—those in which the customer chooses to pay for the requested goods—are isolated. Unsuccessful transactions are not. Because First Virtual tracks consumer refusal, the result of a customer refusal on one transaction depends on the outcome of her previous transactions. Too many refused transactions eventually result in a refusal of service to the customer—that is, First Virtual no longer validates the customer's account identifier and password when a merchant presents them, so merchants presumably no longer send merchandise to her. Thus the lack of isolation is not a flaw in this system, but the result of a considered business strategy.

First Virtual transactions are consistent. Both the merchant and customer know whether the merchant has been paid. There is not consistency, however, with respect to goods delivery. The merchant may believe that the customer has the goods and expect payment, but the customer may not pay. If the protocol were goods atomic, goods consistency would also be expected.

After the final email from the customer to First Virtual confirming her willingness to pay, First Virtual transactions are durable. The customer cannot change her mind about the quality of merchandise after having approved payment of a charge.

Security

First Virtual assumes that the Internet is inherently without security and thus does not send credit card information over the Internet.

First Virtual is not secure. An attacker need only trap a packet that has the account identifier of a First Virtual account holder to be able to use the customer's account information to make purchases. Since there are well-known locations that receive many of these packets (for example, the First Virtual Infohaus), finding such a packet is unlikely to be difficult. Thus the very lack of widespread interoperability between forms of network commerce is an advantage for First Virtual, since you cannot trade First Virtual account authorization for any other financial instrument—only for purchases made through First Virtual. Even that use will eventually run out, after the customer has refused to verify the charges and the theft is discovered. Since a customer's credit-card number is never transmitted through the Internet, obtaining a First Virtual account identifier does not provide the attacker with access to the customer's line of credit.

Merchants likewise can get First Virtual customer account information, but not customer credit card information. Thus merchants do get the information necessary to authorize further purchases within the First Virtual system, including charging their own customers for items they did not select. Merchants themselves will not profit from padding charges, although they can use this information to illegitimately obtain information goods from another merchant.

Merchants cannot protect the information they sell as it travels over the Internet. Attackers may steal information goods by trapping and copying information goods as they are sent to legitimate First Virtual customers.

In sum, First Virtual mitigates risk by limiting interoperability. Although the First Virtual system is not secure, it isolates and limits security failures through business practices.

Privacy
Table 11.1 shows the information available to various parties in a First Virtual transaction. In First Virtual transactions, the merchant gets the customer identification information immediately upon the request for goods, so merchants can easily build detailed consumer profiles. In fact, First Virtual requires merchants to keep detailed transaction records for at least three years after the transaction (First Virtual 1995b).

A customer can choose a pseudonym for her First Virtual account identifier. If the customer takes advantage of this option, a merchant can identify serial purchases by the same customer, but cannot link that information to any non–First Virtual transaction data.

Because messages transmitted in a First Virtual transaction are not encrypted, an observer could easily develop a detailed profile of consumer

Table 11.1
Information available to various parties in a First Virtual transaction

	Information				
Party	Merchant	Customer	Date	Amount	Item
Merchant	Full	Partial	Full	Full	Full
Customer	Full	Full	Full	Full	Full
Law enforcement with warrant	Full	Full	Full	Full	Full
First Virtual	Full	Full	Full	Full	Full
Observer	Full	Full	Full	Full	Full

habits. Observers can even more easily profile a merchant's on-line business by watching only one server location.

Governance
First Virtual can provide all the information necessary for any regulatory purposes concerning any transaction made through its system. In fact, First Virtual maintains more information than it would legally be required to provide.

Banking laws cover neither First Virtual merchants nor First Virtual itself, so legal requirements for maintaining customer transactional data do not apply. The multiyear retention period for transactional data required of First Virtual merchants by First Virtual reflects the time frame of interest to law enforcement rather than businesses, since for a given charge the customer's right to dispute is contractually limited to weeks.

First Virtual makes no attempt to control the use of data about customers maintained by First Virtual merchants. The system's crypto-free nature means that consumers and merchants who use it to transact business have no privacy from even casual observers. This makes the careful choice of and frequent changes in customer pseudonyms important. First Virtual supports such changes.

First Virtual requirements on merchant data retention reflect the need for broader controls on consumer records. Because the provision of consumer credit reporting is not the primary business function of either First Virtual or its merchants, their customer records are not covered under the Fair Credit Reporting Act. Thus First Virtual and associated merchants can sell detailed data on customer preferences.

Secure Sockets Layer

There are multiple versions of secure protocols for use on the World Wide Web and with many browsers. These include S-HTTP, encrypted telnet, encrypted ftp, and the Secure Sockets Layer. These protocols can be used for Internet commerce, and in fact, Netscape has long advertised Secure Sockets Layer as an Internet commerce tool (Netscape 1996). The option addressed here is that offered by Netscape for use with its own browser: Secure Sockets Layer (Freier, Karlton, and Kocher 1996). Version 3.0 is the focus here, as described in the appropriate Internet Draft.[53]

The Secure Sockets Layer is built to enable secure peer-to-peer communication over the Internet, not to enable electronic commerce per se. Electronic commerce is, however, the most obvious, and possibly most frequently used, application of SSL, although it is not an electronic commerce protocol. Rather SSL is a handshake protocol[54] for establishing a secure channel that can then be used for commerce. Possible uses include confidential email, real-time contract negotiation, and transmissions of sensitive data within or between institutions. The Secure Sockets Layer can be combined with other protocols that would be strengthened by the use of an encrypted channel, such as First Virtual. SET (the Secure Electronic Transaction protocol proposed by Visa and Mastercard) assumes the use of the Secure Sockets Layer for customer address information (Lewis 1996).

The Secure Sockets Layer replaces the telephone line in the credit card transactions described in chapter 10 with an encrypted Internet

---

53. An example of such advertising is Netscape's LivePayment, http://home.netscape.com/comprod/products/iapps/livepayment.html. Internet Drafts are descriptions of open standards that are being promoted to the Internet community.

54. A handshake protocol enables machines to introduce themselves and begin communications. In the case of SSL, part of the handshake is the creation of a cryptographic key. Recall the TCP three-way handshake for initiating a connection.

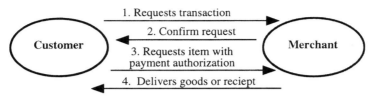

Figure 11.2
A Secure Sockets Layer transaction

connection. The Secure Sockets Layer has an extremely limited scope: it offers only an encrypted tunnel through the Internet that enables the secure delivery of financial information.

The Secure Sockets Layer enables traditional credit card transactions over the Internet. It is most useful for charges sufficiently large that they do not need to be aggregated. Thus the lower bound on transaction scalability in terms of transaction size that exists with traditional credit card purchases also applies to transactions using the Secure Sockets Layer. (Recall the discussion of the costs of credit card transactions.) The Secure Sockets Layer requires that merchants be credit card merchants in the traditional sense: each merchant that uses Secure Sockets Layer must have a merchant credit card account with an acquiring bank.

A Transaction

The Secure Sockets Layer protocol begins with an exchange of certificates and ends with an exchange of keys. The information transmitted in further exchanges has no relationship with the SSL handshake, just as the development of a human relationship is not determined by the introduction. Figure 11.2 illustrates a Secure Sockets Layer transaction. The bank is not shown because communication with the bank takes place according to the predetermined association with the merchant and the bank. It may take place off-line (i.e., not on the Internet but over a private leased line), or over the Internet in an encrypted connection. The connection between the bank and the merchant is not in any way determined by the Secure Sockets Layer.

There are options within Secure Sockets Layer for authentication and key exchange for users with and without certificates. For consistency across protocols included in the discussion here, the customer and merchants are assumed to have certificates.

In the first two steps, the customer and merchant who authenticate themselves to one another generate a shared key. Although authentication and key generation require more than two messages, this exchange can reasonably be modeled as two functional steps. There is a message for use by the customer for requesting the merchant's certificate, and thus the customer is assumed to have the certificate. The customer uses the merchant's public key to initiate a transaction. The merchant replies and may request the customer's certificate. The customer and merchant use the public keys contained within their certificates for authentication of their respective identities and the generation of a symmetric key. Secure Sockets Layer as implemented in Netscape's Navigator assumes that the customer has a certificate from a given number of public-key providers, with the first and earliest being Verisign and RSA (Verisign 1996).

In the third step, using the protection provided by symmetric encryption, the customer sends her credit card number. In the fourth step, the merchant delivers the goods.

After step three the merchant will almost certainly obtain authorization from the customer's credit card provider and therefore could authorize the amount of the transaction through the bank at any time after that step. Because the communication with the bank is not included in Secure Sockets Layer, this is not shown in the figure.

The Secure Sockets Layer provides a handshake for authentication and the generation of a shared key. Thus it clearly cannot provide atomicity. Since credit card companies treat Internet purchases as telephone orders, the customer can refuse payment to the merchant. Thus the lack of money atomicity in the off-line financial system suggests that there is no money atomicity in a transaction using the Secure Sockets Layer, either. There is also neither goods atomicity nor certified delivery.

Consistency, durability, and isolation are as in a telephone order, as described in the first example in chapter 10.

Security
The greatest security threat with the Secure Sockets Layer is that merchants who use the protocol must keep servers secure in order for credit

card numbers to remain secure. Thus the customer must trust not only the merchant and his employees, but also his technical acumen in computer security. The theft of 20,000 credit card numbers from Netcom in the early 1990s illustrates that extending this trust is a problematic proposition. If a merchant's employees are dishonest, his organizational security procedures inadequate, or installation of his software faulty, the consumer is at risk for credit card fraud.

Even if the merchant is honest, his employees may present a security problem. Replay attacks are simple to initiate for a dishonest employee with no access to the information provided to the merchant.

The effective regulatory limitation of key length to forty bits is a weakness, because the payment authorization information is not transaction-specific. (Recall the discussion of cryptography policy in chapter 8.) Forty bits does not provide adequate cryptographic protection against today's processing power. Thus observers could obtain credit card authorization information using attacks as described in the introductory chapters on security.

Privacy

The Secure Sockets Layer provides not financial services, but rather software to create an encryption-secured connection through the Internet. The off-line bank is the financial service provider, and Netscape is only the transmission security software provider; it provides no cryptographic certificates and initiates no financial transaction authorization. Netscape neither receives not maintains any information about any transaction conducted using the Secure Sockets Layer.

Table 11.2 shows information available to various parties in a transaction using the Secure Sockets Layer. Identity information is available as shown in the table because the certificates for customer and merchant authentication are sent without encryption.

An asterisk marks the observer as being uncertain about the date of the transaction. This is because the observer cannot determine if a transaction actually took place—only that there was communication between the customer and the merchant.

Information concerning transactions is concentrated at the off-line financial services provider, the acquirer bank. The bank has the abilities

Table 11.2
Information available to various parties in a transaction using Secure Sockets Layer

Party	Information				
	Merchant	Customer	Date	Amount	Item
Merchant	Full	Full	Full	Full	Full
Customer	Full	Full	Full	Full	Full
Law enforcement with warrant	Full	Full	Full	Full	Full
Netscape	None	None	None	None	None
Bank	Full	Full	Full	None	Full
Observer	Full	Full	Full*	None	None

* Observer can determine only that communication took place between merchant and customer, not whether a transaction actually took place.

to correlate and distribute this information as it would for information in any other kind of transaction.

Governance

The Secure Sockets Layer sets up secure connections through an open network. Netscape as an entity does not have any information about what data has passed through a Secure Sockets connection, so there is no central repository of information for governance.

In a Secure Sockets Layer transaction, the merchant retains the authorization information it receives when processing the customer's credit card payment. Thus the merchant has responsibility for protecting all customer information. This has proven problematic in the off-line payment world, with disbarred merchants and dishonest employees using credit card information to make unauthorized charges to a customer's credit card.

Finally, the amount of consumer information held by the merchant and financial services providers after a customer participates in a transaction that involves the Secure Sockets Layer strengthens the argument that limits on secondary financial information need to be expanded. As Internet commerce becomes increasingly common and long-standing, merchants will build extensive computerized records of consumer purchases. A clear business opportunity exists for the merchants in selling these records.

Secure Electronic Transaction

The Secure Electronic Transaction protocol (Mastercard 1996) is a combination of Mastercard's Secure Electronic Payment Protocol (SEPP) (Mastercard 1995) and the Visa Secure Transaction Technology (STT) (Visa 1995) protocol.

The Secure Electronic Transaction protocol does not necessarily aggregate purchases, although a merchant may choose to send requests for verification and payment in batches. This is feasible for the obvious reason that there is no more need to aggregate large purchases made over the Internet than large purchases made anywhere else. The same customer support, order processing, administration, and promotion savings that can be obtained by other purveyors of electronic commerce can be obtained by traditional credit card acquirers. The Secure Electronic Transaction protocol may not compete with so much as complement the approaches of the previously mentioned Internet commerce providers.

Internet commerce using the Secure Sockets Layer is modeled, in terms of risk, on mail order and telephone commerce. The merchant, rather than the acquirer, takes the risk for invalid purchases as in mail and telephone orders because a physical card is not presented to the merchant in the transaction—only the information on the card is used. Internet commerce using the Secure Electronic Transaction protocol, however, is modeled as a card-present transaction. In card-present transactions, the merchant is guaranteed payment by virtue of having a physical imprint of the customer's card. In case of the Secure Electronic Transaction protocol, the merchant has a digitally signed record that guarantees payment. Thus although the Secure Sockets Layer and the Secure Electronic Transaction protocol use the same credit card clearing system, the risk allocation is fundamentally different.

The Secure Electronic Transaction protocol allows only traditional merchants to sell goods. This means that small publishers, small manufacturers, independent programmers, and professionals working at home cannot use the Secure Electronic Transaction protocol, because they are not likely to have merchant accounts with an acquirer authorized to clear the customer's requests for credit card purchases.

The Secure Electronic Transaction protocol was developed using an open process of issuing drafts and requesting comments. Originally, Visa proposed a proprietary system with Microsoft, possibly in an attempt to leverage the dominance of the Microsoft operating system to popularize Visa's proposed proprietary technology. Visa's decision to pursue an open process is significant in terms of the promise of future interoperability. However, in contrast to open source, in this case the ownership of the open Internet standard is retained by Visa and Mastercard.

The weakness of the Secure Electronic Transaction protocol in terms of interoperability is that a requirement for credit card ownership sharply limits the pool of consumers for Internet commerce. In addition, the requirement that merchants have traditional merchant accounts in order to accept funds seriously limits its potential for Internet commerce use by limiting the merchant population to traditional merchants. Contrast this with the low barriers to being a merchant at Ebay, and consider the rate at which Ebay has grown in comparison with the far slower adoption of the Secure Electronic Transaction protocol.

The probability that the Secure Electronic Transaction protocol will eventually emerge as a common standard for Internet commerce is supported by simple observation of the financial strength of its founders, Visa and Mastercard. CyberCash, American Express, and Europay also have the Secure Electronic Transaction protocol as a standard.

A Transaction
The Secure Electronic Transaction protocol offers multiple protocols for electronic commerce that reflect the different types of Internet access available. Transactions are possible for customers with email connectivity and Web connectivity. Transactions can be implemented by customers with or without certificates. In the discussion here I consider transactions in which a customer has public key certificates and Web access. This is the appropriate model for maintaining consistency across comparisons of different protocols. An alternate version assumes that customers can only calculate hash values of payment information. This protects payment information from merchants.

The Secure Electronic Transaction protocol uses the standard language in the credit card industry. I use slightly different language in the discussion here, to be consistent with other descriptions. Normally credit card verification is referred to as *authorization* and payment is called *capture*. Since the words "authorization" and "capture" have other,

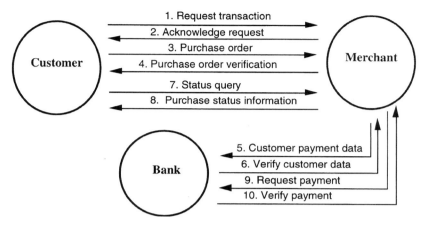

Figure 11.3
A Secure Electronic Transaction protocol transaction

specific meanings in computer security, however, the terms verification and payment, respectively, are used here instead. The bank as shown in figure 11.3 is an *acquirer gateway*, a service provider for acquirer banks. That is, the gateway is the Internet presence of the bank or of a set of banks. With these changes in terminology, the figure corresponds to the description in the Secure Electronic Transaction protocol specifications.

Since the Secure Electronic Transaction protocol specifications permit batching of verification and payment of multiple transactions, the contents of a specific message may vary slightly from the single transaction model shown here. In fact, steps 5, 6, 9, and 10 can precede steps 4, 7, and 8. However, this does vary the distribution of risk, so I am illustrating a single transaction in which verification and payment both occur at the time of the transaction.

Figure 11.3 shows a transaction using the Secure Electronic Transaction protocol for an interactive medium. Notice that browsing and price negotiation are not included in the Secure Electronic Transaction protocol. A corresponding diagram can be found in the Secure Electronic Transaction Technical Specifications (Mastercard 1996, p. 133).

In step 1 the customer identifies her desire to make a purchase to the merchant. This first message includes a customer-specific message identifier (LID_C), a corresponding nonce (Chall_C), the customer-selected payment method (BrandID), and a list of certificates with the appropriate hashes for verification. (Recall from the description of cryptography that a nonce is a random number included in a message to prevent replay attacks.) There is no encryption used to protect this information; however, one presumes that only the cardholder has any interest in sending the cardholder's certificate (because only the cardholder has the secret key that corresponds to the public key about which the certificate attests). Thus after step 1 the merchant (and an observer who may be lurking) know the customer's identity, the merchant to whom the message was directed, the item the customer has requested, and the item's price. The merchant now knows the customer's credit card type, limits on the customer's account (e.g., credit limit, acceptable company pruchases, etc.), and any customer attributes implied by this credit information.

In step 2 the merchant acknowledges the customer's request to begin a transaction. The merchant begins a record that includes the customer's transaction identifier (a unique number assigned to the transaction so it doesn't get confused with other simultaneous transactions) and brand (credit card type) in the database. Presumably the customer's email address (for responses) is also included, although this is not noted in the specifications. According to the Secure Electronic Transactions documentation, the merchant is supposed to obtain the customer's billing address *out of band*. (The merchant must know the customer's billing address for authorization.)[55] The message that contains this information is not specified, although the Secure Sockets Layer is an obvious choice, since it is provides confidentiality and is ubiquitous.

The message in step 2 includes the shared transaction identifier,[56] a response to the first challenge, a time stamp, and a new nonce from

55. Out of band is not defined in the specifications—it is usually transmitted over the Web using SSL according to development discussions on the set-discuss list.

56. The customer may have one transaction identifier for her own records, the merchant another, and the bank a third. All three parties, however, must also share a transaction identifier designed so that no two transactions have the same identifier. It does not matter if two customers or two merchants use the same record number internally; it is the shared identifier that must be unique in the entire market.

merchant to customer. The merchant also sends his digital certificate with the second message, so that after this message the customer has the merchant's certificate.

Step 3 is the customer's purchase request. This is the customer's conditional commitment to completing the transaction. From the perspective of the customer, the customer is not committed, and the payment is not durable, for some weeks after this step. As soon as the customer commits, however, the merchant is ensured payment. The customer maintains the right of dispute in the transaction until after she reviews her monthly credit card charge account summary.

The purchase request is the most complex message: it includes payment and order information. The payment information is encrypted so that the merchant cannot read it, but the bank can. The customer's digital certificate proved that the customer had a credit card and provided information about the customer's credit limit, but in this message the customer provides the information necessary to actually authorize a charge. The order information and purchase amount are sent in verifiable but unreadable form, that is, they are hashed. The merchant obtains the order information external to the protocol, again using an out-of-band technique. The purchase request is digitally signed by the customer. The message includes a general description of goods ordered, transaction amount, and nonces in the clear. The payment information includes account number, transaction identifier, transaction amount, and card expiration date encrypted for the bank.

In step 4 the merchant sends a message verifying the receipt of the purchase order sent in step 3. The fourth message is from the merchant to the customer. The merchant may choose to obtain verification first or to respond to the customer immediately and batch verification later with other transactions. (The former is assumed in both the figure and the discussion.) In this case the merchant sends the customer the results of his attempt to obtain payment verification.

The next message is the merchant's indication to the customer that the merchant will complete the transaction, contingent on authorization, and possibly payment. This message is signed by the merchant. This message includes the transaction identifier, the customer's transaction identifier, and the status of the transaction. The status indicates if the merchant has requested verification, payment, or has made no request to the bank. If credit card verification has been completed previously, then the verification amount would be included. If the transfer of funds (e.g., payment) had been completed, the payment status, payment amount, and the ratio of amount paid to purchase price would be included.

In step 5 the merchant request verification from the bank. (Recall that the bank as represented here is actually a gateway to the clearance system.) This message is encrypted so that only the bank can read it. The message is digitally signed for authentication, then encrypted using a one-time DES key. The DES key itself is then encrypted in the bank's public key.

The verification request includes transaction-specific and merchant-specific data. Transaction-specific data include the transaction identifier, the date of the transaction, and the order information. The order description, the transaction amount, and nonce are hashed together and also included. The merchant's transaction identifier, the customer's transaction identifier, the date, merchant identifying information and the brand identifier are hashed together for inclusion. The merchant-generated data transmitted include the amount, the merchant's business area, and one byte identifying a specific purchase area. This single letter is referred to as the MarketSpecData and identifies the industry involved, whether hotel, auto, etc. The customer's billing address is included in the verification request, and there is also an option for requesting additional verification, above the purchase amount, called AdditionalAmount. Finally, there is a flag to identify the message as part of a batch and fields for associated batch information.

Step 6 is the bank's response to the merchant's verification request. Before responding, the bank authenticates the customer using her digital signature and the signatures of the hash values signed by the customer and sent by the merchant match. The verification response is encrypted and signed by the bank.

In step 7 the customer may contact the merchant to determine the status of the transaction. Only the merchant's transaction identifier and the customer's transaction identifier are included in this message.

In step 8 the merchant responds with a signed message of the same form as the message in step 4. That is, the merchant reiterates his commitment to completing the transaction and notifies the customer of status of the transaction.

In step 9 the merchant requests payment from the bank. Payment is not equivalent to verification. In verification, a certain amount is reserved on the credit line of the customer. In payment, a lesser or equal amount is transferred to the merchant. Payment is reversible in telephone and mail order transactions from the perspective of the merchant, but not in transactions using the Secure Electronic Transaction protocol. The payment messages are both signed and encrypted using a one-time DES key, which is then protected using the recipient merchant's public key.

As part of requesting payment in step 9, the merchant sends the transaction identifier, the transaction date, transaction-specific data (from the verification request), and the amount of the transaction. Data are added for ease of processing if the order is batched. This message is the merchant's commitment to the bank to complete the transaction.

In step 10 the bank confirms payment.

Consider now the transactional characteristics of the Secure Electronic Transaction protocol. The Secure Electronic Transaction protocol does not assure isolation because of the inclusion of an AdditionalAmount field in the verification request from the merchant to the bank. The customer neither approves nor has knowledge of this field. This fact has proven problematic with physical card transactions, as described in chapter 10.

The ability of electronic customers to travel between merchants at a much higher rate than physical customers may exacerbate this lack of isolation. If a consumer visits many web pages, making a purchase request at each one, and each merchant blocks off an amount through the verification process that assures maximum possible payment (using the AdditionalAmount field), the consumer may quickly be drained of available credit.

Credit card transactions using the Secure Electronic Transaction protocol are normally consistent in that the customer and merchant agree on the amount paid. They are also durable. The Secure Electronic Transaction protocol provides money atomicity, but does not provide either goods atomicity or certified delivery. It could be strengthened by the addition of certified delivery by increasing the level of atomicity, particularly for information goods.

Security

The most dramatic improvement of the Secure Electronic Transaction protocol over the mail order and telephone protocol for Mastercard is that the merchant gets only enough information for only one purchase. Merchants cannot use the Secure Electronic Transaction protocol information for replay attacks. Not only are transaction identifiers unique to a transaction (and never repeated), the date and time of the transaction are included in the verification. A merchant cannot produce a purchase order signed with the customer's private key with different time and transaction identifiers than the one the customer originally transmitted.

The Secure Electronic Transaction protocol does not include negotiation or verification of delivery of information goods. A customer can claim not to have received goods already consumed, and a merchant can claim to have provided goods not sent. Therefore the security of the Secure Electronic Transaction protocol depends upon the delivery mechanism used. Nonrepudiation has limited strength when the promise can be verified, but the fulfillment of the promise cannot be.

The Secure Electronic Transaction protocol's lack of goods atomicity creates the potential for fraud. The addition of certified delivery could address this for information goods.

The Secure Electronic Transaction protocol includes the possibility of using a pseudonym in terms of the account number. That is, the customer can choose to use a fake account number rather than her real one. Since the merchant's possession of a real account number creates the possibility for fraud, the use of fake numbers should be a standard feature. Requiring that all account numbers be pseudonyms is a low-cost technique for increasing security. Having pseudonymous identities linked to the pseudonymous account numbers would increase privacy as well as security.

Customer address and order data are provided to the merchants in a separate channel from the Secure Electronic Transaction protocol by the customers. Thus this information is potentially available to observers.

Table 11.3
Information available to various parties in a SET protocol transaction

Party	Information				
	Merchant	Customer	Date	Amount	Item
Merchant	Full	Partial	Full	Full	Full
Customer	Full	Full	Full	Full	Full
Law enforcement with warrant	Full	Full	Full	Full	Full
Bank	Full	Full	Full	Full	Full
Observer	Full	Full	Full	Full	Full

How problematic such an information leak would be depends upon the importance of customer base information to the merchant and the importance of transactional information to the customer.

Customer address information is used for verification of the credit card used in the transaction. Thus one element of verification information is sent in a way that is neither secure nor private. This is similar to the separate channels used for purchase and verification in First Virtual.

Privacy
Table 11.3 shows the information available in a transaction using the Secure Electronic Transaction protocol.

The Secure Electronic Transaction protocol provides more privacy than standard credit card transactions outside the Internet, since the customer can choose a pseudonymous account number. This implies that the capacity for using pseudonyms is built into the Secure Electronic Transaction protocol, although it is not currently explicit. Note that the fact that financial information is hidden from the merchant increases security, not privacy.

An electronic observer can obtain complete knowledge about a transaction using the Secure Electronic Transaction protocol because the certificates containing identity information of the transaction parties are transmitted in the clear. Encryption is used to obscure payment information, not order information. Messages in the Secure Electronic Transaction protocol could be sent over a connection protected from observers using the Secure Sockets Layer.

Recall that the merchant in a transaction using the Secure Electronic Transaction protocol knows not only the customer identity but also other customer attributes, including address. Possession of this information has the potential to be more than just a privacy violation. The availability of this information, and the ability to correlate it in real time with other ethnographic and economic data, create the potential for electronic red-lining. (Red-lining is the denial of services to certain neighborhoods. It is called red-lining because of the practice of drawing a red line on a map to identify "unacceptable" regions, and is traditionally associated with racial discrimination.)

The Secure Electronic Transaction protocol offers a medium level of privacy because the bank (through the acquirer gateway) knows the item(s) purchased. It offers more privacy than First Virtual because the merchant is not apparently required to maintain records of customer purchases for any length of time after payment, as opposed to First Virtual's requirement that records be kept for three years. The nonrepudiation enabled with public key cryptography, the contractual limits on merchant loss, and the statutory limits on customer loss make this retention of customer data unnecessary.

Governance
The Secure Electronic Transaction protocol is an open standard that provides all information necessary for regulatory purposes. The Secure Electronic Transaction protocol is not optimized primarily for privacy in that the customer's name and address are required from the merchant for verification. With the use of certificates and public keys, the security advantage gained by requiring inclusion of such information is questionable for items not requiring physical delivery. In fact, the use of a pseudonymous certificate with no physical customer information would require no change in the protocols and would offer a vast improvement in consumer privacy.

The concentration at the bank, actually an acquirer gateway, of information obtained in transactions using the Secure Electronic Transaction protocol reinforces the need to extend the legal constraints on secondary use of information beyond credit reporting agencies.

According to the Secure Electronic Transaction Business Strategy documentation, the stated reason that privacy is limited in the Secure

Electronic Transaction protocol is the desire to export this protocol and the current controls on the export of cryptography. That is, the amount of privacy the protocol currently offers is limited by the credit card companies' desire to export the technology and the legal restrictions on encryption used to protect private information. This regulatory-driven limit on privacy reflects a need to recognize in regulatory guidelines that transactional information correlated with identity is itself valuable and worth protecting. The limit on the export of cryptography to the purely financial weakens not only the privacy but also the security of the Secure Electronic Transaction protocol, since information that is not strictly financial but that would be useful for identity theft is sent in the clear.

Token Currencies

In token currency the strings of bits transferred in a transaction are themselves legitimately valuable, in comparison to the notational examples in which the value is altered in ledgers and the string of bits in the transactions entails instructions to alter the ledger. A dollar has value in and of itself and is not a promissory note for a particular transaction from a specific account, like a credit card purchase slip. Because of this independence, in value token currency need not be linked to specific transactions or identities.

Digicash was the first and remains the canonical token currency system for Internet commerce. Digicash introduced the concept of *blind signatures,* which allow the bank to verify currency for users without being able to identify the currency verified as it is later spent. (Currency is verified as valid and not yet spent.) Prior to the innovation of blinded signatures, any token currency provided by a bank to a customer could have been identified by the bank at the time it was returned for deposit. The invention of blind signatures created the possibility of anonymous electronic token currency.

Electronic token currency is particularly interesting in that each new token proposal presents a novel mathematical technique or a novel application of a known technique. The most difficult problem remains the prevention of double-spending of coins, which are easy to duplicate —and when a bitstring is itself token currency, then there is universal motivation to do so. In the absence of secure hardware, the dominant approaches to solving the problem of double-spending have involved limits on anonymity and on-line clearing.

The issue of double-spending is related to the issue of isolation. If a token can be spent more than once, then the transactions involving that token are not isolated. This creates a race condition among those who received the token in transactions: whoever gets to the bank first is paid, and the second to arrive is unpaid, along with any subsequent arrivals. With on-line clearing, the payee can clear the token before accepting it. (Clearing refers to a payee's ability to confirm the validity of a token before accepting it and attempting to deposit it. It is comparable to the verification/authorization process in credit cards.) Clearing enables something akin to two-phase commit to occur: clearing is the customer's commitment nested through the merchant, deposit is the merchant's commitment, and acceptance of the deposit is the bank's global commitment. A token thus cleared is locked and cannot be used again until the transaction for which was cleared is complete, so no race condition is possible.

Atomicity in the token currencies is complicated by both the nature of token currency and its anonymity. In a transaction involving token currency, restoration to the previous consistent state can be quite difficult precisely because tokens are not necessarily linked to a specific transaction. Anonymous restoration of a previous state is particularly problematic: what would happen if any anonymous individual could present a claim to the money in other person's wallet?

Consider the three classes of atomicity with respect to token currency. For a token transaction to be money atomic, a customer's payment must be linked with the merchant's payment. That is, it must be the case that if the customer loses the value of a token, the merchant gains the value of the token, and the merchant gains the value of a token only if the customer loses it. For a token transaction to be goods atomic, the merchant must obtain the token from the customer only if some merchandise has been delivered to the customer. For a token transaction to provide certified delivery, the merchant must obtain the token from the customer if the specifically promised merchandise has been delivered to the customer.

To illustrate the issues of security, reliability, and privacy in electronic token currency, chapter 10 included a discussion of a remote transaction with physical token currency: sending cash through the mail.

Here we consider these same lines for several electronic versions of token currency; the original Digicash proposal, a description of MicroMint, and finally, Millicent.

Digicash

In Digicash (Chaum 1985), customers hold the monetary value in the form of electronic tokens. Customers and merchants exchange tokens, and these tokens are validated by a bank. The bank validates that the signature on the token is valid (i.e., that it was approved by the bank) and that the token has not been previously spent.

Digicash provides only a mechanism for electronic payment. Digicash protocols do not provide mechanisms for discovery, negotiation, delivery, or conflict resolution. The scope of Digicash is both its strength and weakness. The advantage is that Digicash can provide an elegant and simple protocol. The disadvantage is that Digicash cannot offer to decrease the cost associated with collection and dispute resolution. In fact, Digicash is specifically designed to mimic cash so that only the purchase itself and the detection of counterfeits are properly the business of Digicash.

A Transaction

Figure 11.4 shows the steps in a Digicash purchase. This digital cash protocol was the first use of blinded tokens for electronic cash. Recall that with blinded tokens, any party X has asymmetric public keys with public key K and secret key k.

Before a Digicash transaction begins, the customer selects a random number (r) and constructs a token (t). She then encrypts the random number with the public key of the bank's asymmetric key and multiplies it with the token and send it to the bank for validations: $r^B t$. (Recall from the table of notation in chapter 10 that this means the random number r is encrypted in the bank's public key B and multiplied by the token, t.) The bank signs the token with its corresponding secret key, and returns: $(r^B t)^b = (r^B)^b t^b$. (As explained in chapter 3, anything encrypted with a

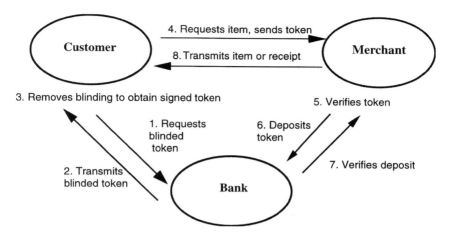

Figure 11.4
A Digicash transaction

public key is decrypted by the private key. Thus the random number is decrypted by the bank's signature with its secret key.) In the third step the customer divides by the random number she originally selected and gets a token: $(r^B)^b t^b)/r = (rt^b)/r = t^b$. This token has been signed by the bank and will be recognized by the bank as valid. The bank has never seen the token, however, and could not distinguish it as the token given to the customer.

In the fourth step the customer sends the request for an item and the token (as payment) to the merchant. In the fifth step the merchant confirms that the signature of the bank is valid. The token is expected to have some specific form, and validating the bank's signature using the bank's public key verifies that the token has been signed by the bank.

In the sixth step the merchant deposits the token. In the seventh step, the bank confirms the deposit. That the token has a valid signature does not mean that the token inherently has value, because it is easy to duplicate a digital token. Thus it is possible that the token has already been redeemed. This would make the copy of the token deposited by the merchant worthless. In the eighth step the merchant delivers the items requested and paid for by the customer in step four.

The token received by the bank in step 6 cannot be identified as the same token sent out in step 2. This is the critical element that makes

Digicash anonymous. Descriptions of many forms of digital cash, including the one referenced here, end at the point where the merchant confirms the deposit.

Digicash as originally designed does not provide the information necessary for conflict resolution or dispute prevention. In fact, if the protocol is interrupted between step 4 and the delivery of goods to the customer, the customer has effectively been defrauded. Because the customer is anonymous, he or she cannot simply contact the merchant and ask for the goods to be resent. Otherwise it would be reasonable for strangers simply to show up and demand goods on the presumption that they belong to them. Imagine a person demanding a dollar from your wallet on the basis that he had once held it. (The partial loss of anonymity resulting from location information has a positive effect here in that merchants could send lost information goods a second time to the same IP address.) The merchant could also claim not to have received a token while cashing the token in at the bank because the bank, has no way of tracing the token to the customer. In this case the customer is again defrauded.

Security

Digicash assumes the privacy of cryptographic keys: the bank's and the customer's. Consider the results if one of these assumptions is invalid. An adversary who gains access to a bank's private key can generate counterfeit tokens that are indistinguishable from valid tokens. These tokens can be generated in any amount desired, so compromise of the key compromises all tokens in circulation.

An adversary who gains access to a customer's private key can create tokens until he drains a customer's account. Including a challenge and response series, where the bank keeps only the hash values of answers for a set of questions, could mitigate the problem.[57] Since digitally signing a token is four orders of magnitude more processor intensive than verifying

---

57. "Challenge and response" is basically questions and answers, but it is more than that since many of the questions are mathematical, so only a person with the correct secret numbers can answer the "question" (recall from chapter 3 that cryptographic keys are numbers). Many people have experienced simple challenge and response, with the standard challenge being, "What is your mother's maiden name?"

a hash value (an unavoidable result of the mathematics involved), this appears to be a reasonable addition to total processor load required of the bank for generating a token.

Two tokens can be multiplied to construct a third counterfeit token, as follows: $(n_1)^b (n_2)^b = (n_1 n_2)^b$. Two signed documents multiplied together result in a signed document. In most cases, such a multiplication results in signed gibberish. In the case of the original token design, the result could be to print money. Notice the counterfeiter still has possession of the original tokens. Tokens can be multiplied to form new valid tokens; that is, consumers and merchants can easily manufacture cash.

Digicash transfers are not money-atomic (Yee 1994). The customer may attempt to resolve this problem by canceling a token (by cashing it in), but if the merchant who has received the token also does this, the result is a race condition. (This also violates consistency and isolation.) Because the bank has no means of determining where a token originated or the agreement between merchant and customer, dispute resolution can be a problem.

One option for addressing issues of customer double-spending and merchant fraud would be to assume that in a dispute between a merchant and a customer, the customer is always right. This would require only keeping the names of customers who complain and the merchants who are the subjects of their complaints. This would maintain the anonymity in a successful transaction of Digicash while reducing the risk to consumers. An aggressive technique of disallowing merchants suspected of fraud might limit the popularity of the system, as consumers and merchants are drawn to popular systems.

A second option would be to assume that the customer is always the fraudulent party in a dispute. This is the option chosen in the a later alternative system also designed by David Chaum, where the detection of double spending is enabled through embedding identity information in the token.

Privacy

Table 11.4 shows the information available to the parties in a transaction using the form of digital cash considered here. Recall that partial identity

Table 11.4
Information available to various parties in a Digicash transaction

Party	Information				
	Merchant	Customer	Date	Amount	Item
Merchant	Full	Partial	Full	Full	Full
Customer	Full	Full	Full	Full	Full
Law enforcement with warrant	Full	None	None	None	None
Bank	Full	None	Full	Full	None
Observer	Partial	Partial	Full	None	None

information trapped by an observer and a seller result from location information, as describing in the section on browsing information in chapter 7.

Digicash is a high-privacy system. The merchant in a transaction using Digicash has only the information necessary to ensure payment, and the bank in the transaction has only the information necessary to credit or debit an account.

Governance
Digicash does not provide any information to law enforcement about the customer in a transaction. This implies that Digicash would thus be an excellent instrument for money laundering or other illicit purchases. This potential drawback is mitigated, however, by the fact that tokens must be verified on-line, and therefore banks can identify someone who makes large deposits or transfers. The Know Your Customer regulations (31 CFR §103) apply no matter what the type of currency a customer deposits, and this ensures that bank transactions above a certain size remain accessible for auditing. This suggests that limits on anonymous account transfers apply as much to Digicash as they do to analog cash. That Mark Twain Bank in the United States has encountered no regulatory resistance to its offering Digicash accounts supports the conclusion that regulators are willing to accept anonymous currency so long as it enters and exits the electronic realm through channels that are as easy to audit as regular channels.

A customer who loses her private key currently has unlimited liability for fraudulent Digicash transactions that result, and this may violate the Electronic Funds Transfer Act. Thus any cost of fraud is transferred to the customer. The Electronic Funds Transfer Acts specifically limits consumer loss in electronic funds transfers to $50 per lost instrument. It is not certain if a Digicash account meets the definition of an instrument under the act.

The lack of any receipt and the ease of merchant fraud seem to create problems with the Truth in Lending Act and Electronic Funds Transfer Act requirements for receipts and billing,[58] as implemented in Regulations E and Z, respectively. A technique exists for providing receipts and certification of a merchant's commitment in an anonymous system (Camp, Harkavy, Tygar, and Yee 1996). This technique, however, significantly adds to the complexity of anonymous exchange of digital tokens. Furthermore, it significantly extends the scope of the transaction beyond that currently considered by many electronic token mechanisms, including the ones under consideration here.

Digicash-based banks can provide aggregate information on deposits and withdrawals and are certainly capable of storing records on individual deposits and withdrawals. Anonymity in Digicash means that the bank cannot link the deposits to the withdrawals. It also means that coins cannot be traced through their path if they change hands more than once. Transferring a coin more than once, however, creates the risk that previous possessors of the coin will return it before the subsequent owners, depriving the subsequent owners of payment.

MicroMint

MicroMint and PayWord are a set of electronic commerce protocols (Rivest and Shamir 1996) that use the difficulty of calculating hash values

58. It is worth noting that the revision of Regulation E noted in chapter 3 would exempt stored-value cards with storage capacity of less than $100 from the receipt requirements. Digicash is suitable for smart card implementations. Secure hardware would remove the tension between atomicity and anonymity because secure hardware provides a secure listing of transactions. Yet my focus here is on Internet commerce, as the infrastructure for secure hardware is far from ubiquitous.

and the birthday paradox to provide electronic currency. Despite their mathematical similarities, however, PayWord is a notational, credit-based scheme and MicroMint is a token, debit-based scheme.

MicroMint is problematic because it assumes the solution to the problem of electronic commerce. That is, there is a bootstrap problem. Once the coins are established and the consumers have coins, the customer purchases with the coins and merchant redeems them. However, the distribution of the first generation of coins—how the coins get established in the first place—remains unspecified.

MicroMint calls the bank involved in MicroMint transactions a "broker." Instead of holding deposits, the broker generates coins and exchanges them with customers. (The broker has the float—the time value of money, or the interest on investing the money while the customer holds it—until the coin is spent.) To defeat double-spending of the coins it generates, the broker must know the identity of the customer to whom it gives the coins. This knowledge requirement, the consumer's need to be able to draw coins, the merchant's ability to deposit them, and the resulting requirement for customer and merchant accounts all suggest that it is a reasonable conjecture that the broker is a bank in all but semantic terms.

The bank mints MicroMint coins by using k hash values and the birthday paradox, as discussed in the chapter 3. Rivest and Shamir (1996) have calculated that to obtain one k-way collision[59] requires calculating expected $2^{(k-1/k)}$ hash values; however, to get c k-way collisions requires expected $c2^{(k-1/k)}$ hash values. Rivest and Shamir compare this to the initial investment in a mint (or an illicit facility in a counterfeiting operation), with high initial costs and low marginal cost for each additional bill printed. A MicroMint coin is a set of numbers that all have the

59. Recall from chapter 3 that when two different values result in the same output of a hash function, that is called a collision (the birthday paradox). For a very simple example, consider a hash function using the $a = 1$, $b = 2$ code used in chapter 3 to illustrate stream ciphers. A simple hash function would be to compress a name by adding up the letter values. In this case Jean (10 + 5 + 1 + 14) and Ken (11 + 5 + 14) would have a collision at the value 30. Jen, Anie, and Ann have a three-way collision at 29. Note that this is far more simple than any hash function in use, but the principle is that a function that alters the input will result in some initial different values resulting in the same output, and these same inputs are said to collide in the case of hash functions.

Table 11.5
Returns to scale in minting money through hash

Number of hashes	Coins produced	Hashes/coin
$2^0 \ldots 2^{26}$	0	——
2^{27}	1	2^{27}
2^{29}	2^8	2^{21}
2^{32}	2^{20}	2^{12}
2^{36}	2^{32}	2^3

same hash value, thus a coin is a set of k numbers $(x_1, x_2, x_3, \ldots x_k)$, where $h(x_1) = h(x_2) = h(x_3) = \ldots = h(x_k)$.

Using hash values, which are publicly known after the coins have been hashed and released, merchants can verify off-line that currency sent by customers is of the valid form. To prevent double-spending, the customer's identity is embedded in the hash values sold to a customer, like so:

$$h(\text{coin}) = h(x_1, x_2, x_3, \ldots x_k) = h(\text{customer identity}).$$

Thus any customer who double-spends would be detected and identified when the tokens were deposited. By using a lower hash value, this becomes computationally feasible. A 16-bit hash value is recommended given the state of computing at the turn of the century. Table 11.5 (as excerpted from Rivest and Shamir 1996) shows the cost of generating coins. This table illustrates that small-scale attacks are not feasible because of the large numbers of hashes required to produce the first coin. The table presents the case where a coin consist of four numbers—that is, a coin requires four collisions. The numbers are 36-bits. Thus there is a tremendous initial investment in preparing the first coin, but as the number of coins created increases, the cost decreases.

The potential for large-scale attacks is addressed by changing the hash value[60] monthly. (This requires that customers submit unused coins for updated coins monthly.) This renders all forged coins invalid at the beginning of the month, and the forger cannot begin generating hash values for the new coins until the hash function for the month has been

---

60. The authors suggest using the same hash value with a different initial condition.

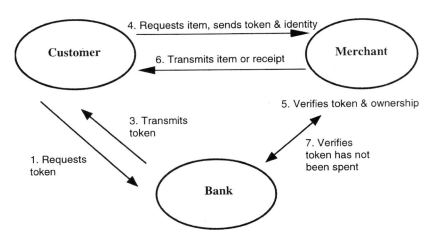

Figure 11.5
A MicroMint transaction

announced. Thus any forged coins have value for only a short time, and the huge initial investment required to mint the first coin must be undertaken not just once, but every month. Furthermore, the broker can detect forged coins, announce a new hash function at any time, and use hidden predicates for daily updating. (A hidden predicate is a special characteristic of a number that is not apparent upon simple examination. To generate a number with hidden predicates, some of the bits in the number are made a function of other, random bits.)

A Transaction
MicroMint transaction begins when the customer obtains a coin from the broker. Figure 11.5 shows the steps in a MicroMint transaction. In step 1, the customer requests a coin. This customer must authenticate her identity to obtain the coin. Exactly how the customer authenticates her identity for purposes of coin generations is not specified in the MicroMint protocol. Thus exactly what information is exchanged at that step cannot be determined. Merchant authentication and broker authentication are similarly unspecified in the protocol. Of course there are many techniques for authentication, ranging from techniques where much information is exchanged (e.g., digital certificates) to techniques where no information but authentication is exchanged (e.g., zero-knowledge authentication).

In step 2 the bank, having obtained the customer's identity in step 1, constructs the coin. The bank then constructs a provably valid coin linked to the customer's identity as described in the previous section. The bank maintains an extremely large database of known hashes from which to construct a coin—it does not begin hashing anew at every customer request.

In step 3, the bank delivers the requested coins to the customer. After the third step the customer can prove that she has a valid MicroMint tokens, and she can prove her ownership of those tokens. Proving ownership, however, requires exposing her identity.

In step 4 the customer transmits to the merchant the information necessary for the transactions: the item, price, token(s), and her identity. At the time of the order the merchant will also have any information transmitted while the customer was browsing. The information the customer transmits includes the customer's identity, which verifies her ownership of the coins she presents.

In step 5, the merchant verifies the token and the customer's ownership of these coins. In step 6, the merchant delivers the item to the customer. The protocol does not include this step explicitly; is assumed to be part of the protocol, however, since the delivery is assumed to be off-line. The deposits can be batched.

In step 7, the merchant verifies that the token has not been already been spent by the customer, by depositing it. The cost of verifying every coin (in terms of processing power, connectivity, and overhead) may not be worthwhile, so a merchant may prefer to batch transactions. Given that MicroMint is designed for small transactions, the assumption of batching is reasonable.

The MicroMint protocol assumes that only users double-spend. As noted, the delivery of merchandise is not included in the protocol. Thus the protocol cannot be money-atomic or goods-atomic.

Off-line transactions are not isolated. If a merchant presents for redemption a coin that has been previously spent, he does not receive payment and is not reimbursed. Thus the outcome of one transaction depends on the existence of another.

On-line transactions in MicroMint are consistent. Since MicroMint coins are not anonymous, the customer can inquire as to whether a merchant to whom she has sent the coins has deposited those coins, and such inquiries do not necessitate the broker allowing anonymous inquiries into merchant records. The merchant can also verify a coin before accepting it. (Given that the customer has no verification of delivery, the option included above where the merchant delivers goods first distributes the risk somewhat more evenly. In the case that the merchant deposits the coins first, the customer has only her claim not to have received merchandise and the merchant take no risk at all.) Although the customer may not have received any merchandise, the money transfer will be consistent.

MicroMint transactions are durable after coin clearance with the broker but not before. If a customer spends the same coins in two locations, this creates a race condition. Again, the party that receives the second coin, and subsequent coins, will not be credited at the broker. Off-line transactions are neither consistent nor durable.

Security
Security parameters in the MicroMint protocol include the strength of the hash value used to construct the coins, the secrecy of a hash value before it is released, and the number of collisions required to create a coin.

If the broker does in fact hold deposits (like a bank), then the issue of customer authentication to the broker needs to be addressed. MicroMint recommends that the broker have a shared DES key with each customer for the purpose of keeping secure the transmission of coins from the broker to the customer. This DES key could be used for authentication as well.

If the hash value chosen for a particular month is leaked to an attacker in the month before it goes into effect, then the attacker can create coins as quickly as the broker. Since the attacker has lower costs than a legitimate broker, presumably the attacker can invest as much as the broker in processing power. (An attacker does not actually have to redeem his coins—he just uses them. A broker has to create only valid coins and redeem them.) If hidden predicates are used in the coin generation, an attacker would need both the predicates and the hash parameters to commit forgery. Thus the use of predicates addresses the security issues of hash values in a cost-effective way.

An increase in the number of collisions required for the creation of a coin increases the cost of manufacturing coins to the broker and the cost of verifying coins to the merchant. Increasing the number of collisions required also increases the security of the coins. In this way the number of collisions required for coin creation is a parallel to certificate lifetime. (Recall the discussion on managing risk by altering certificate attributes. The same principles apply here.)

Observation of traditional paper systems suggests that some proposed security measures against large-scale fraud may be ineffective. The broker can recognize false coins, just as in the physical world the bank can recognize bad checks, but this has not proven effective in preventing check fraud, precisely because checks are verified at the bank, not at the merchant. The merchant in an off-line MicroMint transaction takes the risk of fraud, while the broker has the ability to detect and prevent the fraud.

The broker can also combat fraud by declaring a current hash period to be over and recall all coins. Attackers can invest in computing power equal to the broker, have no customer overhead, and obtain all goods purchased with false coins for no cost. Consumers may pay an attacker for coins at a discount rate, and the attacker does not have to reimburse merchants for coins redeemed or goods purchased with those counterfeit coins. However, the use of daily predicates, the ability of the broker to select the hash function, frequent changes of hash functions, and the computational overhead required to produce the first coin each time this hash function changes all provide strong barriers to potential attackers.

Privacy

The information available to various parties in the MicroMint system is shown in table 11.6. Here again the ability of law enforcement to obtain information about purchases depends on the merchant's record keeping.

MicroMint is a low-privacy system. Since the creator of coins is modeled as simply a broker, it has only a limited ability to provide pseudonymous services. If the broker were in fact an account holder for the various consumers, then the broker could easily offer pseudonymous coins. The cost of pseudonymity would be one search of the consumer database. Consumers could change pseudonyms whenever no coins were held under the previous pseudonym. Because of re-spending, the broker would

Table 11.6
Information available to various parties in a MicroMint transaction

Party	Information				
	Merchant	Customer	Date	Amount	Item
Merchant	Full	Full	Full	Full	Full
Customer	Full	Full	Full	Full	Full
Law enforcement with warrant	Full	Full	Full	*Full*	Full
Bank/Broker	Full	Full	Full	None	Full
Observer	Full	Full	Full	Full	Full

store pseudonyms until the hash value for the pseudonymously released coins was invalidated.

Consumers can spend only their own coins. This means that there is no threat of security loss if one person copies another's coins during a transaction. Because of this security, the MicroMint protocol offers no extension for encrypting negotiation and payment. Thus an observer can obtain all transactional information about a purchase using the Micro-Mint protocol. To eliminate this possibility, MicroMint could be combined with any product or protocol that provides encrypted peer-to-peer communication on the Internet.

By offering pseudonyms and protecting merchant-to-consumer transaction, the information matrix for MicroMint would be changed as shown in table 11.7. Changes from table 11.6 appear in bold. The changes would make MicroMint a medium-privacy system.

Offering pseudonyms would require some changes in authentication for the MicroMint protocol. The broker could either sign pseudonymous keys or provide pseudonymous certificates. Presumably the latter would be preferable because the protocol could then remain off-line from the perspective of the merchant.

Governance
MicroMint offers inexpensive transactions at the cost of anonymity and individual security. It can fulfill all the requirements for information for regulatory purposes.

Table 11.7
Information available to various parties in an enhanced MicroMint transaction

Party	Information				
	Merchant	Customer	Date	Amount	Item
Merchant	Full	**Partial**	Full	Full	Full
Customer	Full	Full	Full	Full	Full
Law enforcement with warrant	Full	Full	Full	*Full*	Full
Bank/Broker	Full	Full	Full	None	Full
Electronic	**Partial**	**Partial**	**None**	Full	**None**

Individual security is lost in MicroMint in that there is limited protection against malicious framing. The arguments against providing such security is that "the known mechanisms for protecting against such behavior are too cumbersome for a lightweight payment system." Given the amount of motivation individuals have to harm one another, as clearly illustrated in the records of law enforcement in every community, I would argue that such harm presents a significant hazard in the Micro-Mint system.

The case of malicious framing presents a clear case where the risks are taken by customers and merchants to save effort on the part of the bank. This is not a system that appears to be prohibited by current regulation: the consumer cannot be made accountable for more than $50 for a lost instrument. Yet this system clearly violates a basic principle of public policy: the risks of loss should fall upon the party most able to prevent those losses. The merchants can lose money; the customers can lose commerce privileges; yet only the broker can prevent such losses by implementing and requiring an extremely strong proof of customer authentication from merchants depositing coins.

In this case, there is a clear policy principle at stake. Presumably the broker is actually a bank, since there must be some deposits against which the customer draws. Either that, or this system is interoperable with other electronic commerce systems. If it is the former, regulators can examine the system and decide if it is acceptable. If it is the latter, then other providers of electronic commerce will decide. If the other providers of electronic commerce provide the user the ability to contest charges, the market may in fact push the final cost of lost money on the broker, as customers object to denial of service or charges for stolen coins. I would advocate including authentication in the protocol.

Millicent

Millicent is an electronic ode to the days of independent banking. It considers the token coins it creates to be scripts because the coins are specific to a bank or merchant. Millicent vendors create their own currency.

Millicent provides merchants with the ability to create their own coins by using hash values to create low-cost digital certificates. Digital certificates are usually associated with public key certificates, although in fact a digital certificate need not be based on public key cryptography. To prevent confusion about this, I refer to digital certificates based on the cryptographic security of hashing rather than on public key cryptography as *hash certificates*.

Tokens in the form of Millicent script are of the following form:

[merchant|value|token specific ID#| customer ID| expiration date| properties][certificate]

where the certificate is:

. hash certificate = H(token, merchant_secret)

Thus a Millicent token is a string of text, validated at issue via hashing with a secret known only to the issuer. Since only the issuer accepts the script, managing this "merchant secret" does not require the key management techniques of public key cryptography.

A Transaction

Figure 11.6 shows a Millicent transaction using a broker, or issuer of a scrip as presented in the Millicent documentation. In step 1 the customer requests merchant-specific script from the broker. In general it would be reasonable to assume that the merchant has such a script. Periodically, however, the broker must obtain additional script from the merchant. Step 2 shows the merchant requesting additional merchant script to fulfill

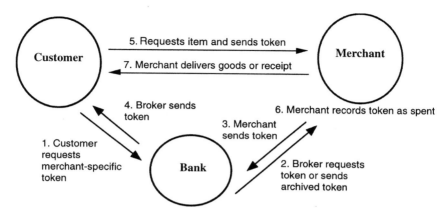

Figure 11.6
A transaction using Millicent tokens

the customer's request. In step 3 the merchant provides script to the broker. In step 4 part of the merchant script is forwarded from the broker to the customer.

At this point the customer has the appropriate script and can transact with the merchant. In step 5 the customer requests items from the merchant. In step 6 the merchant records the script as having been spent (to prevent double-spending). In step 7 the merchant delivers the items requested by the customer in step 5.

In Millicent the customer must trust both the broker and the bank. An explicit decision is made and documented that the most trustworthy party in the party is the broker, and the least trustworthy is the customer. This is borne out by an examination of the transaction—the transaction lacks atomicity.

Millicent is not interoperable. As with First Virtual, the lack of inter-operability is a strength. When using Millicent on-line, customers, merchants, and brokers can all determine the level of risk they will take. Each user determines his or her own risk exposure rather than its level being set by some third party (e.g., a bank or credit card association).

Consider now the transactional characteristics of Millicent. If the message in step 1 fails, there is no transaction—the transaction fails completely. If the message in step 2 fails, the broker may have already debited an amount from the customer's account to cover the tokens she has requested from the broker. In this case the customer may lose funds by beginning again with a new request.

If the message in step 3 fails, the merchant has debited the broker's account for a token that never makes it to the customer and therefore cannot be spent. Thus the vendor has been paid. The broker has been paid by the customer and has paid the vendor. The customer loses money; the merchant gains money. Alternatively there may be an arrangement through which the merchant does not get credited until the broker receives the funds. In this case the broker, rather than the merchant, comes out ahead. If message in step 4 fails, again it is the customer who loses funds.

If the message in step 5 fails, the customer must return the script to the broker to avoid a race condition with a potential thief. Thus the only loss is the cost of token reissue. If the merchant errs in recording the token (step 6) so that the sixth steps fails, then either the customer loses funds or the customer is able to spend the token again. If the message in step 7 fails, than then the customer has no goods.

Clearly the Millicent system lacks atomicity in all its forms. If the customer believes the message in step 5 fails and it has not, this result is a race condition—which will be recorded first, the purchase or the script reissue? Thus the system lacks isolation. Since when step 7 fails the customer can lose funds and the merchant can nevertheless believe the transaction is complete, the protocol lacks consistency. However, once committed (step 6), funds are durable.

Millicent could be made atomic with the addition of an atomicity-generating layer that consists of additional messages to ensure transactional reliability. (An atomicity-generating layer adds a signed contract, merchant receipt of payment, and customer receipt in the case of digital goods.)

Security

Brokers that create their own Millicent currency must keep a secret that if compromised will lead to loss to the merchant. That is, if an attacker obtains the merchant's secret, the attacker can generate merchant-specific

Table 11.8
Information available to various parties in a Millicent transaction

Party	Information				
	Merchant	Customer	Date	Amount	Item
Merchant	Full	Full	Full	Full	Full
Customer	Full	Full	Full	Full	Full
Law enforcement with warrant	Full	Full	Full	Full	Full
Bank/ Broker	Full	Full	Full	Full	Partial
Observer	Full	Full	Full	Full	Partial

funds. The merchant keeps records of what script has been spent, not necessarily what script is outstanding.

Customers are at the greatest risk and have the least control over the security parameters of the system. Merchants are at least risk and have the most control over those system parameters that ensure security. This design encourages underinvestment in security.

Privacy

Table 11.8 depicts the information available to various parties in a transaction using Millicent script. Millicent offers little or no privacy. What Millicent refers to as a private system is in fact merely a system in which all information is not known to observers. Compare this with Digicash, where the customer is anonymous to both the merchant and the bank.

Observers of a Millicent transaction can obtain identity information from the domain name of the customer, as explained in the section on browsing information in chapter 7. Transaction amounts can be determined from observing the site and noting that Millicent is a low-value transaction system, providing an observer probabilistic information about the range of a particular transaction. Similarly, a bank can observe transaction amounts and merchants involved and obtain partial information about a purchase. Law enforcement access depends on merchant record keeping.

Governance

Since Millicent is a low-privacy system, it would appear that information for law enforcement needs would be met. However, Millicent, like cash sent through the mail, provides opportunities for fraud, and fraud prevention is also a law enforcement need. Millicent is not adequate on this count. Millicent's design for low-value purchase means that the record-keeping requirements for large transactions would not be applicable.

Summary

Money takes two basic forms: token and notational. These forms are fundamentally different from one another and imply different trust requirements. Not all forms of money fulfill all the possible functions of money. Differences in scope, duration, and interoperability can increase or decrease risk, depending on the implementation. For example, a long-term notational exchange such as a credit card includes the ability for the customer to dispute merchandise quality after purchase. A cash transaction, on the other hand, ends at the exchange of goods for money.

Internet Notational Currencies

First Virtual offers a low-security system for Internet commerce. First Virtual assumes that the Internet will remain without security and addresses that lack of security through risk management and loss allocation. Unfortunately, this loss allocation (merchant losses) limits the goods suitable for sale using First Virtual. First Virtual is also a low-privacy system that requires merchants to keep extensive records on customers. This reinforces the argument that the controls created on consumer financial data under the Fair Credit Reporting Act should be expanded to cover compilations of nonbank institutions like First Virtual and its associated merchants.

The Secure Sockets Layer is a first-generation Internet commerce protocol that has taken an approach opposite to that of First Virtual. First Virtual assumes that the Internet is without security and merchant losses are negligible; the Secure Sockets Layer assumes that the Internet can be made secure and limits merchant losses by off-line financial management.

It does not attempt to provide atomicity. The Secure Sockets Layer is a medium-privacy system. Its level of security is limited by the constraints on exporting strong cryptography. This provides an argument for the removal of restraints on the export of such cryptography.

The Secure Sockets Layer may create risk as a side-effect in that many merchants keep records of customers' credit card information on machines connected to the Internet and subject to remote attack. There are at least three possible solutions to this problem: security, including cryptography, could be embedded in popular operating systems (and those operating systems could be redesigned to be secure); computer operators with inadequate security practices could be held liable for all losses caused by their negligence; or data could be deleted as soon as possible. Clearly the third solution would be the easiest to implement, and the only option for a single merchant.

Secure Electronic Transactions is a payment protocol that considers all steps in an electronic transaction, excluding account acquisition. Secure Electronic Transactions offers low-privacy system, since purchase information is transmitted in the clear. It provides high level of security by design, as it removes the opportunities for replay attacks and shared merchant terminals that are problematic in the current credit card systems.

The Secure Electronic Transactions standard uses the Secure Sockets Layer for information to be transmitted out of band. Thus the regulatory requirement that limits software for export to using weak cryptography has affected the design of electronic commerce systems. This illustrates the ubiquitous effects of constraints on cryptographic exports on electronic commerce and offers an additional argument for removing these constraints.

The analysis of this set of protocols for Internet commerce illustrates that with notational currency, reliability can be simplified by creating a single ledger where all accounts are finally settled. Creation of a single ledger means concentrated information—thus implying a threat to privacy. One way to address this threat is to accept increased complexity as the cost of protecting privacy. However, the relationship between distribution of information and provision of privacy does not always hold true in that increased centralization does not always imply decreased privacy.

Internet Token Currencies

Digicash is graceful in its simplicity and offers complete anonymity to the customer. Yet Digicash offers this complete privacy at the cost of low reliability. Further, it offers neither money nor goods atomicity.

In the later version of Digicash (not detailed in this book), Chaum attempted to prevent double-spending, thereby increasing system reliability, through encoding identity into each token to be spent. Encoding identity allows double-spenders to be identified, thereby resolving the conflict between anonymity and accountability in the case of double-spending. This addition of integrity provides sufficient information for dispute resolution over issues of payment, but not enough information to resolve disputes over goods delivery.

MicroMint has the potential to create anonymous currency economically for a large number of users. By creating digital currency using a process with decreasing marginal cost, MicroMint can provide anonymous token currency to a large number of consumers. MicroMint would be economical for microtransactions, which are too small for billing or collection using current techniques.

MicroMint in its most simple form offers no money atomicity. To provide money atomicity, MicroMint can be extended so that customer identity is included in every coin. Thus the extension of MicroMint to preclude double-spending depends on the requirement that every consumer identify herself to the merchant to verify the right to spend any coin she sends to a merchant. Millicent creates a lightweight digital token network meant for low-volume transactions. MicroMint, along with the two versions of Digicash, illustrates the trade-off between atomicity and anonymity.

All three token systems meet their design criteria: to create mechanisms for digital token commerce. However, all fail with remote commerce, as does physical cash in the networked world. Thus although all three systems as they are currently described are suitable for secure hardware or smart-card systems, they do not meet the criteria to excel as Internet commerce systems.

The problems with token currency are inherent, and there are three ways to address them: use secure hardware, add identity information, and add atomicity-ensuring steps.

Secure hardware would provide parties to the transaction (at least customers) with records of every transaction that cannot be falsified. Thus customers would no longer have only their word to back their claims: cryptographically verifiable records would support legitimate claims of fraud. This would require physically secure hardware using cryptographic protocols. Although there is much research to be done in secure hardware, IBM currently offers a secure coprocessor card that is safe from even the most James Bond-type exotic attacks. (The processor cannot be attacked with lasers, eaten with acid, or probed in any way to obtain cryptographic key information. Of course it can be destroyed.) Thus secure hardware is a viable option in theory; however, it will only be viable in practice when the infrastructure (including card readers) is widely available. The Internet is the opportunity that it is because it grew organically, by consensus. Adoption of secure hardware may not follow so naturally.

A second option for improving token currency systems is to add identity information to the token. Embedding customer and merchant identity information in the would at least prevent other customers from spending it. Of course, tokens would then no longer be anonymous

Alternatively, vendors of token currency systems could add a layer to provide transactional atomicity and a document trail to better detect the source of fraud (e.g., Camp, Harkavy, Tygar, and Yee 1996). This is simply a set of steps that provides certain types of documentation. Money atomicity would require that there be a step that guarantees a receipt for funds provided to the customer. Goods atomicity would require that there be steps that provide to the merchant documentation of receipt of goods from the customer. Certified delivery would require a receipt that includes a description of the goods promised and of the goods received. All this documentation would need to be secured with strong cryptography, meaning its validity could not be denied assuming no cryptographic keys were lost. This is both possible and processor-intensive.

A final approach would be changing the placement of fraud risks so that brokers and merchants would have no incentive to produce bogus funds. Widespread fraud will drive adoption of additional measures to prevent transactional fraud—even if the widespread fraud is from the loss of a system secret.

12

The Coming Collapse in Internet Commerce

Every currency must come to an end. Some currencies end more spectacularly than others. It is a reasonable assumption that there will be some failures of currencies used in Internet commerce.

Consider all the monetary mechanisms enabled by paper and printing: standardized bookkeeping, derivatives, checks, paper money, stocks, and bonds. Every type of paper commerce is subject to its own unique form of collapse. For example, hyperinflation was not possible before the advent of paper money; entire nations have been thrown into disarray by this phenomenon. That paper money has had many collapses, however, has not killed it. (This may be small solace, of course, to someone holding the wrong pieces of paper.) Paper money has proved to be too powerful and too important to abandon. Similarly, digital moneys are too powerful to reject. Internet commerce will see failures and falls, but electronic commerce on a packetized[61] stupid network will happen.

I would argue that what some may view as failures or collapses are not: they are simply neglected offerings, undesired products. As an analogy, consider the Susan B. Anthony dollar. Because of design flaws, this dollar looked and felt much like a quarter. It is still legal tender, but it was never adopted. Consumer hostility or uncertainty can be identified as a key

---

61. In chapter 1, I described how the Internet delivers information in small chunks, or packets. Also, the Internet protocol does not distinguish types of information, and IP routing includes only the next hop for a message. In contrast, telephone switches handle much more complex tasks than IP routers. Thus the Internet is a "stupid" network compared to the "smart" network of telephones, where the intelligence is in the switch in the center of the network, not in the telephone at the edge of the network. With the Internet, the intelligence is in the endpoints, at the computer, and the switches are rather "stupid."

ingredient in the failure of the Susan B. Anthony dollar. This does not constitute a collapse. The "vendor" still stands behind the value of these dollars, but few want to use the coins. Although these dollar coins have never been embraced by the populace, they still have value, and that value can be transferred. This is analogous to an offering from an established vendor and not a collapse.

That something is a failure and not a collapse does not make it unworthy of mention. The trick in avoiding electronic currencies that will not be adopted is determining which elements will prove to be unacceptable to the consumer. Given the discussion in the foregoing pages, in which I argue that trust and risk are the critical variables, it will come as no surprise that mechanisms that seem ideal to the merchant may not suit the customer. It is the merchant's goal to put the risk inherent in a transaction on the consumer, and the consumer's desire to place that risk on the merchant. Markets have proven quite effective in striking the balance between these opposing desires, although consumer protection is required beyond what the market itself may offer. The point in all this is that a commerce system need not be subject to collapse to be one to avoid.

Predicting the when, why, and where of commerce failures is quite impossible. The examination of systems in this book, however, has made clear that failures have various possible sources. At least two of those failure modes are new to Internet commerce. The possible modes of failure for Internet commerce systems include:

- corporate or vendor failure,[62]
- failure of the integrity of a cryptographic secret,
- widespread fraud resulting in a loss of trust, and
- network failure resulting in a loss of trust.

Consider each of these four modes of failure. Corporate or vendor failure in Internet commerce will be not unlike previous failures of money vendors. With those electronic systems using credit cards, one trusts that the managers of risks in banks can avoid the cost of a sudden collapse due to insolvency. The organization offering the cash, the vendor, should be

62. By implementing commerce technologies in open source, a single corporate failure need not cause the merchants and customers to lose their investments, since the open code is malleable to be interoperable with other extant systems.

the organization at risk should the commerce mechanism suffer technical failures. Vendors offering Internet commerce would of course prefer failures to be paid for by the banks, who view these vendors as specialized merchants.

The second and third modes of failures—failure of the integrity of a cryptographic secret and widespread fraud resulting in a loss of trust—may be indistinguishable if the loss of a cryptographic secret allows widespread but not ubiquitous fraud. Consider the systems examined here in which loss of cryptographic integrity would not result in collapse, but rather widespread failure. A collapse occurs when valid currency cannot be distinguished from bogus currency, or when assets backing a currency system fail. The failure modes of the systems analyzed here should provide a guide for analyzing those of the other commerce systems being offered. There are more than 100 commerce mechanisms currently developed to the point of being accepted for peer-reviewed publication, being implemented, or being presented as a corporate standard.

In determining how a commerce system may fail, one should evaluate whether there is a distributed failure mode as well as a catastrophic failure mode. To consider an engineering example, elevators fail by ceasing to move, not by crashing into the ground, thanks to safety designs, which depend only on the laws of physics. Ideally a commerce system would fail by grinding to a halt in the face of bogus currencies and their transactions, rather than by accepting bogus transactions as valid. Some systems are built so there exists some category of failure other than catastrophic. Systems with distributed failure modes that have been discussed in this document include Millicent, MicroMint, and the Secure Sockets Layer. Digicash may also have a distributed failure mode—if there are multiple root keys. SET has both catastrophic and distributed failure modes. First Virtual has only a catastrophic failure mode, but the implications of such a failure would be limited.

How might these systems fail? The loss of a "secret"—whether this is a root key, a password file, or a seed value for a hash function—can cause failure. A failure would enable multiple copies to be made of false instruments, indistinguishable from valid currency. This type of failures would cascade through the different systems in different ways. In some systems (such as centralized token-based systems), failure would come either from fiscal collapse of the currency supplier, or from hyperinflation when the generation of fraudulent new instruments causes the value of the extant instruments to collapse. In other systems the fraud may be widely distributed but immediately detectable (at high levels), thereby leading to a distribution of risk across the system. If there was a rash of fraud, merchants as well as banks would have to write off a large number of losses.

One researcher found a quick way to break the key-generating mechanism in an early version of the Secure Sockets Layer.[63] The encryption had not been generated entirely from random numbers, but used more predictable values (and could be affordably and easily broken). Suppose a criminal rather than a researcher had found this failure and used it to obtain customer credit card information. In this case, the failure would be detected by credit card issuers and merchants, who would pay for an increase in fraud.

Now consider SET. For SET to be successful, the acquirers must spend significant funds to build a public key infrastructure. Webmasters offering electronic commerce must support more processor-intensive transactions. SET-ready Web sites will cost more to merchants than those that do not support the comprehensive payment mechanism. As a result of these expenditures, the acquirer will have responsibility for fraud. What could drive the expenditure necessary to adopt any heavy electronic mechanism but widespread fraud?

Thus I do boldly predict that if there is a failure of SSL, there will be a transition period of very high fraud followed by widespread adoption of acquirer safeguards, such as adoption of SET or other heavy-duty transaction mechanisms. An alternative may be the development of secure hardware, so that additional encryption in the application would be less necessary. Alternatively, secure hardware might complement encryption at the application level. (For more on this possibility, see the arguments for "end to end" encryption.) In general, when a system begins to have high fraud levels, there will be a move to secure hardware, to more carefully engineered software, or to a more processor-intensive version of the system.

63. This was immediately addressed and the weakness no longer exists.

However, should SET fail, consumers would be responsible for payment. SET could fail if the root keys are compromised, that is, if someone obtained them (other than those authorized to have them). (The root keys are extremely well guarded and well distributed, so this is unlikely.) A criminal who obtained the root keys could assume the identity of a bank and collect funds until discovered. This could result in extremely large institutional losses and be the equivalent of a major bank failure. Conversely, acquiring banks could continue the process of signing up merchants with questionable records. In this case customers would bear the cost. This could lead to a decline in the trust necessary for Internet commerce to thrive.

Should an attacker obtain less-trusted SET keys, he could assume the identity of a false merchant. Customers and merchants could suffer losses, so it is uncertain how long this would remain undetected—but possibly long enough to be profitable for the criminal. However, this corrupt criminal could lend his key to others as easily as he lends his credit card privileges in real life. The problem of merchant fraud is not uncommon and can therefore be assumed to be manageable by the charge clearance system. Since replay attacks would not be useful under SET, this would limit the efficiency of merchant-based fraud.

Consider a failure in First Virtual. The effects of a failure in First Virtual would be limited by its lack of interoperability. First Virtual would not be required to pay merchants when consumers refused payment. Merchants would suffer the losses and move to a different commerce system.

With some systems a failure would result in detectable fraud, and there would be an option to adopt other mechanisms to correct the problems with trust. Thus, despite the novelty of the source of the failure, these cryptographic and trust failures would be of an evolutionary, not of a catastrophic, sort.

Now consider the possibility that collapse would lead to catastrophic loss of a commerce system. Recall the previous examples. In systems without atomicity and adequate receipts, fraud would not be traceable, and therefore the levels of fraud could quickly rise to the intractable. This is not a function of whether a system is notational or token, although token systems are more prone to fail with respect to atomicity than are notational systems, as a result of token systems' concentration of trust in a single or a few frequently used cryptographic keys.

The circulation of bogus moneys would cause merchants to lose funds, or banks would be called upon to honor funds that they did not possess. Three obvious possibilities suggest themselves for a merchant in the case of currency failure. The first is to pass on the cost of fraud to customers; the second possibility is for the merchant to accept the fraud costs; and finally, cost may be placed on a third-party provider.

If the cost is passed on to the customer, merchants will lose customers. Customers will not return to the same commerce system after detecting fraudulent charges and still having to pay for them. Unlike the case of rude service at the corner store, customers will not return to a virtual merchant who mistreats them because there are no geographic advantages to doing so. Hopefully the prospect of such fraud will inspire customers to appreciate the value of investment in secure hardware.

If the second option is chosen and the cost is passed on to the merchant, the merchant may be subject to fraudulent charges and as well as forced to drop the currency mechanism. This will result in lost funds and loss of some customers.

Should the cost of the bogus funds be passed on to the bank or acquirer (i.e., choosing the third option)? There are again two possibilities (this repeated branching of failure possibilities is indeed not unlike a decision tree). The acquirer either itself fails or the system is abandoned. In either case, customer and merchant will know the source of failure. The wise choices are to limit exposure in one system, that is, consumers should use only one credit card on the Internet and not use debit cards. For merchants, this implies embracing many systems to ensure customer service after a failure, and to prevent a one-to-one correspondence between all profit and a single mechanism. For customers, it means embracing fewer systems to limit exposure.

The final mode of system failure is a large-scale collapse. This would require the collapse or a failure of the infrastructure, resulting in a complete loss of trust, rather than the loss of a single instrument. In such a case, information on the endpoints of the network as well as in the network would be corrupted, and denial of service may be the order of the day.

Incidents that foreshadow such an event of this magnitude are the Morris worm incident and the recent explosion of Macro viruses.[64] The Morris worm incident was instigated by a computer science student. On the more theoretical end of the scale, information warfare scenarios are frequently played out as an exercise in paranoia or preparedness, or perhaps both. Information warfare scenarios offer a few useful suggestions.

The major suggestion gleaned from information warfare survival scenarios is that electronic safe havens or subnetworks should be created. This translates into protecting data, internal connectivity, and at the most extreme, temporary disconnection from the external net. This might work for large organizations, but for individuals and small businesses who will not know of widespread attacks until their machine is cut off, this is not useful. However, there is an important concept: save the core business information in the case of collapse by backing up any critical data.

The ability to segregate systems is important for the small computer as well as the large. Designing inventory systems so that purchases be can read without updating the inventory is one way to segregate—that is, be clear in separation of authority to read and write data. Another is to provide inventory information on a daily basis, while leaving the core machines separate. For small businesses this may mean purchasing two machines—consider it a one-time insurance payment. One, the web server, can be seen in the near term as a single cash register. A cash register would not be used for accounting, inventory, etc. The second machine will be connected only occasionally.

64. The Morris worm incident refers to the software written by Robert Morris and released on the Internet on November 2, 1988. A worm is a complete program—an autonomous agent comparable to, well, a worm. A virus is software that attaches to another program and runs only if that program is available. Thus "Word Macro virus" attaches to MSWord and runs only if the program is available. The Morris worm infected thousands of computers within hours, and infected approximately 5 percent of the machines on the Internet. Those machines then committed themselves to worm reproduction, coming to a screeching halt in terms of useful work. Many organizations cut themselves off from the net as soon as the attack was identified. At the time of the attack the damage done was estimated at $98 million; however, there were no measures of certainty attached to this estimate. For more information on the Internet worm, see Spafford 1989.

A difference between a paper collapse and an electronic collapse would be the speed at which each happens. The Morris worm incident took perhaps five days. Yet the worm incident identified a critical need for centralized support for systems under siege—what has become an international network of incident response teams. These incident response teams are the best source of information on the status of any network with respect to security. At the Computer Emergency Response Team site, current information about the latest attacks and defenses are available at no charge. Note that any attacks can be reported to an incident response team and confidentiality will be respected.

Having listed the myriad ways a radical collapse could occur, it is important to note that reactionary paranoia to the threat is not only a waste of time, but also bad security policy. Should there be a crippling attack on the infrastructure, it will be critical to act fast to take countermeasures. It will also be important not to act unless necessary, or there will be a ridiculous amount of unnecessary thrashing. Overreaction can create a denial-of-service attack as effectively as genuine hostilities. Hoaxes must be identified and ignored, while attempts at attack must be recognized.

Electronic commerce will be as critical to business in the next century as paper has been in this century (and the previous three). At this point the risks in transacting over the Internet may seem high, but adoption of some sort of Internet commerce by society is inevitable. This book has focused only on the risks in these first years of Internet commerce.

Internet commerce is happening, and will continue to happen, until it is so varied and interwoven with daily life that the phrase "Internet commerce" will seem as academic as the phrase "paper commerce."

What part will you play?

References

Legislation

5 USC §552 Privacy Act

12 USC §1829 Money Laundering Act

12 USC §2903 Community Reinvestment Act

12 USC §3403 Financial Privacy Act

15 USC §1601 Truth In Lending Act

15 USC §1691 Equal Credit Opportunity Act

15 USC §1692 Fair Debt Collection Practices Act

15 USC §1694 Electronic Funds Transfer Act

18 USC §1029 Computer Fraud and Abuse Act

22 CFR §121 International Traffic in Arms Regulation

22 USC §2571 Arms Control Act

26 USC §6103, 31 USC §3711 Debt Collection Act

31 CFR §103 Know Your Customer Requirements

35 USC §3401 Right to Financial Privacy Act

42 USCS §3608, 15 USC §1681, 12 USCS §1708 Fair Credit Reporting Act

49 USC §1666 Fair Credit Billing Act

50 USC 2401 Export Administration Act

Books and Articles

Alderman, E., and Kennedy, C. 1995. *The right to privacy.* New York: Alfred A. Knopf.

Anderson, R. E., Johnson, D. G., Gotterbarn, D., and Perrolle, J. 1993. Using the ACM code of ethics in decision making. *Communications of the ACM* 36: 98–107.

Anderson, R. H., and Hearn, A. C. 1996. *An exploration of cyberspace security R & D investment strategies for DARPA: The Day after . . . in Cyberspace II,* MR-797-DARPA. URL: http://www.rand.org/publications/MR/MR797/summary.html.

Baird, Z. 1996. How have other nations balanced legal and national security threats and responded to a changed world? American Bar Association Standing Committee on Law and National Security Law Enforcement and Intelligence Conference, 19 September.

Baker, A. 1994. *A concise introduction to the theory of numbers.* New York: Cambridge University Press.

Bernam, J. 1991. Establishing a legal framework for freedom and privacy on the electronic frontier. Conference on Computers, Freedom, and Privacy. Washington D.C.

Bickford, D. 1996. The changed threat to U.S. national security—new problems and priorities. American Bar Association Standing Committee on Law and National Security Law Enforcement and Intelligence Conference, 19 September.

Bloustein, E. 1968. Privacy as an aspect of human dignity: An answer to Dean Prosser. *New York University Law Review* 39: 962–970.

Brands, S. 1993. Untraceable off-line cash in wallet with observers. In *Advances in cryptology—CRYPTO '93,* 302–318. Berlin: Springer-Verlag.

Brennan, J. 1989. *Florida v. Riley.* 488 U.S. 445, 466 (J. Brennan, dissenting).

Brickell, E., Gemmell, P., and Kravitz, D. 1995. Trustee-based tracing extensions to anonymous cash and the making of anonymous change. *Proceedings of the Sixth Annual ACM-SIAM Symposium on Discrete Algorithms,* San Francisco, 22–24 January, 457–466.

Britt, P. 1994. Moving forward with smart cards. *Savings and Community Banker* 3(11): 6–7.

Business Week. 1994. ATM shouldn't stand for "artfully taken money." *Business Week* (Industrial/Technology Edition), 31 May: 110.

Camp, L. J., Harkavy, M., Tygar, J. D., and Yee, B. 1996. Anonymous atomic transactions. 2nd Annual Usenix Workshop on Electronic Commerce, Oakland, California, November.

Camp, L. J., Sirbu, M., and Tygar, J. D. 1995. Token and notational money in electronic commerce. Usenix Workshop on Electronic Commerce, New York, NY, July.

Camp, L. J., and Tygar, J. D. 1994. Providing auditing while protecting privacy. *The Information Society* 10: 59–71.

Cerf, V. 1993. How the Internet came to be. In B. Aboba, ed. *The on-line user's encyclopedia.* New York: Addison-Wesley.

Cerf, V., and Kahn, R. E. 1974. A protocol for packet network interconnection. *IEEE Transactions on Communications* 5: 637–648.

Clark, G., and Acey, M. 1995. Mondex blows users' anonymity. *Network Week* (U.K.) 1(8): col. 1.

Chaum, D. 1985. Security without identification: Transaction systems to make big brother obsolete. *Communications of the ACM* 28: 1030–1044.

Chaum, D. 1989. On-line cash checks. In *Advances in cryptology—EURO-CRYPT '89*, 288–293. Berlin: Springer-Verlag.

Chaum, D. 1992. Achieving electronic privacy. *Scientific American* 267: 76–81.

Chaum, D. 1994. *Prepaid smart card techniques: A brief introduction and comparison*. Holland: Digicash.

Chaves, C. 1992. The death of personal privacy. *Computerworld*, January: 25–27.

Cohen, J. 1996. The right to read anonymously. *Connecticut Law Review* 28(4): 981–1039.

Coleman, J. S. 1990. *Foundations of social theory*. Cambridge, MA: Harvard University Press.

CommerceNet. 1995. The CommerceNet/Nielsen Internet demographics survey: Executive summary. Cited 30 October. URL: http://www.commerce.net/information/surveys/toc.html.

Compaine, B. J. 1988. *Issues in new information technology*. Norwood, NJ: Ablex Publishing.

Computer Science and Telecommunications Board. 1994. *Rights and responsibilities of participants in networked communities*. Washington, D.C.: National Academy Press.

Cox, B. 1994. *Maintaining privacy in electronic transactions*. Pittsburgh: Information Networking Institute, Carnegie Mellon University.

Cox, B., Tygar, J. D., and Sirbu, M. 1995. NetBill security and transaction protocol. Usenix Workshop on Electronic Commerce. New York, NY, July.

Crosby, A. W. 1997. The measure of reality: Quantification and Western society, 1250–1600. New York: Cambridge University Press.

Cross Industry Working Group. 1995. Electronic cash, tokens and payments in the national information infrastructure. Cited September. URL: http://www.cnri.reston.va.us:3000/XIWT/documents/dig_cash_doc/ToC.html.

Davies, D. 1981. *The security of data in networks*. Los Angeles: IEEE Computer Society Press.

Davis, D. 1995. Kerberos plus RSA for World Wide Web Security. *Proceedings of the First USENIX Workshop on Electronic Commerce*, 11–12 July, New York, 185–188.

Davis, P. 1995. Senate Republicans say the Earned Income Tax Credit is becoming too expensive. Broadcast on National Public Radio Morning Edition, National Public Radio. Number quoted by Margaret Richardson, Commission of the Internal Revenue Service, 17 August. Also http://www.realaudio.com/contentp/npr/nb0817.html.

Denning, D. 1982. *Cryptography and data security*. Reading, MA: Addison-Wesley.

Diffie, W., and Hellman, M. E. 1976. New directions in cryptography. *IEEE Transactions on Information Theory* 7: 644–654.

Diffie, W., and Hellman, M. E. 1979. Privacy and authentication: An introduction to cryptography. *Proceedings of the IEEE* 67: 18–48.

Diffie, W., and Landau, S. 1997. *Privacy on the line*. Cambridge, MA: MIT Press.

Douglas, J. 1974. *California Bankers Association v. Schultz*. 416 U.S. 21,85, 94 S. Circuit, 1494, 1529, 39 L. Ed. 2d 812, dissent.

Draper, S. 1989. Security aspects of smart cards. In Caelli, ed. *Computer security in the age of information*. Amsterdam: Elsevier.

Duncan, G., and Lambert, D. 1986. Disclosure-limited data dissemination. *Journal of the American Statistics Association* 81: 10–27.

Duncan, G., and Lambert, D. 1989. The risk of disclosure for microdata. *Journal of Business and Economic Statistics* 7: 207–217.

Echikson, W. 1994. French risk it all on a smart card. *Boston Globe*, 28 February.

Economist. 1996. Who's who on the Internet. *The Economist*. 340.7976.

Edwards, P. N. 1997. *The closed world: Computers and the politics of discourse in cold war America*. Cambridge, MA: MIT Press.

Eisenstein, E. L. 1979. *The printing press as an agent of change: Communications and cultural transformations in early-modern Europe*. Vols. 1 and 2. New York: Cambridge University Press.

FAIR. 1996. FAIR media bias detector. Cited 15 April. URL: http://www.igc.apc.org/fair/media-bias-detector.html.

Federal Bureau of Standards. 1977. *Federal information processing standards publication 46: Announcing the data encryption standard*. Washington, D.C.: U.S. Government Printing Office.

Federal Communications Commission. 1995. *Telephone subscribership in the United States*. Washington, D.C.: U.S. Government Printing Office.

Federal Reserve Bank of New York. 1996. Regulation E—electronic funds transfer—revisions to regulation and official staff commentary. *Federal Register* 61.86.

Feige, U., Fiat, A., and Shamir, A. 1987. Zero knowledge proofs of identity. *Proceedings of the 19th ACM Symposium on Theory of Computing*, 210–217.

Fenner, E. 1993. How mortgage lenders can peek into your files. *Money*. April: 44–48.

Financial Service Technology Consortium. 1995. Electronic payments infrastructure: Design considerations. Cited November. URL: http://www.llnl.gov/fstc/projects/commerce/public/epaydes.htm.

First Virtual. 1995a. Information about First Virtual. Cited 8 October. URL: http://www.fv.com/info.

First Virtual, 1995b, The fine print. Cited 24 June. URL: http://www.fv.com/info/terms.html.

Fischer, M. J. 1988. Focus on industry. *Journal of Accountancy*: 130–134.

Freier, A., Karlton, P., and Kocher, P. C. 1996. *The SSL protocol. Version 3.* Mountain View, CA: Netscape Communications Corporation. Also URL: ftp://ietf.cnri.reston.va.us/internet-drafts/draft-freier-ssl-version3-01.txt.

Froomkin, A. M. 1995. Anonymity and its enmities. *Journal of On-line Law* 1.1.

Froomkin, A. M. 1996. Addressing law enforcement concerns in a constitutional framework. SAFE: Security And Freedom through Encryption Forum. Palo Alto, California, 1 July.

Fukuyama, F. 1995. *Trust: The social virtues and creation of prosperity.* New York: Simon and Schuster.

Garfinkle, S., and Spafford, G. 1986. *Practical UNIX security.* 2d ed. Sebastopol, CA: O'Reilly and Associates.

Godwin, Mike, and Smith, T., eds. 1997. *Cyber rights: Privacy and free speech in the digital age.* New York: Times Books.

Goradia, V., Kang, P., Lowe, D., Magruder, P., McNeil, D., Mowry, B., Panjwani, M., Somogyi, A., Wagner, T., and Yang, C. 1994. *NetBill: 1994 prototype.* Pittsburgh: Carnegie Mellon University. Also INI technical report INI TR 1994-11.

Gray, J., and Reuter, A. 1993. *Transaction processing: Concepts and techniques,* San Francisco: Morgan Kaufmann Publishers.

Griswold v. Connecticut, Supreme Court of the United States, 380 U.S. 947; 85 S. Ct 1081; 1965 U.S.

Hagel, J., and Armstrong, A. G. 1997. *Net.gain.* Boston: Harvard Business School Press.

Halpern, S. W. 1991. Rethinking the right of privacy: Dignity, decency, and the law's limitations. *Rutgers Law Review* 43(3): 539–563.

Hansell S. 1995. Mastercard joins banks to plan card that works like cash. *New York Times.* 17 August: D2.

Hanushevsky, A. 1995. Electronic commerce page. Cited November. URL: http://abh.cit.cornell.edu/ecom.html.

Harrison, C. 1994. Shoppers urged to guard against credit card fraud. *Atlanta Constitution.* 27 December: C4.

Hart, A. S. 1996. Personal communication, 16 May.

Harvard Law Review. 1991. Addressing the new hazards of the high technology workplace. *Harvard Law Review* 104: 1898–1916.

Heggestad, A. 1981. Regulation of consumer financial services. Cambridge, MA: Abt Books.

Henry v. Forbes. 1976. 433 F. Supp. 5.

Herlihy, M. P., and Tygar, J. D. 1987. "How to Make Replicated Data Secure." *Advances in Cryptography—CRYPTO '87*, ed. Pomerance. Berlin: Springer-Verlag.

Herlihy, M. P., and Tygar, J. D. 1991. "Implementing Distributed Capacities without a Trusted Kernel." *Dependable Computing for Critical Applications*, ed. A. Avizienis and J. C. Caprie. Berlin: Springer-Verlag.

Hodges, A. 1983. *Alan Turing: The enigma*. New York: Simon and Schuster.

Hoffman, L., and Clark P. 1991. Imminent policy considerations in the design and management of national and international computer networks. *IEEE Communications Magazine*. February: 68–74.

Hoffman, L., Kalsbeek, W. D., and Novak, T. P. 1996. Internet use in the United States: 1995 baseline estimates and preliminary market segments. Project 2000 Working Paper. Also URL: http://www2000.ogsm.vanderbilt.edu/baseline/1995.Internet.estimates.html.

Ingramham, D. G. 1991. Coming of age in cyberspace. Conference on Computers, Freedom, and Privacy, Washington, D.C.

Internet Domain Survey. 1998. Connected to the Internet. Cited March. URL: http://www.nw.com/zone/WWW//top html.

Jennifer, G., Steiner, B., Neuman, C., and Schiller, J. I. 1988. Kerberos: An authentication service for open network systems. *Proceedings of the USENIX Winter Conference*, 191–202.

Johnson, B. S. 1989. A more co-operative clerk: The confidentiality of library records. *Law Library Journal* 81: 769–804.

Johnson, D. 1989. Documents disclose FBI investigations of some librarians. *New York Times*, 7 November: A1.

Johnson, K. 1993. One less thing to believe in: Fraud at fake cash machine. *New York Times*, 13 May: A1.

Kailer, 1995. Reasoning about accountability in protocols for electronic commerce. *Proceedings of the IEEE Symposium on Security and Privacy*. Oakland, California, May.

Kalven, 1966. Privacy in tort law: Were Warren and Brandeis wrong? *Law and Contemporary Problems* 31: 326–332.

Kaplan, E. H. 1991. Needles that kill: Modeling human immunodeficiency virus transmission via shared drug injection equipment in shooting galleries. *Reviews of Infectious Diseases* 11: 289–298.

Karasik E. 1990. A normative analysis of disclosure, privacy, and computers: The state cases. *Computer Law Journal* 10: 603–634.

Katz v. United States. 1967. 389 U.S. 351, 369 F2d 130 (9th Cir).

Kaylin, J. 1992. When the needles do the talking. Yale. April: 34–37.

Kohnfelder, L. M. 1978. Towards a practical public-key cryptosystem. Bachelor's thesis, MIT.

Lamont v. Postmaster General. 1965. 381 U.S. 301, 301.

LaPlante, A. 1994. Citibank's smart move. *Information Week* 492(12): 42.

Lewis, T. 1996. Personal communication.

Low, S., Maxemchuk, N. F., and Paul, S. 1993. Anonymous credit cards. First ACM Conference on Computer and Communications Security. Fairfax, Virginia, 3–5 November.

Madsen, W. 1992. *Handbook of personal data protection.* New York: Stockton Press.

Markoff, J. 1995. Security flaw is discovered in software used in shopping. *New York Times*, 19 September: A1, D21.

Marx, G., 1986. The iron fist and the velvet glove. *The Social Fabric: Dimensions and Issues*, ed. J. E. Short. Beverly Hills, California: Sage Publications, pp. 135–162.

Mastercard. 1995. Secure electronic payment protocol specification draft. Version 1.1. Pt. 2. Cited November. URL: http://www.mastercard.com/Sepp/sepptoc.htm.

Mastercard. 1996. Secure electronic transaction technology, draft. URL: http://www.mastercard.com/SETT.

Mayland, P. F. 1993. EFT network risk begs CEO attention. *Bank Management* 69(10): 42–46.

McClellan, D.1995. Desktop counterfeiting. *Technology Review.* Cited February/March. URL: http://web.mit.edu/afs/athena/org/techreview/www/articles/feb95/mcclellan.html.

McGraw, D. 1992. Facing the specter of AIDS. *Boston Globe*, 13 March: 3–5.

McKnight, L. W., and Bailey, J. P., eds. 1997. *Internet economics.* Cambridge, MA: MIT Press.

Medvinski, G., and Neuman, B. C. 1993. NetCash: A design for practical electronic currency on the Internet. First ACM Conference on Computer and Communications Security, Fairfax, Virginia. 3–5 November.

Miller, B. C., Neuman, C., Schiller, J. I., and Saltzer, J. H. 1987. Section E.2.1: Kerberos authentication and authorization system. Project Athena. Cambridge, MA: MIT.

Miller, M. W. 1992. Data tap: Patients' records are treasure trove for budding industry. *Wall Street Journal.* 27 February: A1.

Morgan, G. 1992. Balancing national interest. *The Institute* 16.

Mosteller, F. 1965. *Fifty challenging problems in probability with solutions.* Toronto: General Publishing Company, Ltd.

Mundt, K. H. 1992. New dimensions in data security. *Proceedings of the 15th National Computer Security Conference.* Baltimore, MD, 438–447.

NAACP v. Alabama. 1958. 357 U.S. 449.

National Bureau of Standards. 1977. *Federal information processing publication 46: Specifications for the digital encryption standard.* Gaithersburg, MD: U.S. Government Printing Office.

National Center for Supercomputing Applications. 1995. NCSA mosaic web index. Cited November. URL: http://www.ncsa.uiuc.edu/SDG/Software/Mosaic/Docs/web-index.html.

National Computer Security Center. 1985. *Trusted systems evaluation criteria DOD-5200.28-STD.* Gaithersburg, MD: U.S. Government Printing Office.

National Computer Security Center. 1990. *Trusted network interpretation environments guideline NCSC-TG-011.* Gaithersburg, MD: U.S. Government Printing Office.

National Institute of Standards and Technology. 1991. Proposed federal information processing standard for digital signatures. *Federal Register* 56: 42980–42982.

National Institute of Standards and Technology. 1994. *Federal information processing standards publications 185: Escrowed encryption standard.* Gaithersburg, MD: U.S. Government Printing Office.

National Research Council. 1996. *Cryptography's role in securing the information society.* Washington: National Academy Press.

Netscape. 1996. Netscape commerce server. Cited May. URL: http://home.netscape.com/comprod/netscape_commerce.html.

Newberg, P. 1989. *New directions in telecommunications policy.* Durham, NC: Duke University Press.

New York Times. 1995a. Woman missing bank card finds she is overdrawn $346,770. *New York Times,* 12 February: 1, 36.

New York Times. 1995b. Credit union's error is thieves' delight. *New York Times,* 9 February: B9.

Nimmer, R. T. 1992. *The law of computer technology.* Boston: Warren, Gorham, and Lamont.

Office of Technology Assessment. 1985. *Electronic surveillance and civil liberties. OTA-CIT-293.* Gaithersburg, MD: U.S. Government Printing Office.

Office of Technology Assessment. 1986. *Management, security, and congressional oversight.* OTA-CIT-297. Gaithersburg, MD: U.S. Government Printing Office.

Office of Technology Assessment. 1995. *Information technologies for control of money laundering.* OTA-ITC-630. Gaithersburg, MD: U.S. Government Printing Office.

Okamoto, T., and Ohta, K. 1991. Universal electronic cash. *Advances in Cryptology—CRYPTO '91,* 324–336. Berlin: Springer-Verlag.

O'Keefe, M. 1994 Portable POS debit terminals mean greater convenience. *Bank Systems and Technology* 31(11): 35–37.

Olmstead v. United States. 1928. 277 U.S. 438, 48 SCt 564, 72 LEd2d 944.

Pfleeger, C. P. 1989. *Security in computing.* Carmel, IN: Prentice-Hall.

Pool, I. 1983. *Technologies of freedom.* Cambridge, MA: Harvard University Press.

Privacy Protection Commission Study. 1977. *Personal privacy in an information society.* Washington, D.C.: U.S. Government Printing Office.

Prosser W.L. 1941. *Handbook of the law of torts.* St. Paul, MN: West Publishing Co.

Rabin, M. O. 1978. *Digital signatures, foundations of secure communication.* New York: Academic Press, 155–168.

Randell, B., 1983. Recursively structured distributed computing systems. *Proceedings, Third Symposium on Reliability in Distributed Software and Database Systems.*

Randell, B., and Dobson, J. 1986. Reliability and security issues in distributed computing systems. *Proceedings, Fifth Symposium on Reliability in Distributed Software and Database Systems.*

Reid, M. A., and Madam, M. S. 1989. IC card design: Technology issues. *Information Age* 11(4): 211–216.

Rivest, R. L., and Shamir, A. 1996. PayWord and MicroMint: Two simple micropayment schemes. Submitted to Eurocrypt '96.

Rivest, R. L., Shamir, A., and Adleman, L. 1978. A method for obtaining digital signatures and public-key cryptosystems. *Communications of the ACM* 21: 158–164.

Rodman, P. 1996. Loss of national sovereignty and control by nation states. American Bar Association Standing Committee on Law and National Security Law Enforcement and Intelligence Conference. 19 September.

Rubin, L., and Cooter, R. 1994. *The payment system: Cases, materials, and issues.* St. Paul, MN: West Publishing Co.

Sandberg, J. 1995. Netscape software for cruising Internet is found to have another security flaw. *Wall Street Journal.* 25 September: B12.

Schambelan, B., 1992. *Roe v. Wade: The complete text of the official U.S. Supreme Court decision, annotated.* Philadelphia, PA: Running Press.

Schlossberg, H. 1993. Victims tired of researchers getting away with murder. *Marketing News,* 16 August: A16.

Schneier, B. 1995. *Applied cryptography.* 2d ed. New York: John Wiley and Sons.

Schnorr, C. P. 1990. Efficient signature generation of smart cards. *Advances in Cryptology—CRYPTO '89,* 239–252. Berlin: Springer-Verlag.

Schuba, C. L., Krsul, I. V., Kuhn, M. G., Spafford, E. H., Sundaram, A., and Zamboni, D. 1997. Analysis of a denial of service attack on TCP. 1997 IEEE Symposium on Security and Privacy, Oakland, California, 4–7 May.

Shamir, A. 1979. How to share a secret. *Communications of the ACM* 22: 612–613.

Simpson. 1996. The effects of electronic credentials lifetime on the risks and costs of electronic commerce. Qualifier report, Carnegie Mellon University.

Sirbu, M., and Tygar, J. D. 1995. NetBill: an Internet commerce system optimized for network delivered services. IEEE ComCon. San Francisco, California, 6 March.

Smith, S. 1992. A theory of distributed time. Ph.D. text, Carnegie Mellon University. Also CMU technical report CMU-CS-92–231.

Spafford, E. H. 1989. The Internet worm: Crisis and aftermath. *Communications of the ACM* 32(6): 678–687.

Speiser, S. M., Krause, C. F., and Gans, A. W. 1991. *The American law of torts.* New York: Clark Boardman Callaghan.

Sproull, L., and Kiesler, S. 1991. *Connections.* Cambridge, MA: MIT Press.

St. Laurent, S., 1998. *Cookies.* New York: McGraw-Hill.

Trubow, G., ed. 1991. *Privacy law and practice.* New York: Times Mirror Books.

Trubow, G. 1992. When is monitoring e-mail really snooping? *IEEE software* 9(2): 97–98.

Tunstall, J. 1989. Electronic currency. In Chaum, D. and Schaumuller-Bichl, I., eds., *Smart card 2000: The future of IC Cards: Proceedings of the IFIP.* Amsterdam: Elsevier.

Turn, R., and Ware, W. 1976. Privacy and security in information systems. *IEEE Transactions on computers.* C-25: 1353–1361.

Tygar, J. D. 1996. Atomicity and electronic commerce. *Proceedings of 1996 Symposium of Principles of Distributed Computing.* Philadelphia: ACM Press.

Tygar, J. D., and Yee, B. 1991. Strongbox: A system for self securing programs. In Rashid, R., ed., *CMU computer science: A 25th anniversary commemorative.* New York: Addison-Wesley and ACM Press, 163–198.

United Nations. 1995. *The United Nations and human rights, 1945–1995.* The United Nations Blue Book Series, 7. New York: United Nations.

United States v. Miller. 1976. 425 U.S. 435.

United States v. Payner. 1980. 447 U.S. 727, 100 S. Ct. 2439, 65 L. Ed. 2d 468.

U.S. Bureau of Census. 1995. *Statistical abstracts of the United States.* 115th ed. Washington: Department of Commerce.

U.S. Council for International Business. 1993. *Statement of the United States Council for International Business on the key escrow chip.* New York: U.S. Council for International Business.

U.S. Department of Defense. 1985. *Department of Defense trusted computer system evaluation criteria.* Fort Meade, MD: National Computer Security Center.

U.S. District Court. 1992. *United States v. Julio Fernandez, John Lee, Mark Abene, Elias Ladopoulos, and Paul Stira.* Indictment 92 CR S63.

Van Natta, D. 1995. Five phone marketers arrested in credit card sting. *New York Times,* 15 August: A14.

Verisign. 1995. Verisign expands digital ID offerings to leading web servers. Cited November. URL: http://www.verisign.com/pr/pr_servers.html.

Verisign. 1996. Frequently asked questions about digital ID's. Cited 26 May. URL: http://digitalid.verisign.com/id_faqs.htm.

Visa. 1995. Secure transaction technology specifications. Version 1.1. Cited November. URL: http://www.visa.com/visa-stt/index.html.

Wacker, J. 1995 Drafting agreements for secure electronic commerce. *Proceedings of the World Wide Electronic Commerce: Law, Policy, Security, and Controls Conference.* 6.

Walden, I. 1995. Are privacy requirements inhibiting electronic commerce. *Proceedings of the World Wide Electronic Commerce: Law, Policy, Security and Controls Conference,* 10.

Warren, S., and Brandeis, L. 1890. The right to privacy. *Harvard Law Review,* 4: 193–220.

Waters v. Fleetwood. 1956. 91 SE2d 344.

Wood, J. C., and Smith, D. S. 1991. Electronic transfer of government benefits. *Federal Reserve Bulletin* 77(4): 203–217.

Woodyard, C. 1991. Lungren joins suit accusing TRW of illegal practices. *Los Angeles Times,* 9 July: 1.

Yee, B. 1994. Using secure co-processors. Ph.D. text, Carnegie Mellon University. Also CMU technical report CMU-CS-94–149.

Ziegler, R. F., Brodsky, D. E., and Sanchez, C. M. 1993. U.S. securities crime. *International Corporate Law.* Criminal Investigations Supplement: 69–74.

Zimmerman, P. 1995. *The official PGP user's guide.* Cambridge, MA: MIT Press.

Zuckerman, G. 1994. Insider trading is back. *Investment Dealers Digest* 60(2): 12–15.

Index

/